CHANNEL TUNNEL VISIONS

CHARING CROSS
❀ To BAGDAD ❀

AN ACCOUNT BY VARIOUS EXPERTS OF THE GREAT AFTER-WAR COMBINED RECONSTRUCTION SCHEME, INCLUDING

(1) The proposed London improvement—the transfer of Charing Cross Station to the south of the Thames, under conditions which would make it the leading terminus in Europe; (2) The construction of the Channel Tunnel on a larger scale than hitherto contemplated; and (3) The opening of a new trans-continental highway from Charing Cross to Bagdad, thence to India. This, one of the greatest of all inter-Allied post-war Reconstruction reforms, would promote the common interests of the Allied nations in Europe and the East and for ever destroy the German dream of Oriental conquest

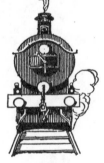

1917

Edited by the Editor of "The Daily Chronicle"

'Charing Cross to Bagdad',
Daily Chronicle, special supplement, 1917

CHANNEL TUNNEL VISIONS

1850-1945

DREAMS AND NIGHTMARES

KEITH WILSON

THE HAMBLEDON PRESS

LONDON AND RIO GRANDE

Published by the Hambledon Press 1994

102 Gloucester Avenue, London NW1 8HX (U.K.)
P.O. Box 162, Rio Grande, Ohio 45674 (U.S.A)

ISBN 1 85285 132 5

A description of this book is available from
the British Library and from the Library of Congress

Typeset by York House Typographic Ltd, London W13 8NT

Printed on acid-free paper and bound in Great
Britain by Cambridge University Press

Contents

Part II: 1914-1945

Illustrations

14 Sir Arthur Fell

15 General H.H. Wilson and Marshal Foch

16 Maurice Hankey and David Lloyd George

Text Illustrations

End-Papers

Abbreviations

CAS	Chief of Air Staff
CID	Committee of Imperial Defence
CIGS	Chief of the Imperial General Staff
DMO	Director of Military Operations
EAC	Economic Advisory Committee
HPDC	Home Ports Defence Committee
JIC	Joint Intelligence Committee
SAC	Scientific Advisory Committee

Acknowledgements

The main debt to be acknowledged is to Sally Scott, who from the outset saw this subject as deserving of treatment on a large scale, and who encouraged me to persevere with it. I am most grateful to Martin Sheppard, of Hambledon Press, for all his suggestions as to how to extend and improve the original version. Professors John Gooch and Edward Spiers, of the University of Leeds, have seen certain chapters, and let me have their views. An award from the Small Grants Fund of the University of Leeds allowed me to pay a visit to the Lansdowne Papers at Bowood House. The Earl of Balfour was kind enough to allow me to quote from Balfour Papers in the Scottish Record Office. Crown copyright material in the Public Record Office is reproduced by permission of the Controller of Her Majesty's Stationery Office.

The author and the publisher are both grateful to Michael Heath and the *Independent* for permission to reproduce his cartoon 'We Apologise for the Late Arrival of this Tunnel . . . ' as the end-papers to this book (*Independent*, 21 April 1993); and to the following for permission to reproduce illustrations: Eurotunnel (plates 1-6); the Press Association (plate 11).

This royal throne of kings, this scepter'd isle,
This earth of majesty, this seat of Mars,
This other Eden, demi-paradise;
This fortress built by Nature for herself
Against infection and the hand of war;
This happy breed of men, this little world,
This precious stone set in the silver sea,
Which serves it in the office of a wall,
Or as a moat defensive to a house,
Against the envy of less happier lands;
This blessed plot, this earth, this realm, this England,
This nurse, this teeming womb of royal kings,
Fear'd by their breed and famous by their birth,
Renowned for their deeds as far from home, –
For Christian service and true chivalry, –
As is the sepulchre in stubborn Jewry
Of the world's ransom, blessed Mary's Son;
This land of such dear souls, this dear, dear land,
Dear for her reputation through the world,
Is now leas'd out, – I die pronouncing it, –
Like to a tenement or pelting farm:
England, bound in with the triumphant sea,
Whose rocky shore beats back the envious siege
Of watery Neptune, is now bound in with shame,
With inky blots, and rotten parchment bonds:
That England, that was wont to conquer others,
Hath made a shameful conquest of itself . . .

Shakespeare, *Richard II*, Act 2, Scene 1

Introduction

A tunnel under the English Channel could have been constructed in the course of the last two decades of the previous century, or before the First World War, or during the inter-war decades of the 1920s and 1930s. Engineering opinion was, on the whole, in no doubt that it could be done. There was, after all, no difference in principle between the seven mile long Severn Tunnel of the 1880s and one three times that length. This was not a case where differences of scale, or of degree, created a difference in kind that would have put the project beyond the bounds of the possible. No doubt problems would have been encountered in the construction. In all probability the members of those great generations of engineers would have overcome them. By 1934 there were two tunnels under the Mersey estuary, one for trains and one capable of sustaining four lanes of motorised transport.

Since the late 1860s, moreover, promoters and entrepreneurs from the railway world had put themselves forward, backers and bankers (particularly the Rothschilds) had been found, pressure groups had been formed, and several schemes had been assiduously and seriously pushed. On several occasions, a majority of Parliament had appeared to be in favour of one of the schemes, as indicated by the polls of both Houses of Parliament made by the House of Commons Channel Tunnel Committee in 1919, 1924 and 1929; in 1906 the Foreign Secretary, Sir Edward Grey, had thought the then House of Commons would raise no objections. The bulk of the British press, especially in 1919–20 and in 1928–30, had also been in favour. Mr Gladstone believed in the early 1880s that, had the issue been presented to the British public as a whole in the form of a plebiscite or referendum, they would have approved the scheme. He remained of this opinion until his death in the mid 1890s. The chairman of a Joint Select Committee of both Houses of Parliament in 1883, Lord Lansdowne, came down in favour. So did four out of five members of a non-parliamentary committee appointed by Stanley Baldwin in 1929 to consider economic aspects of the project. Throughout the seven decades dealt with here the governments of France, on whose territory one end of the tunnel would be, were never less than enthusiastic. They were not the problem. The obstacles lay elsewhere.

Had a tunnel been built in the late Victorian period, or in the Edwardian age before the First World War, or before the Depression of the early 1930s or the appeasement policy of the late 1930s, there is no doubt that it would have had enormous consequences – for Britain, for Europe, and for the world. These consequences would have been evident on every plane – economic, cultural, intellectual; in terms of trade and commercial policies; in terms of foreign policy; in terms of defence policies and of strategic policies. Communications would have been different; patterns of trade and travel would have changed; attitudes to other countries, towards the peoples both of Europe and of the British Empire, would have altered and developed in different ways. The number of adjustments that would have had to be made would have been countless.

This book seeks to explain why it was that no Channel Tunnel was built between 1870, which saw the end of the period of national unification in Western Europe, and 1940, which saw the defeat of France in the third Franco-German war, the British retreat from Dunkirk, and the German occupation of northern France and of the Channel coast which was to last for four years. The book examines in the necessary detail those occasions, in Gladstone's time as in the time of Lloyd George and of Ramsay MacDonald, when the decision on a Channel Tunnel rested on a knife-edge, and could have gone either way.

Because everything depended on the British Government sanctioning one or other of the proposed schemes, attention must be paid to the views of successive political administrations, to the role and influence of certain advisers, such as Sir Maurice Hankey of the Cabinet Office, and to the evolving machinery of government, such as the Committee of Imperial Defence. The Channel Tunnel question affected many fields of government, and could not be answered by any one Department of State. Any study of how proposals were received and why they were dealt with as they were must also examine its connection with the defence field, in terms of fears and possibilities of invasion, for instance; with the foreign policy field, in terms of relations with the states of continental Europe; with the arguably far more important imperial policy field, in terms of relations with the British Empire as opposed to relations with the Great Powers of Europe, and must explore the constant tension between those two fields; with the economic field, in terms of government liabilities and expenditure, the boundaries of the State and the relation of the power of the State to private and commercial enterprises.

On close examination, all of these fields turn out to be full of vested interests and of departmental, inter-service, and individual rivalries. There never was a golden age when this was not the case. Nor was there ever a time when the process of decision-making did not include a huge amount of internal manipulation, with the British people as a whole largely excluded on the perennial grounds that they could not be trusted to know how or why decisions were reached. When there was so much to play for, in terms of power and influence, nothing could be taken for granted or left to chance. Then as now, rules tended to be thrown out of the window, or to be made up to suit themselves by the governmental participants as they went along. It does no harm to be reminded, through this extended example, of these simple truths and truisms.

The possibility of a Channel Tunnel, for the promoters and for those within the ruling elite whom they won over, was a dream. For those within the ruling elite who opposed it, the prospect of a Channel Tunnel was a nightmare. The possibility and the prospect brought out the best in some and the worst in others. An effort has been made here to present the arguments for and the arguments against in such a way as to enable and encourage the reader to participate in what was, in effect, a recurrent debate, against a constantly changing backdrop of world developments, both political and technological. This debate contained much ingenuity and some very special pleading on both sides. Beyond the actual, or real, merits and de-merits of the issues being ostensibly debated were secret agendas such as the promotion of conscription or the avoidance of immigration which were far too sensitive and revealing to be deployed openly or frequently. Readers would do well to bear in mind, as they become familiar with the issues raised, the positions taken, the justifications put forward and the arguments presented, what one of the French commentators, Valbert, wrote in 1882 of those who ranged themselves against the project to the extent of trying to engineer a general panic in the popular mind:

> Those who reduce everything to mathematics and who wish to reckon only with facts forget that the popular imagination is a fact in its own right, and one that has to be taken into consideration . . . If it was up to (some), they would enlarge the Channel, they would put twenty more kilometres between Dover and Calais. Their frightened imagination believes it sees pass through this tunnel

many things which they do not like, institutions which displease them, geome-
tricians whose square is suspect to them, artists whose fantasies they dread, the
radicals of Menilmontant, the socialists of Berlin, the nihilists of Moscow, every
kind of political epidemic and subversive paradox, revolutions, calamities. Pure
dreams, one might say! Dreams or the truth, nerves are anathema to reason,
and nerves once stimulated often determine the events of the world.

In large part, the contest was one between instinct and reason, between
the gut and the head, between the heart and the mind. It was a contest
with elements of all these things on both sides. The story of this contest
illustrates and illuminates a great deal about the outlook and working of
the British establishment, and about the attitudes and psyche of those
who undertook to speak for the British people, who claimed to know
them and to know what they thought, what they would say, and how they
would react. The contest is far from over, even now.

CHANNEL TUNNEL VISIONS

PART I

1850–1914

Chapter 1

Prologue, 1850–1906

Throughout the nineteenth century three ways of making easier and quicker the crossing of the physical gap between England and the continent of Europe were under consideration: ferries that would transport whole trains, as distinct from simply their passengers; bridges; and tunnels. The growing expertise, experience and above all confidence of the engineering profession was the motive force behind all these projects. Engineers connected Anglesey to Wales, Italy to Switzerland, the Mediterranean to the Red Sea, the Atlantic to the Pacific. Engineers, like the architects of the middle ages, became international figures. They regarded the achievement of a crossing of the English Channel in a dispassionate way: to them it represented a professional challenge – no more, no less. For many decades, their interest in this particular challenge resulted only in beautiful drawings which never progressed beyond the drawing-board or portfolio.

Giving something of the flavour of some of these projects will help prepare the ground for what comes later. In 1851 Britain was connected to the Continent by the laying of a submarine electric telegraph cable between England and France. With a view to consummating the international union thus far achieved, as the *Illustrated London News* put it, the French engineer M. Hector Horeau, who had an address in Queen Anne Street, Cavendish Square, London, proposed a tubular tunnel, made of strong plate iron, which would rest on the sea bed, and which would contain two lines for trains and a pathway for the surveyors. Horeau believed that a slope could be given to his railway which would enable it to dispense with steam engines: 'the greatest depth of the sea in the middle of the Channel will admit of the construction of inclined planes, by means of which the train would be enabled to reach a point where a stationary engine or atmospheric pressure might be employed in propelling the train to the level of the land railways of France and England'. The contemporary account goes on:

> These tunnels beneath the sea would not prevent navigation: two lighthouses might be erected at the entrance of the tubes; also several smaller ones between the lighthouses of France and England. These beacons, which may bear the names of the different nations of the earth, should be lighted up at night, and would indicate outwardly the position of the submarine railway, so that mariners should not cast anchor near it, as the tube might be damaged.
>
> The day and night lights of the lighthouse should be transmitted through the tube (covered internally with coating of enamel or lead) by means of reflecting metal plates. The upper part of the tube should have some strong glass windows placed at equal distances, and gas, which would complete the lighting between the beacons; the carriages might also be open, or have glazed roofs, to enable the passengers to profit by the various lights.

Horeau estimated the cost as £87,000,000, and invited 'the cooperation of men of science, by instituting experiments to test the practicability of what must be considered a plan as ingenious as it is novel'.[1]

Four years later Mr James Wylson C.E., put forward a scheme which he costed at only £15,000,000. He wrote:

> I propose to situate [the tunnel] at a uniform depth from the surface by means of ties below and buoys above, if necessary, at suitable intervals. The continuation of the tunnel into the shore on either coast I should dispense with, and, in order that it should have a partial freedom of motion, it should terminate with solid ends before reaching the shores.[2]

With a bridge one might be on rather firmer *terra* than with such schemes as those already mentioned. In 1889 M. Schneider, of the French firm Creuzot, and M. Hersent, a former president of the French Civil Engineers' Society, produced a design which owed something to the input of the British engineers Sir John Fowler and Sir Benjamin Baker. The details were given at a meeting in Paris of the Iron and Steel Institute. A line from Cap Grisnez to a point near Folkestone was selected, because such a line passed over the shallow parts of the Channel, the Colbart and Varna banks. A million tons of steel would be required. The cost was estimated at £34,000,000 and the time needed for construction at ten years. Spans would vary from 320 feet at the narrowest to 1,638 feet at the widest. (The largest span of the Forth Bridge is 1,640 feet.) The columns would rest on massive masonry supports and would be 130 feet high. The calculation was that at high water the lowest height of the bridge above the water would be nearly 180 feet.[3]

The trouble with bridges was the huge initial cost. This was compounded by the cost of maintenance. The whole of the steel construction would have to be repainted every four years, at an annual cost of £40,000; after twenty-five years 5,000,000 of the 20,000,000 rivets would have to be replaced annually, at a cost of £52,000; 'gradual renovation' of beams, girders, superstructure, would add another £48,000 per year. Over and above all this was the maintenance of the lighting apparatus to warn shipping of the presence of the piers of the bridge. Finally, there were the problems that the piers would cause for shipping in that they would alter the currents and thereby create new sandbanks and shallows. All nations concerned in maritime commerce would be affected, and international questions would be raised that could be settled only with great difficulty.

Nevertheless, one company formed to promote a bridge over the Channel devised a variant design for a submerged bridge, or submarine barrage. This would rise to about 48 feet below the level of the water, and form a roadway for a transporter wagon weighing several thousand tons, the platform of which would emerge above the highest tides, and which would be capable of carrying four railway trains at the same time. Such a structure would certainly have altered the currents in the Straits, perhaps to the extent of irreversibly silting up Dover or Folkestone, or Boulogne, Calais or Dunkerque. One critique pointed out some of the other risks attached:

> The preservation of this submarine bridge, which could not be maintained nor even inspected, would be most difficult, if not impossible, to hope for. One wonders to what risk of running off the rails the wagon rolling along would be exposed. It is also true that this wagon would have been exposed to meet many other hindrances on its way. Without considering the danger that would arise in case of a drifting wreck becoming entangled in the bridge, there is also the possibility of a ship's anchor let down in rough and stormy weather parting, as even the most solid of anchors have been known to do, at the bottom of the Straits, dashing against the bridge, and obliging the ship to abandon part of its chain, thus forming a most dangerous obstacle. Granted the said wagon were sufficiently elevated and heavy enough not to be displaced by encounter with the waves, what can be said of its chances of running foul of any obstacle? Two vessels having a clear course, and capable both of manoeuvring properly, very often have difficulty in not fouling each other in the Straits; there are such instances every day. What would it be if some day a wagon unable to perform evolutions were substituted for one of the boats?[4]

1. De Gamond and Sir John Hawkshaw

Given the above flights of fancy, the development of ideas for a tunnel that was not only beneath the sea but beneath the sea-bed itself, is all the more understandable. The first such project was presented in 1802 to Napoleon Bonaparte by the French mining engineer Mathieu. Mathieu suggested transforming the Varne bank, which was only 49 feet under water, into a large artificial island – so large in fact that an international town could be built upon it, together with a 'harbour of refuge' for shipping. From this new international town, almost at the midway point of the Straits, one tunnel would go to England, and one to France. In each tunnel a paved way would be laid down, lighted by oil lamps. and ventilated by shafts emerging from the water into the open air.

Mathieu's project preceded any serious study of the geology of the Straits. It was Thomé de Gamond (1807–75), hydrographic and mining engineer, military officer, LL.D and M.D., who laid the scientific foundations in this respect. Gamond first studied under Walter Staat, the Waterworks Engineer at Brussels. Thereafter, he devoted his professional life to devising means of communication between Britain and France. In 1834 he envisaged a submerged tunnel constructed of metallic tubes on the principle of the telescope; in 1835 a submerged tunnel in the form of a concrete arch on the sea-bed; in 1837 a ferry boat floating on the Straits and connecting with the cliffs on both sides by means of hydraulic masonry; in 1840 an artificial isthmus projected from Dover and consisting of sunken blocks of concrete, with three passages for navigation. His gathering of geological information involved considerable risks: in order to obtain samples of submarine clay, for instance, he had to descend over 100 feet without any diving apparatus, fastened only to a rope and with bags of pebbles weighing 160 pounds as ballast. In 1856 he presented both to Napoleon III of France and to Queen Victoria and Prince Albert a provisional solution to the problem he had set himself, and announced, 'I have carried my studies to the limits of my personal powers. This work must now be taken up by other intellects well skilled in the physiology of rocks and in the working of subterranean strata'. The publicity given to his ideas inspired others, and he himself received encouragement from Isambard Brunel, Joseph Locke and Robert Stephenson. The revised plans which he presented to the Universal Exhibition of 1867 in Paris envisaged a tunnel on a line from Eastwear Bay, east of Folkestone, to Cap Grisnez,

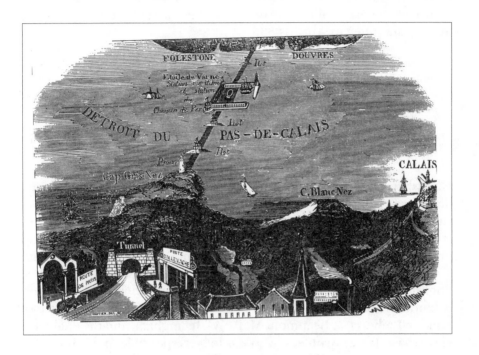

One of de Gamond's schemes,
including an 'international city' on the Varne bank

and included a proposal to make some thirteen islands in the Channel, so as to begin the tunnel at many points by sinking shafts in them.

The work of de Gamond was complemented and completed by that of Sir John Hawkshaw, who went on to build the 4½ mile long Severn Tunnel in the 1880s. In 1865 Hawkshaw began, at his own expense, a private enquiry to acquire as accurate a knowledge as was possible of the nature of the material under the sea-bed. As he told the Parliamentary Select Committee in April 1883:

> So far back as 1865 I began to consider the question: at that time it was with me simply an engineering problem, and . . . myself, the late Mr Brassey, and the late Mr Wythes, during 1865, 1866, and 1867, carried out considerable investigations in the Channel. We bored through the chalk on the French coast, and on the English coast; and by means of a steamer, and suitable apparatus, examined the bottom from side to side, the object of that being to ascertain, first, the thickness of the chalk, and next its continuity across the Channel . . .

Hawkshaw came to the conclusion that the problem could be solved, and that it was practicable to make a tunnel across the Channel. He convinced de Gamond to abandon the line of the latter's projected tunnel, and to become a member of an Anglo-French committee which would press ahead with the forming of companies in England and France, with a view to obtaining the concessions for the proposed work. On the English side, this committee consisted of Lord Richard Grosvenor, Admiral G. Elliot, Thomas Brassey M. P., W. Hawes (Director of the East London Railway), F. Beaumont M. P., W. Bellingham, and the engineers Hawkshaw, James Brunlees (who was to be responsible in the 1880s for the tunnel under the Mersey) and William Low. On the French side it consisted of Michel Chevalier (Inspector-General of Mines), P. Talabot (Chief Engineer of Roads and Bridges, Director of Paris-Mediterranean Railway), E. Blount (banker), W. B. Buddicom (former Constructor of the French Western Railways), and de Gamond.

Hawkshaw had interviews with Lord Clarendon, the Foreign Secretary, and with Mr Gladstone, Prime Minister for the first time. Having formed a company, the committee applied in March 1870 to the French Government for a perpetual sole concession for the construction of a submarine railway. The French Government immediately asked the British if it was disposed to approve of this enterprise in principle and whether, if so, it would regulate, by a diplomatic agreement, the conditions for the construction and working of such a line. This enquiry inaugurated a new, and diplomatic, phase in the history of the Channel Tunnel question.

'Hopes and Fears, or a Dream of Tunnel',
Punch, 25 February 1882

2. Towards an Anglo-French Treaty, 1871–76

Lord Clarendon was happy to vouch for 'the respectability and *bona fides* of the parties in this country who are concerned' in the enterprise. Prompted by the French Government and by Lord Richard Grosvenor, who had become chairman of an Anglo-French company for the construction of a Channel Tunnel, Clarendon asked the Board of Trade to look into the nature of the concession required and to provide him with an early reply. Grosvenor believed that Clarendon was on the point of declaring that the British Government had no objection to the carrying out of the preliminary inquiries for which Grosvenor's company was seeking permission from the French. Clarendon, however, died on 27 June 1870, and the French Empire's declaration of war on Prussia and the North German Confederation on 19 July meant the interruption of these embryonic negotiations for the duration of the hostilities.

It was exactly twelve months later, and with Clarendon's successor Lord Granville, that Grosvenor next raised the issue. He wrote to Viscount Enfield on 11 July 1871:

> We are now informed by our friends in France that the time has arrived when we may continue our negotiations, and . . . I write to you to ask if HM's Government would write to Lord Lyons [British Ambassador in Paris] to inform him that the British Government is notified that the Tunnel Committee desire to renew their demands in France, and that Lord Lyons is authorised to declare to the French Government that the British Government has no objection to bring forward; but, on the contrary (this addition would be of great service to us) sympathises with the undertakers.

Although he immediately referred this to the Board of Trade for observations, Granville was not so amenable, or susceptible, as Clarendon had been. Towards the end of the year Grosvenor, whose Channel Tunnel Committee had taken offices at 5 Victoria Street, Westminster, tried again, sending Granville a full account of the efforts made since 1867. This elicited from the Foreign Office the reply that

> considering that other parties have schemes for facilitating the intercourse between this country and France, Lord Granville thinks that as matters now stand HM's Ambassador at Paris could not properly be instructed to advocate the interests of any one in particular. If the Lords of Trade should consider one scheme preferable to the rest, and the Board of Admiralty should concur in

their views, it would then rest with HM's Ministers to determine what support it might be proper to give to it before the French Government.

The competing schemes, at the time, were for steam ferries of 450 feet in length, capable of carrying entire trains of passengers or goods, in order to accommodate which it would be necessary considerably to enlarge the harbours on both sides of the Channel. There were modest ferry proposals also, which required more moderate extensions of harbour facilities. When at the end of November the French Government did ask the British for their opinion on the principle of the Channel Tunnel scheme, making it clear that the scheme could not be carried out without the concurrence of the British Government, the Board of Trade was given an opportunity to pronounce on the relative merits of the competing schemes. The Board of Trade adopted the criteria that 'schemes which obviously present very great difficulties ought not, on account of their possible ultimate advantages, to be allowed to stand in the way of schemes which will satisfy immediate wants and which are more clearly practicable'. As regards a submarine tunnel, they noted that 'many engineering enterprises which at first appear impracticable have been carried into effect'. However, they thought it right to point out 'that it is, to say the least, doubtful whether either Government ought to give its consent to the establishment of a perpetual monopoly of tunnel communication between England and the Continent in the hands of private persons'. They were in fact quite adamant that such an undertaking must not become 'a perpetual private monopoly'. After examining the alternatives, the Board of Trade concluded 'that the tunnel scheme, even if admitted to be practicable, ought not to be allowed to interfere with or delay the navigation schemes'.

The Channel Tunnel Company was formally incorporated and registered in London on 15 January 1872. Because permission from the French Government depended on their receiving a declaration of agreement in principle from the British Government which the latter was not prepared to provide, the Channel Tunnel Company sought in April the permission of the Board of Trade to test the practicability of its scheme by sinking a shaft near St. Margaret's Bay and driving a temporary driftway a mile under the sea. The Board of Trade had no objection to this, but the situation was still dominated by the conclusions they had arrived at on 23 December 1871. That this was so was underlined again when in June 1872 the promoters once more applied to the Foreign Office for an expression of acquiescence in the principle of the scheme. Granville made it clear, both to the promoters and to the French

Government, that it was only subject to the Board of Trade's observations concerning the dangers of the tunnel's becoming a perpetual private monopoly that the British Government had no objection in principle to the proposed tunnel. Well might a French Government committee conclude, as it did at the end of the year, that since the original scheme of 1868 had been brought forward, the study of the question appeared to have gone backwards rather than forwards.

The tide turned in June 1873, following a personal approach by Lord Richard Grosvenor to Mr Gladstone. The Prime Minister appreciated that two questions were intertwined. The first was, how far new means of communication were desirable; the second, how far the government could go in giving an opinion as between the various ways of providing new means of communication. As Gladstone put it:

> On the second question it is for us to say as little as possible. Still it occurs to me that the Tunnel is free from an objection to the Ferry plan viz. that it [the Ferry plan] might give an excuse for a great naval harbour on the French side at the narrowest point of the Channel.
>
> But on the first question I suppose we really whilst renouncing all interference regard with a friendly and lively interest all schemes formed with this object [new means of communication] and open to no just objection, which is the case of the Tunnel.

Gladstone thought that it would do no harm to state all this openly, which is what Lord Richard Grosvenor wanted, and would appear to have overruled Granville, who had reminded him that a scheme for improving Dover Harbour had just been sanctioned by the Cabinet and did 'to a limited degree compete with the Tunnel scheme.'[5] As a result a way out of what had appeared to be the impasse of a perpetual private monopoly was found. Both the Foreign Office and the Board of Trade were amenable to a compromise, on the following lines:

> Whilst firmly opposed to any monopoly, HM Govt. would not be inclined to offer objections to a concession being granted to a public company in France, provided that, either by fixing reasonable limits as to time, or by reasonable conditions as to purchase of the undertaking by the respective Governments, or in any other way, the concession were prevented from operating hereafter as a monopoly injurious to the public.

The British Ambassador in Paris was told on 23 July to communicate this to the French Government. The prospect was thus opened of ultimate ownership of a Channel Tunnel by the two governments. The French Government immediately responded to pressure from Lord Richard

Grosvenor and opened an enquiry in August 1873 into the possibilities of the Pas de Calais area. This enquiry was completed in December 1873.

At this stage the French Government set up a committee under the Minister of Public Works to consider the application made to it by the Channel Tunnel Company. This committee did not complete its report until July 1874. The report concluded that the case thus far made by the promoters was not quite convincing or detailed enough. Partly for this reason, and partly because the international character of the undertaking required a prior agreement between the British and French Governments, they were not prepared to make at this stage a declaration of the public usefulness of the scheme. Before that could be done, further investigations had to take place with a view to demonstrating the viability of the scheme, and the approval of the Ministers of War and Marine, and of the National Assembly, had to be obtained. If the above conditions could be met within five years, the French were prepared to grant the promoters a definite concession for ninety-nine years, and a monopoly of it for thirty years.

This French report was sent to the new British Foreign Secretary, Lord Derby, who sent it on to the Board of Trade, saying that 'it is very desirable to support any well-considered scheme, the result of which may be to increase the facility of communication between the two countries', provided however that such support was not confined to any one undertaking. The Board of Trade's reply, of 9 December 1874, represented a real turning-point. What they registered, and what Lord Derby may not have registered, were the implications of a crucial move already made by the promoters. This was their giving notice of a Bill to enable them to acquire lands at St. Margaret's Bay. The implication of this was that the Government might have no further control over the project as a whole. As the Board of Trade spelled it out:

> The immediate object of this Bill is to enable [the promoters] to acquire land for the purposes of making their experimental shafts and driftways. But if they acquire sufficient land it is difficult to see what further powers they will require from HM Govt or from Parliament in order to make the Tunnel. On the one hand, HM Govt will be bound by no concession; on the other, the Company will be bound by no conditions, except such as Parliament may introduce into the Bill. It will therefore be expedient, if not necessary, for HM Govt to decide before the Bill in question passes, whether it is desirable to make any and what terms with the promoters.

Another danger was that, procedurally, the French and British Governments were not quite in step in their dealings with the promoters. Since the works on either side of the Channel, when completed, would necessarily form one work, it was important that the conditions imposed by the two Governments should be the same. The Board of Trade was quite firm: it was 'desirable that HM Govt. should, at the present moment, make up their minds whether they will encourage the undertaking, and if so, on what terms'. It had no objections to the terms proposed by the French Government, and suggested that they be adopted. It made one further point:

> Reference is made in the papers to the military necessities of either country. This is a question for the War Office rather than for the Board of Trade. But it is clear that HM Govt must retain absolute power not only to erect and maintain such works at the English mouth of the tunnel as they may deem expedient, but also whenever they apprehend danger of war, or of intended war, to stop traffic through the tunnel. And it is for consideration whether they should not have the right to exercise this power without claim for compensation.

Subject to those observations the Board of Trade saw no reason why Lord Derby should not approve the course proposed by the French Government. Nor did Lord Derby. He wrote immediately to the French Minister for Foreign Affairs, the Count de Jarnac, on 24 December 1874, in the sense recommended by the Board of Trade.

Developments followed rapidly. On 18 January 1875 the Minister of Public Works, M. Caillaux, laid on the table of the National Assembly a Bill relative to the French section of the proposed tunnel. (Caillaux went on to become a share-holder in the French company that was formed on 1 February 1875; he was on the committee representing that company in 1906. 50 per cent of the shares of the French company were taken by the Northern Railway Company of France, 25 per cent by Rothschilds, and 25 per cent by engineers and others connected with the project; as Rothschilds had a controlling interest in the Chemin de Fer du Nord they thoroughly controlled the new company.) On 20 January a copy of the English Channel Tunnel Bill, due to be dealt with in the next parliamentary session, was sent on to the Foreign Office by the Board of Trade, who reminded Derby that there would be opportunities so to modify it during its passage through Parliament as to secure the public interest involved in the construction of the tunnel. On 5 February Lyons in Paris informed Derby that the fifteen members of the French Assembly elected to serve on the Committee on the French Bill were all favourable to the tunnel scheme.

On 9 February Queen Victoria made an effort to stop these developments in their tracks. She wrote to the Prime Minister, Disraeli, that 'She hopes that the Government will do nothing to encourage the proposed tunnel under the Channel, which she thinks very objectionable'. Her private secretary wrote in the same sense to Lord Derby. The Foreign Secretary, who believed that the Queen was 'in an excited condition', did his best to calm her down. He wrote:

> The Queen is probably aware that the Channel Tunnel scheme is got up by private promoters. No assistance in the form of subsidy or otherwise is asked from the State. All that the promoters desire at present is leave to take land and make other necessary arrangements for preliminary experiments with a view to ascertain whether the undertaking is practicable. It is obvious that we cannot reasonably object to such investigations being made. To say – 'We will have no closer intercourse with the Continent, and therefore all schemes for a tunnel shall be discouraged' – is a policy which neither the House of Commons nor the public would tolerate, and which I am sure Her Majesty would not wish to adopt.

In case this was not quite enough, Derby went on to say that he had discussed the subject in the previous year with the First Lord of the Treasury (i.e. Disraeli) who had entirely agreed as to the general course to be adopted. The Queen was not mollified. She considered it all '*very unsatisfactory* . . . If England is to be connected with the Continent, we shall have to keep up double Army, which we so *unwillingly* afford now'. She asked her private secretary to write something to that effect. General Ponsonby, however, took the same relatively relaxed line as the government, and ignored her.[6]

The next development was a suggestion from the Secretary to the Treasury, W. H. Smith, that, in advance of the passing of the Bill, a small committee of representatives of the British and French Governments should meet to draw up a provisional code of regulations. Amongst other things, there was the question of the limits of jurisdiction between the two countries: 'if a crime were committed in the tunnel, by what authority would it be cognizable? Or, again, if one country were to adopt a different code of law with regard to the management of railways from that adopted by the other, by which of them would the Company be bound?' Derby welcomed this suggestion, and so did his opposite number, now the Duc Decazes. By the 1st of March the French had appointed their three representatives – Kleitz and Droeling (both Inspectors-General of Roads and Bridges) and de Lapparent, the Engineer of Mines. The British representatives, selected by 15 March, were Captain Tyler (Board of Trade), Horace Watson (Solicitor to the Department of Woods) and Mr Kennedy (Foreign Office).

The absence of Service Department involvement at this stage is worth remarking upon, as both Admiralty and War Office had been asked to express views. On 5 March the Admiralty had written that, 'as the proposed tunnel does not in any way interfere with Admiralty interests, their Lordships have no remarks to offer on the subject'. The Secretary of State for War, Mr Hardy, was not quite so disinterested, but adopted an unfortunate turn of phrase. An official wrote on his behalf to W. H. Smith:

> I am to request that you will inform the Lords Commissioners of HM's Treasury that Mr Secretary Hardy is of opinion that due attention should be paid to defensive considerations in the instructions to the Commissioners, who will be appointed in conjunction with the French Government, and that the promoters of the project for a tunnel should be informed that such defensive works as may be required are to be provided, without cost to the Government, in accordance with plans to be approved by the Secretary of State for War.

Hardy may have expected a member of his department to be selected, but his failure to nominate any one did not serve the War Office well, and left it out in the cold. The Treasury went ahead and itself selected the British representatives. Although the terms of reference they were given included the paying of attention to 'the question of closing or otherwise neutralising [the tunnel] in time of war or apprehended war', the War Office, the more it thought about the matter, became distinctly unhappy. On 13 March the War Office sent a memorandum to the Treasury. It began:

> There appears to be no military objection to the proposed tunnel provided due precautions be adopted. Should this country in alliance with France be at war with another continental power, the existence of the tunnel might be advantageous.
>
> Should this country be at war with France the proposed tunnel could no doubt be readily closed. Having regard, however, to the possibility of the tunnel being unnecessarily injured under the influence of panic, and to the probable cost of repairing such injury, it is desirable to obviate, as far as possible, the necessity for adopting extreme measures, and with this object to pay due regard to defensive considerations in the construction of the tunnel.

Warming to his theme, the writer went on:

> Moreover, unless proper military precautions be taken, it might under some circumstances happen that France might be able, in anticipation of a decla-ration of war, to send a body of troops through the tunnel, and thus obtain an

important military advantage. Such a body of troops could readily intrench themselves, and could be rapidly reinforced.

If, however, suitable defensive arrangements are made, such an undertaking would be impracticable, and even in case of war being imminent, no fears need be entertained, which might lead to the partial destruction of this costly work.[7]

Clearly there were still some within the War Office who did not feel that they had to justify their existence by imagining the unimaginable, and devising ways to deal with it.

By 1 April, the line had hardened to the extent that the War Office decided to protest to the Treasury against its exclusion from the Joint Commission, stating that 'the questions involved (in consideration of the measures to be taken in the event of war to close the tunnel or to render it neutral) are most important, and are essentially military, and the Secretary of State for War is convinced that much inconvenience and delay will arise if the consideration of them is deferred until the leading features of the arrangements have been settled by the Commission.[8] The Treasury replied, a week later, saying blandly that it was too late to make any changes in personnel, and that, moreover, there was no representative of the French War Department on the Commission. The Treasury trusted that the Secretary of State for War 'will not press this point further'. This incensed those officials at the War Office who maintained that War Department interests could not be satisfactorily entrusted to the Commission, and that the War Office should reserve to itself an independent position with respect to the provisional code of regulations. With regard to the Treasury's point that the French War Department was not represented, one official said that 'the importance of military representation thereon is not so pressing to the French as to the British Government – It is conceivable that France might invade England by means of this Tunnel, but it is scarcely possible to conceive the circumstances under which Great Britain would contemplate an invasion of France . . . ' Moreover, 'it is absurd to suppose that the neutrality of this Tunnel can be maintained in the event of a war between this country and France – should such a war break out it may be necessary to destroy it, at least in part and it will certainly be necessary to close it to traffic for a considerable time . . . '

The same official returned to the attack almost immediately:

It should be borne in mind that this Tunnel will put an end to the insularity upon which Great Britain so relies for defence and it will do so at or in close proximity to our most important strategical Harbour; I do not apprehend any danger from this provided proper precautions be taken, yet this fact I think raises the scheme from a mere commercial undertaking, and invests it with a political character, and this character is still further stamped upon it by the action of the two Governments in the appointment of the Commission, and by the magnitude of the undertaking . . . I foresee great difficulties in the future if the Department of State whose province it most affects sits outside as adviser merely to one half of the Commission – in such a position its views may or may not be accepted, probably they will not in their entirety because they will seem hostile to the interests of the undertaking – and what trouble and endless delay will there not be hereafter in weaving these views into the regulations drawn up by the Commission which will emanate from that body with much of the authority of both Governments of England and France.[9]

This counter-attack so far retrieved the ground lost initially by the War Office that the three British members of the Joint Commission invited it to send a representative to be interviewed by them on 29 April. Nugent was chosen, and went along with a view to registering the reservations he had already expressed. The documents that Nugent lodged with the British Commissioners were drawn up by the Solicitor of the War Office, C. M. Clode, who had when drawing them up observed:

> The subject is one so novel that no ordinary experience will guide us. The committee has been formed without any element of that which in an English point of view is the essence of the scheme, viz. its effect on the insular position of Great Britain in relation to national defence. However, we must do the best under the circumstances in which the War Department is placed, and the Treasury should be requested to give the Secretary of State access to all the proceedings of the committee, and the fullest information with regard to the scheme as it is developed.

In a preliminary Report of 10 May 1875 Tyler, Kennedy and Watson responded to this by proposing the reservation of full rights for the War Department. They went on:

> We consider that the promoters should be bound to construct or provide, at their own expense, all such defensive works or appliances as may be required by the War Department; and that the British Government should have the power, without assigning cause, of stopping the traffic through the tunnel at any moment . . . We would . . . call attention to the consideration that, whatever precautions may be taken in connection with defensive works, the construction of the tunnel must necessarily, to a certain extent, impair the insular position of Great Britain.

The British and French Governments had intended to suspend legislation until the Joint Commission reported. At the beginning of July, however, strong representations having been made to them by the promoters, they relented. As a result, the Bills in question received the assent of the unhappy Queen Victoria and of President MacMahon on the same date, 2 August 1875. The two measures were by no means identical. The French one was a definite concession of the right to make a tunnel towards England, provided certain conditions were met; the British Act of Parliament merely authorised the Channel Tunnel Company to acquire lands at St Margaret's Bay and carry out such operations as might be authorised by the Board of Trade, under the proviso that the company should be bound by any conditions which might be imposed in consequence of negotiations with the French Government.

The two halves of the Joint Commission worked separately until the end of the year. Under pressure from Lord Derby, who wanted their conclusions to be embodied in a protocol which might then form the basis for a treaty to be concluded between the British and French Governments, they came together at the end of January 1876 and again in the last week of May. There was a hiccup in May, before the final sessions of the commission, when the French promoters published a pamphlet challenging the principle on which the governments were proceeding. These promoters asserted that they had a vested interest in the concession made to them by their own government, and they repudiated any further terms which might be imposed on them as a result of any agreement between the two governments. The Board of Trade dealt with this as follows:

It is impossible that the English Government should for a moment admit the validity of this objection. The tunnel must be regarded as a whole, and the French Company must have known from the beginning that any concession made to them by their Government could be of no effect and of no value whatever, unless followed or accompanied by a concession on the English side. It is idle, therefore, for them to allege a vested interest in the terms granted to them by the French concession, and to repudiate the control which the two Governments are now seeking to impose upon them. Whatever claim arising out of their concession the French company may have upon the French Government, they have none upon the English Government, and even as regards their own Government both they and that Government must be taken to have acted with the knowledge that the consent of the English Government must be obtained.

The Report of the Commission was ready at the end of May 1876. They agreed that the jurisdiction of each Government should cease at the centre of the proposed tunnel, and recommended the appointment of an international commission of six members to advise the two Governments on the construction, maintenance and working of the submarine railway. They agreed that each Government should have the power to suspend the working of the railway and to damage or destroy the works of the tunnel or railway in its own territory, and also to flood the tunnel with water, without being liable to any claims for compensation. Within five years from 2 August 1875, the French company should be bound to conclude an agreement in writing with an English company, and vice versa, for the construction, maintenance and working of a submarine railway; and the works of exploration should be started within one year from 1 July 1876.

Considerable momentum in the cause of the tunnel had been generated by mid 1876. All seemed set fair for the incorporation into an Anglo-French Treaty of the conclusions of the Commission. Had a treaty been signed, the War Office would have had to accommodate itself to a *fait accompli*. At this point, however, the promoters' energy fell away. Whilst the French company did all that was required of it, the English one did not. The latter issued a prospectus proposing to raise only £80,000 for experiments at St Margaret's Bay. Although Sir John Hawkshaw, Sir Thomas Brassey and some other engineers took shares, sufficient capital was not forthcoming, partly because of a deepening commercial depression, and the year allowed for the purchase of land expired in August 1876 with the work in abeyance. As a result, no efforts were made at the level of governments to proceed with the ratification of the treaty of which the Report of the Joint Commission was to have been the basis.

By August 1880 the French company, according to the terms of its concession, should have come to terms with a duly authorised English company. As this had not transpired the French promoters needed, and obtained, a presidential decree prolonging for another three years the time given for completing the preliminary works.

At the same time, another English scheme was brought forward. This new scheme was initiated by Sir Edward Watkin. Watkin, born in 1819, had gone into his father's cotton merchandising business in Manchester. Having raised money for the opening of public parks in Manchester and Salford he helped found the *Manchester Examiner* in 1845. In the same year he had begun his main career, that of railway promoter, as secretary to the Trent Valley Railway. He negotiated the sale of this, and his own transfer, to the North Western Railway Company. In 1853 he was appointed general manager of the Manchester, Sheffield, and Lincolnshire Railway. In 1861 he was commissioned by the Secretary of State for the Colonies, the Duke of Newcastle, to go to Canada to investigate the means of confederating the five British provinces there into a dominion, and to consider the feasibility of transferring the Hudson Bay territory to Government control. He severed his connection with the Manchester, Sheffield and Lincolnshire on his return, and was briefly president of the Grand Trunk Railway of Canada. In 1863, however, he became director of the Manchester, Sheffield and Lincolnshire Railway, and served as chairman of this from 1864 to 1894. He combined this with the chairmanship of the South Eastern Railway Company, from 1866 to 1894, and with the chairmanship of the Metropolitan and East London Railway Company from 1872 to 1894.[10] One of his main objectives was to create a through route, under a single management, from Manchester to Dover; this, the Great Central line, was opened to traffic in March 1899. Another through route in which he was interested was that between Liverpool and Cardiff, with a view to bringing South and North Wales into direct railway communication with Lancashire via the Mersey Tunnel, which was opened in 1886. He also proposed a railway tunnel between Scotland and Ireland, and a ship canal between Dublin and Galway. In 1889 he became chairman of a company to erect in Wembley Park, Middlesex, a tower modelled on the Eiffel Tower in Paris. Only a single storey of the 'Watkin Tower' was completed; it was opened to the public in 1896, and demolished in 1907.

Watkin's parliamentary career began in 1857, when he was returned as Liberal Member for Great Yarmouth. He sat as member for Stockport from 1864 to 1868, and as Member for Hythe from 1874 to 1895. Watkin had discussed the question of saving time crossing the Channel and avoiding sea-sickness with Richard Cobden in Paris during the negotiation of the Anglo-French Commercial Treaty of 1860, with which one of the French promoters, Chevalier, had also been involved. Watkin later claimed that it was at his suggestion that de Gamond had first spoken to Napoleon III. Watkin's scheme was based on the results of experiments made by sinking shafts on the property of the South Eastern Railway Company in the neighbourhood of Dover, something sanctioned by the South Eastern Railway Act of July 1874. A gallery at the foot of Shakespeare cliff, extending about a mile under the sea, had been built. At an Extraordinary General meeting of the South Eastern Railway Company held at London Bridge Railway Station in June 1881, Watkin announced to the shareholders that the results showed the possibility of completing an experimental tunnel seven feet in diameter within five years, if the work was carried on simultaneously from both ends. He had already come to an understanding with some of the original French promoters.

This meeting had been covered by *The Times* of 17 June, and the ensuing correspondence on the subject prompted the Board of Trade to suggest to the Service Departments the desirability of appointing a Departmental Committee consisting of War Office, Admiralty, and Board of Trade representatives, 'in order to consider what steps, if any, should, under present circumstances, be taken by H.M. Government'. The Admiralty, still in its 1875 mode, did not see the point, and was of the opinion 'that the time has not yet arrived for the appointment of such a Committee', and that 'the subject in its present stage appears scarcely to rest within the functions of this Department'. Childers at the War Office was more alert than his predecessor had been, and immediately agreed to act as proposed by the Board of Trade. This placed the Admiralty in an embarrassing position, and the Board of Trade pressed the point, stating

> that they find the work of forming a subway under the Channel is making considerable progress, and that they may be asked at any time to sanction the extension of the subway under the sea, and they therefore feel that they ought to be prepared to state the conditions on which consent may be given to such a work. It is on this account, and also owing to public susceptibility having been aroused as to possible danger to this country from a tunnel under the Channel, that the Board of Trade desire to be fortified with the opinion of the military and naval authorities, so as to be in a position to know what, if any, conditions are to be made in respect to these considerations.

The Admiralty gave way, and appointed Vice-Admiral Phillimore to the committee. The other members were Mr Farrer, of the Board of Trade, and Colonel J.H. Smith, Royal Engineers.

3. Adye *v.* Wolseley

Farrer, Phillimore and Smith interviewed Sir Edward Watkin on 13 December 1881 and, three days later, Sir John Hawkshaw. They next met on 25 and 26 January 1882 when they interviewed Lieutenant-General Sir Garnet Wolseley, the Adjutant-General, and Lieutenant-General Sir John Adye, the Surveyor-General of the Ordnance. Both had, in the meantime, supplied memoranda as requested by the Secretary of State for War.

Wolseley did not mince his words:

The proposal to make a tunnel under the Channel may . . . be fairly described as a measure intended to annihilate all the advantages we have hitherto enjoyed from the existence of the 'silver streak', for to join England to the Continent by a permanent highway, will be to place her under the unfortunate condition of having neighbours possessing great standing armies . . . The construction of the tunnel would place us under those same conditions that have forced the Powers of Europe to submit to universal service.

Wolseley next invoked the name and memory of the Duke of Wellington, whose published correspondence was full of efforts to rouse the nation 'to a sense of its helpless condition and its powerlessness to resist a formidable invasion',[11] words that should be read, marked, learned and digested by that benighted school of primarily British historians who still believe that the nineteenth century was the century of the 'Pax Britannica'. Wellington, Wolseley recalled, had viewed the development of steam power as, in effect, joining England to the Continent by 'an isthmus of steam':

Were he now able to speak, what would he say if it were proposed to connect England with France by a permanent and almost indestructible 'isthmus' when all the Continent bristles with bayonets, and the first desire of every Continental Power is to be strong on land and to keep the great military machine, its army, in a state of perfection and complete readiness for active operations upon the shortest notice?

The 'isthmus of steam' that he [Wellington] dreaded was still a floating one . . . but it is now proposed to burrow this tunnel some 200 feet beneath the surface of the ground. It will in fact be, if made, more indestructible than any other possible form of roadway, and the possession of it by a Continental enemy for 24 hours would place this country completely at his mercy. Those who know Wellington's power of thought, the soundness of his military judgement, his clearness of perception upon such questions, will not require to be told what his advice would now be upon this question . . .

For Wolseley, only if England had a great standing army like that of France, only if 'the whole manhood of England was organised into regiments, and so into a great military machine', could she afford to create 'this new danger to our national existence'. The Volunteers and the Militia were no substitute for defending the country against invasion. For Wolseley, who went on to claim that England 'never can have [a great army] under our form of government', it was a case, with those in favour of a tunnel, of 'Those whom the Gods wish to destroy, they first drive mad'.

He discounted the neutralising value of a convention with France. He insisted that it was ridiculous to imagine that any civilised Power would never, under any circumstances, disregard the terms of such an agreement. Having invoked Wellington, he now invoked the first Napoleon. He wanted people to realise 'that the thing on which they propose to stake their national existence is the character of the man who may at any time hereafter have the means of wielding the power of France':

> Is human nature so utterly changed that it has become certain that what has been may never be again? What is the nature of the treaty that a man of the great Napoleon's turn of mind and morality would respect or care anything for the moment he felt that the interests of his nation would be advanced by breaking it? . . . What guarantee have we that another Napoleon may not again direct the destinies of France?

He followed this up by a very particular interpretation of works currently under way across the Channel:

> The construction of a splendid harbour at Boulogne, designed to admit the largest class or warships, is now being pushed forward rapidly. Great harbour works are also in progress at Calais and at other French ports on the Channel. These works would enable a large army to be embarked there at any time of tide, and would afford a safe anchorage for the two or three steamers that would be required for the conveyance of the few thousand infantry intended for the sudden descent upon our end of the tunnel. The construction of these great harbours, so close to our open and unprotected shores should, I think, cause us to review our military position at home very seriously, and to make us pause ere we discarded the only real armour we possess, namely, the protection which the 'silver streak' has hitherto afforded us.

2,500 men, ably led by 'a daring, dashing young commander' might, felt Wolseley, 'some dark night, easily make themselves masters of the works at our end of the tunnel, and then England would be at the mercy of the invader' – 'this is', he maintained, 'no wild dream of an impossible undertaking'. Moreover,

> Remembering the stakes to be won in case of success, it is quite certain that, sooner or later, the attempt would be made. The existence of the tunnel would, therefore, I contend, be a constant inducement to the unscrupulous foreigner to make war upon us, as it would hold out to him hopes of a conquest the like of which the world had never known before. With such a bait at the end of the tunnel always dangling before the foreign ruler who was anxious to strengthen his own position or to immortalise his name, and the knowledge of how little he would risk by the attempt, it is scarcely begging the question too much to say that it would be made at some period or other.

Wolseley maintained that in all the discussions there had been on the question of an invasion, 'no sane man' had ever held it to be impossible that a few thousand infantry could be landed in calm weather at some

'The English Tunnel Bugaboo',
American cartoon (1883) featuring Wolseley riding the British lion away
from the French cockerel

selected point. To his mind, 'the main argument against the construction of the tunnel is based upon this fact, for it is felt that our end of the tunnel could be thus seized, and that its seizure would place England at the mercy of the invading army that could then be passed through it' and supplied by means of it. Should that happen, he envisaged Britain having to make peace on terms which stipulated not only a crushing indemnity but the permanent occupation of the British end of the tunnel – 'Metz and Strasbourg were exacted from France in 1871'. He denied that Dover could be made impregnable: 'the strongest fortress in the world may be taken by surprise, or may be surrendered through cowardice or treachery'. He ended:

> Surely, John Bull will not endanger his birth-right, his liberty, his property, in fact all that men can hold most dear, whether he be a patriot or merely a selfish cosmopolitan, and whether this subject be regarded from a sentimental or from a material point of view, simply in order that men and women may cross to and fro between England and France without running the risk of sea-sickness.
>
> Even now when protected by our 'silver streak' we suffer from periodic panics, which are as injurious to trade as they are undignified; this tunnel would render their recurrence much more frequent, thereby increasing the loss they occasion. The night does not follow the day more surely than will a vastly increased annual military expenditure follow upon the construction of the tunnel. Are we to be taxed additionally for these new military establishments in order to save a certain number of travellers and tourists of all nations from sea-sickness?

This was dated 10 December 1881. Clearly Wolseley was in no mood to accept the invitation extended to him on 7 January 1882 by Sir Edward Watkin, who offered to provide a special train for a visit to and tour of the works between Folkestone and Dover, which had in the previous month formally been incorporated as the Submarine Railway Company.[12]

Sir John Adye's view was diametrically opposed to Wolseley's. Adye began from the more generous standpoint that a tunnel would bestow great advantages on both France and Britain as a result of improved facilities for general intercourse and for extended commerce. He stated 'that the idea of any great danger to this country being created by the completion of a submarine tunnel did not come across my mind when I heard of it, nor after more careful consideration of the circumstances has my opinion changed'. It was evident to him that Britain could not be attacked successfully by a direct advance through the tunnel; considering the ease with which the invading troops could be destroyed as they emerged, that idea could be dismissed: 'it hardly requires argument'.

Possession of the English end of the tunnel was the prerequisite to a successful invasion and that, so far as Adye was concerned, could only be obtained either by force or by treachery. He dismissed both. Force was not a problem, because if an invasion took place in such force as to be able to seize the British end of the tunnel, that force would be much more inclined to march on London and end the whole campaign: 'Why . . . should an enemy, having successfully invaded England, turn aside to capture a very doubtful line of communication, when the main object of his efforts was straight before him?' As for treachery, this seemed hardly possible:

> Unless it were seized by a party of sufficient strength to hold it for a time, such an attempt would be useless; and where are the men to come from who would have it in their power to exercise such treachery? I do not quite follow the arguments of those who urge that treachery is practicable in such a case, that is, how a sufficient body of foreign troops is to be brought over and placed in possession of our end of the tunnel.

Just as the defence of the tunnel exit was, for Adye, 'a simple operation', so was the general destruction of the tunnel as a whole; as to its dangers in a military sense, he said that with the taking of 'the most ordinary precautions, I am unable to perceive them'. He went far beyond this position, however, and far beyond that of Wolseley:

> Even supposing that a certain amount of danger were caused to this country by the construction of a submarine tunnel from France, I do not think that circumstance in itself would be a sufficient argument against its construction. The advantages of increased means of intercourse between the two countries, and the facilities for commerce etc., may be so great as to overbalance the possible disadvantages.

Where Wolseley saw a tunnel as a bait tempting France to invade, Adye saw one as a way of so cementing Anglo-French relations as to remove that temptation altogether. The argument that because a certain course might lead to a possible danger in war one should peremptorily put a veto on that course, and therefore be deprived of the advantages available in peacetime, was in his view not a sound argument. He also pointed out that the tunnels under the Alps presented greater dangers to the countries concerned than one under the Channel would present to Britain (he was referring here to the seven miles long Mont-Cenis tunnel, which had opened in 1872; the St-Gothard tunnel was nearing completion, and was opened to traffic in June 1882) and that the nations on both sides of those mountains remained confident that they could prevent the adverse use of those tunnels in wartime. His final paragraph illustrated this point:

> I would point out that all the great Continental Powers of Europe are united, as it were, by a net-work of railways, roads, and river communications, all of which afford ready means for invasion in case of war; dangers far and away greater than any we can incur by one long tunnel from one country necessarily terminating at a fixed point or exit in the other. The Continental Powers, however, do not dream of interdicting or blocking these international highways in peacetime, because they feel, and rightly so, that the remedy would be far worse than the disease . . . Consequently, whilst alive to the possible dangers, they confine themselves to minimising them in time of war by obvious military precautions. This is exactly what we shall have to do when the tunnel is completed, but the precautions to be taken by us are fortunately of a very simple character as compared to those entailed on the Continental Powers.

Farrer, Phillimore and Jones were in no position to arbitrate between two such heavyweights as Wolseley and Adye, and immediately said as much to Joseph Chamberlain, the President of the Board of Trade. Chamberlain agreed – decisions on a question that was clearly becoming a question of some magnitude could not rest with a committee appointed at the instance of one department, but must be settled on the responsibility of the Government as a whole. The committee of three was thanked for the services it had rendered, and was dismissed on 2 February 1882.

On 31 January Admiral Sir A. Cooper Key, a member of the Board of Admiralty, had written to the First Lord, Northbrook, a letter which broke new ground so far as the Navy was concerned. Cooper Key was of the same persuasion as Wolseley. To Wolseley's arguments about increased expenditure and a standing army he added very little. A new argument was the probability that, if a tunnel was built, a large proportion of the goods now conveyed by sea would then be conveyed by land: 'the commercial advantages would be thus obtained at the expense of our shipping interest, one of the chief sources of our greatness and strength'. What really agitated Cooper Key was the future role of the Navy:

> We have hitherto considered it our chief duty to ensure the command of the Channel by an efficient fleet; of what avail will that fleet be if an enemy can go under the Channel? We have hitherto felt satisfied that even if an enemy effected a landing on our shores, while our fleet was engaged elsewhere, it would be impossible for him to maintain and supply his troops if we cut him off

from the base of his operations. These safeguards no longer exist if he can reinforce his troops and supply them with ammunition and stores by land.

In his view, it was not necessary to prove how an enemy could use the tunnel for purposes of invasion – it was sufficient to indicate the mere possibility. He asserted 'most confidently' that a simple fortification guarding the tunnel exit and the apparatus for destroying it would be 'utterly insufficient'. A small force sent through by rail, aided of course by treachery, together with other forces landed on both flanks, and the enemy would have possession. Four hours would then be enough to enable 100,000 men to assemble, who would be joined within a few hours by as many more. That army would then march on London. Behind this scenario lay another one, that of a redundant but expensive Navy, 'looking on as a helpless spectator'. The elements of an unholy alliance with the Adjutant-General were clearly present.

To this unholy alliance should be added the most senior officials of the Foreign Office. Lord Tenterden and Sir Charles Dilke, the Permanent Under Secretaries, discussed the matter at the beginning of March, and wrote notes for the Foreign Secretary embodying their concern. Tenterden was concerned primarily about a war with France or with France and other Powers in alliance: if in such a war England should be defeated, 'the French and their allies would undoubtedly make it a condition of peace that the Tunnel if destroyed should be repaired and placed in French possession'. England would then be 'at the mercy of France', and would face a long struggle to recover her position. Dilke thought there were several difficulties about the tunnel that justified the hesitation of the public and the press. One was the risk of seizure by soldiers disguised as civilians in time of peace. Another was the complications which would arise if in the event of a war between Germany and France the Germans should seize and hold the French end. Yet another was that 'it is certain that when the tunnel once exists people will begin to say "what a shameful waste of money it will be to blow it up or flood it at the bare risk of war. Let us have its neutrality declared under European sanction", and so we might be lulled to sleep, only to wake when it was too late'.[13]

When Tenterden discovered that another official, Sir Edward Hertslet, the Foreign Office Librarian, had very similar views he encouraged him to develop them in a memorandum. Hertslet's memorandum, dated 13 March 1882, emphasised certain contradictions in the current state of affairs. On the one hand there was Lord Richard Grosvenor's Channel Tunnel Company, which had obtained a special Act of Parliament in

1875, and which was bound by the Projet of the British and French Commissioners of 1876 to come to an arrangement with a French Company before 2 August 1880. This, stated Hertslet, they had failed to do, 'thereby admitting the many difficulties which stand in the way'. Moreover, they had not commenced any actual boring of the tunnel itself, although they had acquired land near Dover. They now had another Bill before Parliament, in which they asked for fresh powers to purchase more land, for the purpose of making a railway in connection with the tunnel, and in which they referred to the fact that it was laid down in the Projet of 1876 that they should come to an agreement with the French company before a certain date; however, they had omitted to state the fact that the date for agreement had been fixed, and had expired on 2 August 1880. All they said was that negotiations had taken place. Was this sufficient, asked Hertslet, and could they keep open indefinitely the period within which they were to come to an agreement with the French company, bearing in mind that no treaty upon the subject had yet been concluded between England and France? On the other hand was the South-Eastern Railway Company of Sir Edward Watkin, which had obtained permission, by a clause in their General Act of 1874, to spend money on preliminary investigations with reference to a projected Channel Tunnel, and which had obtained further powers by their General Act of 1881 to purchase land for that purpose. *They* had commenced to make *their* tunnel, and were now asking Parliament for further powers to acquire more land, and for making a railway between Folkestone and Dover in connection with that tunnel. That tunnel, however, was not the one which the Joint English and French Commissioners had alluded to in their Projet of 31 May 1876. As the Joint Commissioners had contemplated the conclusion of an agreement between the English company and the French company, as well as a treaty betwen England and France, *before* the tunnel was made, 'Is it right', asked Hertslet, 'to allow the South-Eastern Railway to go on with their works without H.M.'s Government knowing whether they have any Agreement with a French Company on the other side, and which could only be with the same French Company, represented by M. Michel Chevalier and others, to whom the French Concession was granted in 1875, since the French Government undertook not to grant a similar Concession to any other French Company for the term of thirty years . . . '? Hertslet wanted to know if the Concession granted by the French Government to the Channel Tunnel Company 2 August 1875 had lapsed, in consequence of the English and French companies having failed to conclude an agreement between themselves within the time specified. If it had not lapsed, he wanted to know how much longer the period would be for the making of that agreement. He wanted to know when the Treaty between England and France was to be concluded, and took it that the Projet of 31 May 1876 'would appear to have entirely lapsed'. He wanted to know if the bases recommended on 31 May 1876 had been 'sufficiently well considered to enable the two Governments to conclude a Treaty'. He wanted to know whether there were to be two tunnels, one made by the Channel Tunnel Company under its Special Act, and the other under the South-Eastern Railway Company's General Act. Finally, he wanted to know how far either, or both, of these tunnels were to be allowed to advance towards completion 'before the Government step in and define clearly the bases upon which they are to be constructed'.[14]

Tenterden supplemented Hertslet's memorandum, which he described as 'able and interesting', with one of his own. He maintained that a tunnel would 'materially alter the relations in which this country stands towards the Continent of Europe, and especially France'. He quoted, out of context, a phrase used by the French Minister of Public Works in his Report of 13 July 1874: 'For a long time Great Britain has shown herself proud of her isolation from the Continent as a guarantee of independence'. Next, he quoted a paragraph from the Report of the Committee of the French National Assembly which contained a passage saying that one could not but note that England, far from suffering from her isolation, was happy about it and enjoyed, under the protection of her fleet, a security envied by other peoples. What Tenterden did not say, and what the rest of the Report, which he did not quote, made clear, was that this referred to the years 1805 to 1825. Nor did he quote what the Chairman of the Committee of the National Assembly had told that body on 21 July 1875, namely that the Channel Tunnel project had not produced any difficulty in the breast of the Commission nor anywhere else.

Tenterden's hostile attitude became more explicit as he went on, with clear echoes of both General Wolseley and Admiral Cooper Key. Ignoring the fact that both the British and French War Offices had reserved their positions, he stated:

It does not appear that consideration has at any time been given to the possibility of an European coalition against England, resulting in a successful invasion, and in England being compelled to accept conditions of peace, one of which would undoubtedly be that the Tunnel, if destroyed, should be repaired at the cost of this country, and placed under the control of the conqueror.

Or, the Tunnel might have failed to be destroyed, under some conditions of neutralization into which England might have been deluded.

It is not difficult to suppose a number of contingencies in which the possession of the Tunnel might be the object of secret arrangements among other Powers, which, however improbable they may at present appear, cannot safely be ignored.

At present England is secure because she is out of reach; but once let there be a possibility that by a successful war the conquest of England and the command of her vast resources could be secured, a prospect would be opened to French statesmen which it might be very difficult for a man of genius and ambition to resist.

If the Tunnel is once constructed the immunity of isolation which England has hitherto enjoyed in regard to continental disputes will be at an end. For instance, with reference to contraband of war, we have always contended that our neutrality was sufficiently maintained by the right of capture conceded to belligerents at sea; but it would become necessary to alter our legislation under the penalty of becoming involved in endless complications with regard to the supply to munitions of war or articles such as electric batteries capable of being used in war.

Many other considerations will readily present themselves to any one who reflects on the matter, among which I would especially point out the administrative difficulty of acting with sufficient decision and promptitude in an emergency, should it be necessary to suddenly destroy the Tunnel.[15]

When Tenterden and Dilke had sent the Foreign Secretary their original notes of 5 March, Granville had minuted, 'I am rather in a difficulty about this scheme which I will tell you when we meet'. He embodied his difficulty in an answer to a parliamentary question which he drafted himself, saying that there was to be no publication of any proceedings of committees 'until HMG have decided whether or not to reverse the policy of the late Government which formally approved of the Tunnel scheme and communicated that approval to the French Government'.[16]

Granville's problem, which was a compound of the problem of continuity and of problems with the French if continuity was interrupted, was about to be shelved, if not solved, by the action of the Secretary of State for War.

4. From War Office Scientific Committee to the Duke of Cambridge

At this stage Childers, the Secretary of State for War in Mr Gladstone's Government, decided to seize the initiative from the Board of Trade. Chamberlain was informed that, before the Government considered the Channel Tunnel question on the wider ground of national interests, the War Office intended to appoint a committee of engineers and scientists to consider whether the tunnel and its approaches could be rendered absolutely useless to an enemy, and in what manner. This committee, said Childers, 'should consider what appliances whether of destruction or of obstruction, or of flooding, or all combined including any works defending or commanding the exit should be provided, so that the use of the Tunnel in every imaginable contingency may be, beyond doubt, denied to an enemy'.[17] Childers' words 'every imaginable contingency' were to dog the discussion of this question for decades to come.

The head of the Intelligence Department, Major-General Sir A. Alison, was selected to chair this 'Scientific Committee'. The other serving officers on the committee were Major-General Gallwey, the Inspector-General of Fortifications; Colonel Sir John Stokes, the Deputy Adjutant-General; Colonel Sir Andrew Clarke, Commandant of the School of Military Engineering; Colonel H. J. Alderson, Assistant Director of Artillery and Stores; Colonel V. D. Majendie, the Chief Inspector of Explosives (Home Office). There were also three civilians: W. H. Barlow, a Fellow of the Royal Society; E. Graves, Engineer-in-Chief to the General Post Office; and Professor Abel, Chemist to the War Department. At least one member displayed much sympathy towards the cause of a Channel Tunnel. This was Colonel Sir A. Clarke, who likened the current opposition to a tunnel to the agitation and speculation which had accompanied the building of the railways fifty years earlier:

> It was said by military authorities that the establishment of such improved means of communication and locomotion would tend to weaken and destroy the obstacles nature had given our island home to check the advance of an invader. Those who examined the evidence given before the Select Committee of the House of Commons that sat to enquire into the project for a line of railway from Southampton to London . . . will doubtless find that there were then objectors who asserted that the existence of such a line would offer a tempting invitation to an enemy's fleet for the occupation of the Solent and Southampton water, and to use those places as a base from which to operate on London.

Clarke effectively trumped Wolseley by recalling a note by the Duke of Wellington in the records of the Horse Guards, deprecating the fears expressed about railway development, and showing that this new 'resource of civilisation' added materially to the strength and in no way diminished the defensive power of the country. Bearing this in mind, said Clarke, he was the more surprised that in the present instance the experience of the past did not appear to be a ground of confidence in the present amongst what he called 'the new alarmists': 'It would seem as though any such scheme were to be regarded with the same fear and apprehension on the part of respectable authorities as was the construction of the South-Western Railway'.

Clarke was not disposed to attach much importance to danger arising from French policy or actions. He was actually more impressed with the possibility of an Anglo-Russian clash, in which case a Channel Tunnel would have distinct advantages:

> Preserving our alliance with France – an alliance which, if carried into active operation, would enable the two countries to defy the world . . . – our troops, munitions, and materials could more readily be advanced to any place of attack by the agency which a tunnel would afford; whilst at the same time our fleet, relieved from guarding our commerce in the tunnel, would be free to operate elsewhere. The tunnel would, in fact, be a link literally binding the two countries more closely.

Moving on to a consideration of the actual facility for attack on Britain which it was said the tunnel would afford, Clarke first stated that 'the importance of the protection which "the silver streak" gives has itself been somewhat magnified at the expense of the tunnel scheme'. A French commander, ordered to invade Britain, would use steam transport, rather than any tunnel. A theoretical surprise attack by 2,000 troops was 'a simple impossibility':

> Are these troops to come without arms and without uniforms, so that their passage and arrival may not be suspected? The sudden movement of such a body could not elude suspicion, for we cannot suppose that all this movement could go on without the railway subordinates, the military or the police getting some hint of it. And even if the 2,000 men could be secretly conveyed, it is not to be forgotten that their passage would have to be preceded by the massing of an immense force of troops on the other side, which force, it is supposed, might be brought over after the tunnel was secured. Such a massing of troops would, of course, not be the matter of an hour, and it would, if anything, be as difficult to keep secret as the passage of the 2,000.

On the supposition that 2,000 men had got through, Clarke maintained that it would be impossible for them to achieve anything – the difficulty of passing the main body, with its horses and material through a narrow tunnel in a short time would be 'simply insuperable'. Even allowing for an initial surprise, 'a force which could only issue from the end of a caterpillar-like structure in driblets would soon find itself disseminated'. Furthermore, it was 'absurd to suppose that the art of the military engineer is so exhausted that the tunnel itself could not be secured . . . the resources of military forethought and science are not so used up, but that we could reduce to a minimum, if not obliterate, all possible risk of danger or even of panic from the making of a tunnel . . . ' For instance, there was the suggestion of driving a sub-way from Dover Castle to within 15/20 feet of the tunnel, and placing at that point enough dynamite to destroy any life in the tunnel and effectively prevent its further offensive use. Unless Dover Castle was taken, this sub-way would be secure; others could be made.

Clarke ended on a generous note similar to that of General Adye, a note which contained an admonition to his peers:

> . . . if the industrial and social progress of our country, and the larger interests of humanity can be promoted by a work of this kind, it is not the *rôle* of the soldier to check the aspirations of his countrymen. They rather, ignoring the imputations that may be made as to the promoters and capitalists being guilty of merely ignoble and sordid motives, let him exercise his service and his art for the removal and not the creation of obstacles to enterprise.

Having interviewed Watkin, Grosvenor and Hawkshaw, the Alison Committee reported on 12 May 1882. Their conclusions were, in effect:

1 It was undesirable that the end of the tunnel should be within effective range of the sea.

2 The tunnel should not emerge within any fortification; its exit, as well as the air-shafts, and pumping apparatus, should be commanded by the advanced works of a fortress.

3 There should be means of closing the tunnel by a portcullis; and of discharging poisonous ('irrespirable') gases into it (Professor Abel, Chemist to the War Department, was a member of the Committee which contemplated this early foray into the realms of chemical warfare).

4 There should be provision for producing the temporary demolition of the land portion of the tunnel by means of mining.

5 There should be arrangements for a temporary flooding of the tunnel by sluices.

6 There should be arrangements for a permanent flooding of the tunnel by mines which should open a direct communication between the bottom of the sea and the tunnel.

7 The mechanical arrangements required for temporary obstruction should be capable of being controlled from different points within the fortifications, and the means of destroying the tunnel should be controlled, not only from the central work of the fortress, but also from one or more distant places, which should have independent communications with the mines, separate from those of the fortress.

Neither the Channel Tunnel Company's scheme, nor that of the South Eastern Railway Company, which founded the Submarine Railway Company in December 1881, met all the above conditions, and the Alison Committee could not recommend that either of them, as at present planned, be sanctioned. The Report ended with the following statement to Childers:

It is only by the multiplication of means, which can be placed under the control of independent authorities acting from different localities, that [the] element of uncertainty can be to the greatest extent minimised, and these considerations your Committee have steadily kept in view in the recommendations which they have made. But they cannot disregard the possibility that a long period of peace and uninterrupted tranquillity might engender carelessness in maintaining in good working condition the arrangements applied to the partial or complete destruction of the tunnel, and might lead to fortifications being left so inefficiently armed or insufficiently manned as not to be secure against surprise. They therefore desire to record their opinion that it would be presumptuous to place absolute reliance upon even the most comprehensive and complete arrangements which can be devised, with a view of rendering the tunnel 'absolutely useless to an enemy', 'in every imaginable contingency'.[18]

The Report of the Alison Committee made no difference to Adye. He commented that in his judgement the recommendations were sound and practical, and could be carried out 'without great cost or difficulty'. 'Nothing', he said, 'is more obvious than the facility with which the tunnel can be denied to an enemy, by means which no vigilance on his part could prevent or remove.' Childers sent the Report, and this comment by Adye, to H.R.H. the Duke of Cambridge, Field-Marshal Commanding-in-Chief of the Army.

The voice of the Duke Cambridge was to be the decisive one. At the beginning of the year, on receipt of Wolseley's memorandum, he had written to the Adjutant-General: 'I can assure you I am just as anxious as you can be that the Channel Tunnel should not be carried out as I believe it to be a most dangerous element of attack as the cause of Foreign Wars and complications.' He had gone on to say that the more Wolseley's and his own views were made known the better he would be pleased, 'in the hope that by drawing public attention to the subject this mischievous project may after all be given up'. He had lobbied Childers with a view to getting him to release Wolseley's memorandum from its confidential status, and agreement had been reached that Wolseley's views should be published in an article by Lord Dunsany in the February issue of *The Nineteenth Century*. He had made a further suggestion to Wolseley, writing:

> If there are portions of your Minute which it may be thought safer to leave out such as direct allusion to a *French* invasion, why not leave the present Minute as a Confidential one and write another based upon the precautions to be put forward by the Military authorities to the Chairman of the Company and take care it is sent to the public prints for publication in the shape of an official protest. I am quite prepared to put upon it officially that I fully concur in the views therein expressed, having already done so on your Confidential minute.

Wolseley's vastly extended memorandum of 16 June 1882 was the result of his taking the Duke of Cambridge's advice. The Duke had also suggested, to Childers, that the Alison Committee should be composed purely of military officers; in this he was not successful, as Childers insisted that 'the military opinion must come afterwards, when the means of destroying the Tunnel have been sifted'.[19]

With the report of the Alison Committee in his hands, the time had come for the Duke of Cambridge to pronounce. He claimed, in effect, that the voices of Adye and Clarke were unrepresentative of opinion in the Army. The view of the officers 'on whose judgement I should myself be disposed to rely', he said, were almost unanimous in the sense represented by Wolseley, which was none too subtle a way of leading from the front. He criticised Adye for not strictly adhering to the wording of the Report in commenting upon it. Adye had said that the Alison Committee urged that 'whilst the land portion of the tunnel should be constructed in the vicinity of a fortress . . . ' Cambridge pointed out that the Committee's actual words were: 'it is *imperative* that the tunnel should emerge in the immediate vicinity *of a first-class fortress in the modern acceptation of the term*, a fortress which could only be reduced after a protracted siege by land and sea'. This made all the difference, for 'a first-class fortress in the modern acceptation of the term' meant such a fortress as could not be built for less than £3,000,000, and which would require a garrison equal to the great garrisons on the Continent, i.e. between 7,000 and 11,000 men, which would be another absolute additional cost upon the country.

   The Duke of Cambridge was prepared to insist that all the arrangements suggested by the Report should first be costed in great detail, and that the whole of the money required should be paid over to the Treasury by the promoters before permission was given to begin the tunnel at all. He was happy to think that the Report amounted to 'an absolute condemnation' of all the current proposals, and was determined that any modified proposals be submitted to the very same Committee, rather than be treated as a departmental question, as he gathered Adye wished. He again attacked Adye for treating as 'trivial and insignificant' what the Committee had regarded as 'a grave national danger to be provided against by a vast multiplication of precautions, and on which, moreover, they are unable in any case to place absolute reliance'. Like the Committee, the Duke of Cambridge did not believe that immunity from danger could be engineered. No reliance could be placed on the electrical communication with distant points unless the wires were tested every few hours, he maintained. All therefore depended on the security of the new fortress and on the adoption of precautionary measures when there was a prospect of war. But as the stoppage of the tunnel would be taken as a sure indication of coming war, an English Cabinet would be unwilling to order it. The majority of wars had begun before diplomatic relations had been broken off, according to a paper which he had ordered the Intelligence Department to prepare, and which he enclosed. It was not only the possibility of a rupture with France that had to be considered. Any power at war with France, after taking possession of Belgium might seize Calais, and 'might find it convenient to punish an alliance of ours with France by a sudden seizure of Dover'. He referred to the fact that only a few years ago Chester Castle had been the object of an attack by the Fenians: 'Who can guarantee us that such a seizure of Dover by persons from within might not be made?' The only positive security against the danger of the tunnel would be the maintenance of a vast army, entailing probably a compulsory system of universal military service. His duty, on military grounds, was to protest most emphatically against the construction of the tunnel. This protest was delivered to Childers on 23 June 1882.

5. Parliamentary Joint Select Committee, 1883

Throughout 1882 the Channel Tunnel issue was kept very much in the public eye, in addition to the attention it received at the level of certain government departments. Coverage in newspapers and journals, and in Parliament, greatly exceeded that given in the previous year. The influential monthly *The Nineteenth Century*, which had led the way by allowing Lord Dunsany to pronounce on the merits of the 'silver streak' in its issue of May 1881, devoted its efforts in the spring of 1882 to the registering of a sustained protest. This took the form of a commissioned petition, and the names of the signatories were printed in the April and May issues. James Knowles, the editor of *The Nineteenth Century*, had attempted but had failed to induce the Duke of Cambridge to allow his name to be placed at the head of this 'Protest against this mad project of turning England into a promontory of France'.[20] The signatories included the former Home Secretary R.A. Cross; Cardinal Manning; the Bishop of Gloucester and Bristol; the Poet Laureate, Lord Tennyson; Robert Browning; Herbert Spencer; the Governor of the Bank of England, H. R. Grenfell; the editors of the *Spectator*, the *Morning Post*, the *St James's Gazette* and *Lloyd's Weekly News*. The House of Lords, the Church of England and the magistracy were especially well represented: the columns of Reverends and JPs very nearly equalled those composed of Lieutenant-Generals, Major-Generals, Lieutenant-Colonels, Majors and Captains. In the March issue, John Fowler had been allowed to put forward his Ferry scheme, under the heading 'The Channel Passage: An alternative'.[21] One of the ploys devised by *The Nineteenth Century* rather backfired. The editor appealed to the London Trades Council which represented forty-six organised trade societies and had nearly 15,000 members in London alone, to sign the protest. Instead, the annual delegate meeting held in April 1882 unanimously passed a resolution: 'That this delegate meeting believes that the opposition to the Channel Tunnel is absurd, and expresses its astonishment at such opposition receiving the least countenance from anyone connected with the cause of labour, and considers that instead of such project of industrial progress being prejudicial it would be to the interests of this country if carried out, and tend to unite the sympathies and welfare of the peoples of England and France.'[22] This, as will be seen in due course, was not lost on the Prime Minister of the day.

The proceedings of Parliament were peppered with questions relating to the successive enquiries that were known to be under way, and with requests for the publication of the relevant papers. Concern was also expressed that experimental digging was continuing. The question of the rights of the Crown to the foreshore at Dover was raised, and on 30 March Joseph Chamberlain announced that a case would be submitted to the Law Officers of the Crown. He added that the Chairman of the South Eastern Railway Company (Watkin) had been warned that the Government claimed the bed of the sea below low-water mark, for three miles. On 21 April Chamberlain stated that he had given 'most explicit directions' to the South Eastern Railway Company that its works were not to proceed below the level of low water. On 1 May he stated that 'the Government had come to the conclusion that it was desirable that what is called the experimental boring of the Channel Tunnel should be stopped, and that further expenses should, as far as possible, be avoided, until Parliament has come to a decision whether the Channel Tunnel is to be made or not'. The Board of Trade continued to harass Watkin, who maintained that not only had he every right to continue digging, but that the digging was a continuous process which could not simply be switched on or off. On 26 June Chamberlain accused Watkin's Submarine Continental Railway Company of having 'persistently evaded' the demands of the Board of Trade. Watkin, who had already appealed to Gladstone, and received a reply suggesting that the harassment would cease, strongly denied the charge:

> If the President of the Board of Trade, who several times has been invited to visit the works, and who three times agreed to do so, but in no case joined the special train provided for him, had inspected the works personally, as the Prime Minister and the Minister of War did, it is believed that no difficulty of any kind would have arisen, always assuming that the President is in favour of the construction of the Tunnel, and not opposed to it.

Chamberlain took Watkin to the High Court on 5 July, and obtained a ruling which reinforced his 'explicit directions' of 28 April. Visits by representatives of the Railway Department of the Board of Trade were made to the workings. These established that the diggers had gone at least 600 yards too far. The Solicitor to the Board of Trade accused Watkin of 'a flagrant breach of faith' and reminded him that the Court

Order of 5 July 'must be strictly and literally adhered to'. The South Eastern Railway Company protested once again, their lawyers saying that they did not wish to keep on referring to previous correspondence, 'but when the Government has been asked in vain, and over and over again, to declare its policy on the main question – tunnel or no tunnel – surely my clients might fairly lay claim to more considerate treatment'. The Submarine Railway Company then wrote to Gladstone, asking him to intervene, as the head of the Government, 'to protect us from a course which we believe to be entirely unprecedented in the industrial history of the country'. Gladstone on 31 July would not undertake to interfere with the Board of Trade; he did, however, agree to the request of the directors of the company that their correspondence with the Board of Trade be laid before Parliament, and indicated that this would happen within a fortnight.

Two weeks later, on 15 August 1882, both the above-mentioned papers and others relating to the project since 1870 were published as a Parliamentary Blue Book. They were formally presented to Chamberlain, who announced the two conclusions at which the Government had arrived. The first of these was that 'they cannot advise that the two Bills now before the House should, at all events in their present form, be allowed to proceed any further'; the second was that a Joint Committee of both Houses of Parliament would be set up, at the beginning of the next session, 'to consider the whole matter'.[23] Also on 15 August, the South Eastern Railway Company and the Submarine Continental Company found themselves accused of a breach of the injunction of 5 July, and therefore of a contempt of court, and the object of a sequestration order. In the High Court the following day they undertook not to work the boring machinery for any purpose whatever except on application in writing to and permission in writing from the Board of Trade. The Court ordered that the hearing of the sequestration order should stand over.

The announcement of the Joint Select Committee of Parliament was made by Granville, the Foreign Secretary, in the House of Lords on 26 February 1883. Salisbury, from the Opposition front bench, called this 'a Constitutional precedent of no little Magnitude'. Granville, for his part, said that the question was one 'which must be decided very much upon its general merits, and not in regard to the particular policy of any foreign country at this particular moment'. On 3 April, in the House of Commons, Chamberlain justified the Government's decision on the grounds that the enquiries thus far had been only partial ones:

there had been no attempt to exhaust the evidence, favourable or unfavourable, as to the effect of the Tunnel on commerce; . . . the advantages of greater
facilities of communication had not been brought in any prominent way before
the Committee previously; . . . the general military question had not been fully
discussed . . . it was desirable that further evidence should be taken on the
subject; . . . that the House and the Government should be in a position to
weigh the balance of advantages before they were asked to come to any
conclusions in the matter.

Gladstone followed, and justified the procedure decided upon by argu-
ing that his Government's freedom had been circumscribed by the step
taken by the previous government of entering into communications with
the French Government. The adoption of a common organ for the two
Governments, and the adoption of the scheme in principle by each of
them; the discussion and determination of the conditions on which the
scheme ought to be executed; and the recommendation that a treaty
should be framed, bound all subsequent Administrations. Since that
time, he went on, public opinion 'in certain quarters at any rate', had
taken a new turn. Only one authority was superior to the Executive
Government, and was not bound to recognise the Commission or the
Report of the Commission, and that was Parliament, and that 'Parliament is the master of the situation' was something fully recognised by the
French. Hence the conclusion that 'there is no other course open to us
but to submit the matter to the judgement of the two Houses of
Parliament, and especially of the Representative Chamber, as being now
the only free, competent, independent, and legitimate authority to
declare the judgement of the country on a matter in which it will be
admitted that the judgement of the country ought to be given, whatever
the judgement may be'.[24]

　　Childers, now Chancellor of the Exchequer, put another gloss on this.
He said that the state of affairs when the present Government took
office was that the late Government 'was committed up to the hilt in
favour of the project'. The present Government, having opened their
own enquiries, was now coming to the House, and saying to the Conservatives: 'You have practically committed the country up to the hilt to the
arrangement with France. Is it not right that Parliament should complete the enquiries, which up to this point have not dealt with important
parts of the question, before a decision is taken to break off or to carry on
the negotiations?'[25] Viewed in this perspective, the Board of Trade
committee and the Alison Committee were steps of a preparatory
nature, taken with a view to getting the Liberal Government, ultimately,
off the hook on which its Conservative predecessor had placed it.

One reason why the next step was a Joint Select Committee, however, is that the Conservative Party at the time was engaged in a policy described later by Gladstone as one of 'systematic obstruction' in the carrying on of public business, This is why, said Gladstone, his Government felt that it could not give up the necessary parliamentary time to the Channel Tunnel issue: 'We considered at the time it was not compatible with our duty to press forward an important Bill which would have required that extraordinary facilities should be provided for the discussion of the subject.'[26]

The leader of the Conservatives, Lord Salisbury, who had maintained that the matter of the Channel Tunnel was one on which an executive decision by Government, rather than a reference to Parliament, was appropriate, carried his obstructiveness to the point of insisting that the Government must take the whole responsibility of nominating all the members of the Select Committee. Although the Government had said that it would not consider itself bound by the Report of this Committee, merely that it 'will certainly attach very great weight' to it,[27] it was not to be caught out in quite this way, and brought into play the Committee of Selection to nominate the Joint Select Committee. The latter consisted of Lord Lansdowne (Chairman), the Earl of Devon, the Earl of Camperdown, Lord Aberdare, Lord Shute; Sir H. H. Vivian, Sir M. Lopes, Mr Baxter, Mr Peel and Mr Harcourt. This Committee started its meetings on 20 April and finished them on 21 June 1883. They interviewed the following persons:

Sir E. Watkin, MP, Chairman of South Eastern Railway Company
Sir F. Bramwell, Vice-President, Institute of Civil Engineers
Lord R. Grosvenor, MP, Chairman of Channel Tunnel Company
Sir J. Hawkshaw, Engineer to Channel Tunnel Company
Mr James Allport, Director of Midland Railway Company
Mr James Grierson, General Manager of Great Western Railway Company
Mr Henry Oakley, General Manager of Great Northern Railway Company
General Hutchinson, Railway Inspector, Board of Trade
Mr Samuelson, MP
Mr H. Lee, MP
Mr I. Holden, MP
Mr J. Slagg, MP, President of Manchester Chamber of Commerce
Mr G. Shipton, Secretary to London Trades Council
Mr G. Wedgewood, Senior Partner, Josiah Wedgewood and Sons
Colonel Yolland, Inspector, Board of Trade
Colonel Beaumont, Royal Engineers
Mr James Staats Forbes, Chairman of London, Chatham and Dover Railway
    Company
Mr C.M. Palmer, MP, Chairman, Steamship Owners' Association

Mr R. Giffen, Commercial Department, Board of Trade
Mr H.R. Grenfell, Director of the Bank of England
Mr R. Capper, General Superintendent of Swansea Harbour Trust
Sir J. Lintorn Simmons, Inspector-General of Fortifications (retired)
Vice-Admiral E.B. Rice, C-in-C at Sheerness
Mr G.R. Blanchard, Vice-President of the Erie Railway
Admiral Sir A. Cooper Key, Senior Naval Lord of the Admiralty
Colonel Sir A. Clarke, Inspector-General of Fortifications
Lieutenant-General Sir A. Alison
Sir F. Abel
Sir A. Otway, MP
Mr John Fowler
H.R.H. the Duke of Cambridge
Mr W.F. Ecroyd, MP, Woollen manufacturer
Admiral Sir J. Hay, MP
Mr F. Brady, Engineer-in-Chief, South Eastern Railway Company
Sir G. Elliot MP, President of the Association of Mining Engineers
Mr C.M. Kennedy, Head of the Commercial Department, Foreign Office
Sir J. Behrens, Woollen manufacturer
Colonel Majendie, Chief Inspector of Explosives
Lord Wolseley, Adjutant-General of the Forces
Sir P. MacDougall, Chief of Intelligence Department (retired)

Of the above, ten were military officers, three were naval officers, ten came from manufacturing and commerce, twelve from railways and engineering, and two from Government Departments.

By 10 July Lord Lansdowne had completed his report. It was entirely favourable to the Channel Tunnel scheme. With regard to 'commercial or other' advantages the most important paragraphs were nos 47 to 50:

47 We cannot doubt that the tunnel, once opened, would not only afford a profitable and expeditious route for the conveyance of a portion of the goods traffic already in existence, but would lead to a large expansion of the trade between this country and the Continent. We share the belief expressed, almost unanimously, by the witnesses who have appeared before us as representatives of various commercial interests in this country, that the introduction of improved facilities for communication between one country, or one district, and another, has invariably led, if not to the creation of new trades and new industries, at all events to a development, often far in excess of the most sanguine expectations, of those already in existence.

48 Such an expansion of trade has followed from the introduction of through rates, and from the removal of interruptions of gauges in this country, and from the establishment of improved communication and the overcoming of physical obstacles on the Continent of Europe and in America; and

we have no reason to doubt that it would follow, if the disadvantages occasioned to international commerce by the existence of the English Channel were to be successfully removed.

49 From such a development of the trade between the United Kingdom and the Continent this country would, it can scarcely be doubted, be the greatest gainer.

50 Owing to the peculiar position which it occupies in the commercial system of the world, it has, we believe, more to gain than any other nation by an improvement of its trade routes, and more to lose by the neglect of any opportunities which may present themselves for their improvement. The greatest distributor of commodities in the world, it is, above all nations, interested in the improvement of those channels through which that distribution is effected. This consideration is entitled to the greater weight, because the enterprise of our Continental competitors has, by the improvement of Continental harbours and the facilitation of through traffic in goods throughout the Continent, already been successful in threatening our supremacy in the *entrepôt* trade. We desire to express our belief that not the least material of the arguments in favour of the establishment of submarine communication is to be found in the fact that it would probably tend to retain for us a large amount of business which recent changes upon the Continent are already tending, and may still further tend, to divert from our ports.

The figures provided by Giffen, of the Board of Trade, pointed in one direction only, insisted Lansdowne:

72 We desire to insist particularly upon the importance in the interests of the large depôt trade carried on by this country of neglecting no opportunity which may present itself for the improvement of our trade communications. The figures which we have given show how large a part of the foreign and colonial produce which we import is re-exported to Germany, Holland, Belgium, and France, and that of this a large part follows the short sea route. The evidence which we have received shows that this trade is threatened by the increase of business at places like Antwerp, Havre, and Rotterdam, which are able to receive and distribute goods to the Continent. The fact that the chief manufacturing places on the Continent with which our business in the distribution of raw material is carried on are situated inland, would render it possible for direct railway carriage from this country to compete under favourable conditions with railway carriage between the same places and the continental ports.

Moving on to summarise the 'security as a nation' aspects, Lansdowne remarked that the 'apprehensions' urged against the tunnel were based on assumptions which in turn required conditions which, regarded separately, appeared to him 'highly improbable': 'That the whole of them should concur, we believe to be so nearly inconceivable as to justify us in dismissing from our minds any apprehensions founded upon such an hypothesis'. For instance, with regard to the anticipation that the capture of the tunnel might be helped by treachery, 'it is perhaps sufficient to observe that, happily, the records of this country afford little support for such a conjecture, and that if the existence of treachery be assumed, it would have to operate over an area so extensive as to render its success far from probable'. Finally, Lansdowne disposed of the argument that the tunnel might have to be ceded as a result of British defeat sustained in some other part of the globe. In the first place, he could not bring himself to believe that if the fate of the nation depended upon the destruction of the tunnel, the rulers of the country would refuse to give the necessary orders, or the military authorities refuse to carry them out. Secondly, it had to be pointed out that 'if it be once granted that this country has sustained a reverse so overwhelming as to oblige her to submit to the terms of a peace dictated by a victorious enemy, the presence of the tunnel, even if it were to remain intact, would not materially alter a position already assumed to be desperate:

> It would, we conclude, be a condition precedent to such reverse, that we had entirely lost the control of the sea, and that our armies had sustained a crushing defeat. It might be fairly contended that, under such circumstances the victors being absolute masters of the English Channel, would be able to bring across it, without hindrance, whatever supplies and reinforcements they might need for the subjection of this country. There would indeed, were our case so desperate as it is assumed to be, be nothing to prevent a victorious enemy from exacting the cession of the whole of our fleet and of our dockyards, and the demolition of our national defences, except such as he might himself retain.

Lansdowne pursued this logic to the bitter end: 'Finally, amongst the conditions imposed, it is conceivable that one might be the construction of the tunnel at our expense, and its cession to the invaders.'

This future Foreign Secretary brought together his verdicts on the commercial and security aspects in paragraph 135:

> We are of opinion that a great industrial enterprise, offering a prospect so encouraging, should not be arrested except for conclusive reasons. We have given our reasons for believing that in the case of this enterprise the reasons urged for arresting it are not conclusive. In order to show sufficient cause for interference on the part of the State under such circumstances, it is, in our opinion, not enough to prove that circumstances can be conceived under which the existence of a Channel Tunnel might involve a more or less remote risk to

the country, or that it is impracticable to devise precautions upon which absolute reliance might be placed 'in every imaginable contingency'. This is, however, all that has been done in the present instance by the opponents of the tunnel project. They have, with much ingenuity, assumed the presence of every condition favourable to the view which they entertain, and the absence of every condition unfavourable to it, but they have not been able to show that there is the slightest prospect of the simultaneous presence of the whole of those favourable conditions, and unless this be assumed the whole argument founded upon them falls to the ground.

Accordingly, 'we have no course open to us except to recommend that this enterprise should not be prohibited on merely political grounds, and that it be allowed to proceed, subject to the ordinary Parliamentary examination by Committees'.

The trouble was that only three members of his Select Committee – Aberdare, Baxter and Peel – were prepared to sign Lansdowne's report. The other six were all convinced that the Channel Tunnel should not be allowed to proceed. All six submitted separate reports, and none of these secured the entire approval of a majority of the Committee. It was the case, however, that a majority of the Committee believed that it was 'not expedient that Parliamentary Sanction should be given to a Submarine Communication between England and France'. This did get the Government off the particular hook that it had said it was on. On 17 July 1883 the Second Reading of the Channel Tunnel Railway Bill was deferred at the request of the Board of Trade. On the 24th Chamberlain told the House of Commons that the Government had accepted the six to four verdict of the Joint Select Committee; the following day he wrote to Gladstone, 'I do not think that any encouragement should be given to Sir E. Watkin'.[28] It had been a very close run thing.

In June 1890 Gladstone reflected that 'there are states of feeling which thrive by what they feed on; and that what is true of the love of money is also true of the love of panic . . . '[29] Gladstone's reflection was made in the course of a speech in the House of Commons in favour of a motion for the reading of a Channel Tunnel Bill. His speech closed with the words: 'I must repeat the sentiment which on every occasion I have been ready to express, and say that I believe this to be a considerable measure and a useful measure, and that the arguments opposed to it deserve neither acceptance nor respect.' The motion was lost, by 153 votes to 234. In 1883 Gladstone had maintained that there was no better place in which to establish the opinion of the British people than the House of Commons,[30] and he would have preferred that mode of procedure rather than that of the Joint Select Committee which he had to resort to because of Lord Salisbury's parliamentary obstructionism. In June 1890 Gladstone said that 'if you could get at the feelings of the sensible population of this country . . . the mass of the working population – I believe that it would be found that they look upon the opposition to the Channel Tunnel on the ground of danger as an almost preposterous opposition, and share none of those apprehensions which perplex [Sir M. Hicks Beach, the opposer of the motion]'. In 1883 Gladstone's 'Representative Chamber' had not been consulted; even if it had been, it did not represent 'the mass of the working population', and a majority of its Members would in all probability have been found to have been in the grip of the 'unreasoning panic' manufactured in certain War Office circles. That there had been a degree of manipulation, similar to that involved in the manufacture of the jingoism of 1877–78, when Conservative Party agents were instructed to report that the country wanted war with Russia,[31] is clear. Wolseley had wanted to write an article for *The Nineteenth Century* at the beginning of 1882.[32] With the connivance of the Duke of Cambridge and of Childers he had given his memorandum of December 1881 to Dunsany so that the latter might accomplish that particular mission. As late in the day as 8 August 1883 Mr Holland MP was asking Wolseley whether he should table a parliamentary question as to whether any steps were being taken to prevent the Channel Tunnel Company from continuing their boring operations, 'or do you think that I had better leave it alone? . . . Only one line to say that you advise it or not'.[33] Wolseley's victorious expedition to Egypt, which took place between the end of the Alison Committee and the beginning of the Joint Select Committee, added to Wolseley's reputation. On 5 June 1890 the House of Commons, in voting against the motion for a Channel Tunnel Bill, was still in the grip of the panic he had helped to engender. It always would be so long as he was on the scene and the Duke of Cambridge was Commander-in-Chief of the Army. Unfortunately for the promoters of the Channel Tunnel scheme, Wolseley succeeded Cambridge as Commander-in-Chief when the latter retired in 1895, and held the post himself until 1900.

Sir Edwards Watkin's Submarine Railway Company, which in 1882 had acquired the rights of the South Eastern Railway Company, absorbed Lord Richard Grosvenor's Channel Tunnel Company in 1886, having raised its capital to £275,000 in order to do so. It continued to introduce Bills and Motions into Parliament. All were either defeated or withdrawn. The treatment of one of them, in early 1894, allows an introduction to a figure of some subsequent importance. The Bill in question was the Channel Tunnel (Experimental Works) Bill, which the Treasury sent on to the War Office. There, the Permanent Under Secretary wrote: 'I am strongly opposed to this tunnel and I believe its construction would be a national misfortune'; the Adjutant-General minuted for the Secretary of State: 'I suppose we should continue to oppose?' The Secretary of State for War in Gladstone's final Government was Sir Henry Campbell-Bannerman. The War Office returned the Bill to the Treasury on 19 February, the writer stating:

> I am directed by Mr Secretary Campbell-Bannerman to acquaint you . . . that on each occasion of a Bill being brought forward for the construction of a tunnel between this country and France, his predecessors have, on military grounds, expressed themselves as opposed to the measure; and he sees no reason for adopting a different course as regards the present Bill; which though not purporting to sanction the actual construction of a working tunnel, would be a direct step towards such a result.[34]

6. The Troisième Bureau and French Invasion Plans

There is another figure of subsequent importance who requires an introduction. This is Colonel C. à C. Repington. Between 1890 and 1895 Repington was responsible for the French section of the Intelligence Division. In a secret study written in 1895 he showed that there were twenty-six French ports connected by rail with the interior, eight of which offered first-class facilities for the despatch of an expedition by sea. All told, the French had forty-four miles of quayage that could be utilised for invasion purposes. His conclusion was:

> In the end of all discussions in France upon a war policy against England, the invasion of this country, no matter how difficult or even desperate an undertaking, will probably be decided on, now as in the past, not only as the best solution, but as the only one offering France an honourable, rapid, and favourable issue from the struggle . . . The vital point for us to ascertain, not by abstract theories, but either by direct evidence or by penetrating the enemy's brain through a close study of the problem from his point of view, is *what he intends to*

do for it is only after ascertaining this that we can lay securely the foundations of an opposing war policy, and a national system of defence.[35]

At this time, 1895, the French had no plans for an invasion of England. They had had no such plans for over twenty years.

The first French General Staff study involving an invasion of England is dated June 1897, and was the work of the Troisième Bureau. The study suggested that France might detach 60,000 troops from her field forces even during the early stages of a general European war. These troops would have to be assembled and despatched before the fifteenth day of mobilisation, in order to have any chance of escaping the British Navy, and would be landed between Dover and Newhaven, before marching on London.[36] The French planners admitted that their plan faced grave difficulties, and that in order to be successful 'it will be necessary to plan long in advance', something which clearly had not been done.

During the crisis sparked off by the arrival of a French force at Fashoda on the Nile in autumn 1898, however, a similar plan was brought up. The Commander of the French Mediterranean Fleet, Admiral Fournier, pointed out that British cruisers and destroyers would wipe out any such expedition: 'Even if by an off-chance a first landing can be made, would not the lines of communication and retreat of troops thrown thus on English soil be undoubtedly cut? I do not fear to say such an operation appears to me chimerical in the present circumstances, which are quite different from those which inspired Napoleon the First . . . [To] carry out this operation today would be a folly which would lead only to a naval disaster . . . '[37] Early in 1899, even with the Fashoda crisis still not fully resolved, Fournier only allowed himself to consider *simulating* an invasion as 'the most efficacious means of intimidating England, if all measures were taken simultaneously and openly to make them fear a landing'. Massing troops on the coast and concentrating the French Northern Fleet off Brittany might have the desired salutary effect on British public opinion, which would not be familiar with naval doctrine and tactics: 'the fear of a landing of our troops would produce such an effect that England would perhaps hesitate to push matters to extremes'. Fournier's gallic optimism was the mirror-image of the panic-stricken Wolseley's scenario. Whilst the French War Minister was prepared to consider such a 'demonstration', most of those involved believed that it would immediately produce an English declaration of war. Only Admiral B. de Coulston proposed a real attempt at invasion as opposed to an imaginary one, but even for a feint no preparations were in place.[38]

The Boer War revived French interest in the subject of an invasion of England. Several journals published articles envisaging such a *coup de main*. In December 1900 a former Minister of War, General Mercier, proposed an invasion of England in the course of a debate in the Senate on the French naval estimates. At the same time the first in what was to be a four-volume study of Napoleonic invasion plans commissioned by the General Staff was published under the title *Projets et tentatives de débarquement aux Îles Brittaniques*. As the conclusion put it, these studies 'confirm once more that historical law that the result of a war depends essentially on the precision of preparations for it . . . ' The Supreme Naval Council took matters a little further, and as a result some amphibious exercises were held in autumn 1901, but as much for propaganda as for military purposes, which is, no doubt, why a French officer, Lieutenant-Colonel Delauney, submitted an article on them to the *Pall Mall Gazette*, which published it in November 1901.[39] British military intelligence, which had been present at the exercises, had not been impressed:

> The disembarkation appears to have been more theatrical than practical, and the chief instruction to be derived from it is to regard the experiment as an example of how a thing should not be done. No effort was made to carry out the operations under conditions that would prevail in war. The disembarkation was not covered by the Fleet; there was nothing in the way of surprise; the troops were very slow in getting ashore; and there was great confusion in the way they were landed, the boats coming up haphazard, without any system.[40]

Further studies were undertaken, and the Minister of War ordered that an expeditionary project be planned down to the last detail. This envisaged an expeditionary force of troops withheld from the Reserve, who would first be concentrated in inland garrisons adjacent to railways leading to the Channel Ports. Six hours of darkness would be enough to transfer 48,000 men, 5,200 horses, and twenty-four batteries of artillery, to the coast, arriving at midnight, with a view to landing the following morning on certain selected British beaches. The French General Staff considered such a plan worth having, as long as Britain did not have a truly national army like their own and that of Germany, in case Britain was ever again in the circumstances which prevailed during the Boer War.[41]

Repington was told something of this planning by the French Military Attaché, Major Huguet, on 5 January 1906, by which time Repington was military correspondent for *The Times*, and active in urging that a British expeditionary force be sent to help France if the forthcoming Algeciras Conference broke down and was followed by a German invasion of France. Huguet said that he had just recommended that the officers of the Troisième Bureau stop trying to improve their plans, and turn their attention to a different subject. In November 1907, however, Huguet revealed more – the plan was based upon surprise, and all concerned in the planning were confident that it could be carried out successfully; the intention was to land on open beaches on the south coast on a Sunday morning; all the material required for rapid disembarkation had been collected and stored at the French Channel Ports; the ultimate fate of the transports was of no importance.[42] Only in July 1908 was the Troisième Bureau closed, on the somewhat belated grounds that 'in the present state of our foreign relations such a plan no longer corresponds to any plausible hypothesis'.[43] The equivalent German unit, which had considered landings in the Thames and on the Norfolk coast, had been shut down in 1901.[44]

In 1901 Sir Edward Watkin died. He was replaced as Chairman of the Channel Tunnel Company by Baron Emile d'Erlanger, the Chairman of the Chemin de Fer du Nord. His board of Directors was composed of Lord Burton (of the South Eastern and Chatham Railway), Viscount Ridley (Chairman of the Tariff Reform League), Mr Arnold Morley (former Postmaster-General), Vice-Admiral Sir Charles Campbell (retired) and Major-General Sir Alfred Turner (formerly Inspector-General, Auxiliary Forces). D'Erlanger's son, Emile Beaumont d'Erlanger, succeeded to the chairmanship of the Channel Tunnel Company in 1911. Born in Paris, he had become a naturalised British subject in 1891. An association with Cecil Rhodes had begun in 1892, with the financing of railways in Rhodesia. The younger D'Erlanger had gone on to become chairman of the railway contractors Pauling and Company, who built the Rhodesia section of the 'Cape to Cairo' railway. They also built the New Cape Central Railway, the British Central African Railway and the Rhodesia Katanga Railway. D'Erlanger was also involved with the Victoria Falls Power Company, and a director of the Chartered Company of Rhodesia. His descendant Leo, who took up the cause of the Channel Tunnel after the Second World War, asked before he died that his coffin be dug up and placed upon the first train to cross the Channel through the tunnel.

HANDS BENEATH THE SEA.

Father Neptune. "LOOK HERE, MADAM. I'VE BEEN YOUR PROTECTOR ALL THESE YEARS, AND NOW I HEAR YOU THINK OF UNDERMINING MY POWER."

Britannia. "WELL, THE FACT IS I WANT TO SEE MORE OF MY FRIENDS OVER THERE, AND I NEVER LOOK MY BEST WHEN I'VE BEEN SEA-SICK."

'Hands beneath the Sea', *Punch*, 2 January 1907

Chapter 2

The Committee of Imperial Defence, 1906-7

1. Clarke *v.* Wolseley

The Committee of Imperial Defence was a product of the premiership of A.J. Balfour, and of the recognition, following the shambles of the Boer War, that a thorough review and overhaul was required, not only of the British Army but also of the full range of Britain's imperial and defence commitments. The Prime Minister presided over all meetings of the CID, whose membership was restricted to the political heads of the service departments, the most senior officers, the Ministers for Foreign Affairs, India and the Colonies, and whatever other 'experts' the Prime Minister chose to invite to attend. Proceedings and papers were kept strictly secret by a small secretariat. This committee rapidly assumed great importance, both as a forum where discussion took place and where decisions were taken on imperial, foreign political and defence matters. Although regarded with suspicion by some Liberal politicians, as a challenge to the authority of the Cabinet, it survived the transition of December 1905 from Conservative to Liberal Government.

On 28 February 1907, at its 96th meeting, the CID had before it three papers. The first of these was a memorandum on the Channel Tunnel by the Secretary, Sir George Clarke, dated 18 June 1906, which included an appendix drawn up by the Board of Trade in May 1906. The second was a memorandum from the Board of Trade, 'The Economic Aspects of the Proposed Channel Tunnel', dated 25 August 1906. The third was a note by Sir George Clarke of 31 January 1907 on the Channel Tunnel Bill recently put before parliament. Government departments had picked up reports in the press of the determination of the directors of the Channel Tunnel Company, confirmed at its annual general meeting on

7 June 1906, to submit their scheme to Parliament for consideration at the earliest possible opportunity.[1]

Sir George Clarke had passed first into and first out of the Royal Military Academy, before entering the Royal Engineers in 1868. He had served on Wolseley's Egyptian Expedition of 1882. He had been a member of the Committee on War Office Reorganisation of 1900-3, before serving as Governor of Victoria. The start of his tenure as Secretary of the CID coincided with the signature of the Anglo-French Conventions of the spring of 1904, which removed many outstanding disputes between Britain and France, and which those responsible for foreign policy in Balfour's administration regarded as stepping stones for an all-round settlement with Russia, France's ally and Britain's chief imperial rival. A native of Folkestone (and no relation of Sir A. Clarke), Clarke had written a pamphlet favouring the Channel Tunnel over twenty years before.[2] In June 1906 he relished the opportunity to demonstrate how far from satisfactory, in his view, had been the handling of this question in the past. When drafting his memorandum he wrote to Lord Esher, a permanent member of the CID who was on the closest terms with King Edward VII, that the question had been 'terribly tangled' in the early 1880s. He also said that Sir Edward Grey, the Foreign Secretary, 'thinks the present House of Commons would raise no objections. The Lords might'.[3]

In the memorandum itself Clarke maintained that the main question at issue was whether it was reasonably probable that an enemy continental Great Power could obtain full possession of the approach to and the exit from an undamaged Channel Tunnel.[4] He noted that Anglo-French relations had been placed on a satisfactory footing, and that the CID had recently affirmed the principle that, so long as naval superiority was maintained, invasion of the British Isles was impossible. He also claimed that the idea of French aggression no longer haunted the imagination of the public. There were, therefore, 'grounds for a dispassionate review' of the military objections to the project.[5]

Clarke admitted that the opinion expressed by a War Office Committee on 17 May 1882, that no prearranged measures for rendering a tunnel impassable would satisfy every imaginable contingency, was irrefutable. He then stated:

> In war, however, as in civil business of all kinds, it is futile to attempt to provide against 'every imaginable contingency'. There are no limits to the imagination, and all that can be done is to guard against the reasonably practical operations

of an enemy. We have, therefore, to distinguish between what is feasible and what is purely visionary.[6]

Clarke's first target was Lord Wolseley, who on 16 June 1882 had written:

> The seizing of the tunnel by a *coup de main* is, in my opinion, a very simple operation, provided it be done without any previous warning or intimation whatever by those who wish to invade the country . . . My contention is that were a tunnel made, England, as a nation, could be destroyed without any warning whatever, when Europe was in a condition of profound peace . . .

Clarke's second target was the author of a War Office Intelligence Branch memorandum entitled 'Hostilities without Declaration of War', which listed over one hundred examples from the eighteenth and nineteenth centuries of hostilities preceding declarations of war. Clarke maintained that this memorandum 'was wholly irrelevant to the main issue', that the three cases cited by Wolseley in support of his contention were easily shown 'to have no bearing upon the theory of hostilities "without any previous warning" ', and said that 'it is impossible to find in modern history any case of a premeditated attack by one civilised nation upon another, delivered at a time when their mutual relations were completely satisfactory'. He quoted the draft Report of the Joint Select Committee of Parliament of 1883, chaired by Lord Lansdowne. This said:

> We do not take the view that the contingency of a *coup de main*, struck by a Power with whom our relations had been friendly and unstrained, is one which we have any right, or which experience would justify us, in placing amongst the foremost of the probabilities with which we have to deal. It is our impression, on the contrary, that if such an attack were to be made it would have been preceded by circumstances which would have called for effectual precautions against a surprise . . . We are glad to learn from the whole of the military witnesses who have come before us that, if such precautions were in existence, the risk of a successful surprise would be extremely remote. That this would be so, whether the attempt were made by a force sent through the tunnel or by one landed in its vicinity, there can be little doubt.[7]

Clarke argued that 'Unless we admit "every imaginable contingency" without examination, and unless we further accept as a practical possibility (for which there is no precedent) a deliberately planned attack by France at a time when the relations between the two peoples were unclouded, no plan for securing sudden possession of the tunnel, which

would have the most remote chance of success, can be formulated . . . '
Only by the acceptance of a succession of impossible conditions could
risk to the nation before the outbreak of a war be argued. The *coup de
main* theory 'may be unhesitatingly rejected': 'The witnesses who
advanced this theory showed that they had never clearly thought out the
nature of the operations involved, and were mainly influenced by the
idea that elaborate prearranged mechanical contrivances for obstruct-
ing the tunnel might fail if suddenly required to act at a time of
profound peace – a proposition which is unexceptionable, but which
leaves out of account all the real difficulties of the invaders.'[8] Cases
envisaging the capture of the tunnel in the course of hostilities were
dismissed, as was the cession of it as one of the conditions of a disastrous
peace.

   Clarke believed that six provisions for denying the use of the tunnel to
an enemy would satisfy the most exacting demands. These were: temporary obstruction by mechanical means; means of bringing fire to bear
upon the outlet; means of temporarily flooding; facilities for cutting the
railway line at its exit; exposure of the line after egress on both sides of
the Channel to the fire of warships; means, external to the defences of
Dover, of admitting the sea in the last resort.[9] It was not that Clarke
believed all these measures were absolutely necessary. It was rather that,
the military authorities having adopted 'alarmist views', and made them
public, such measures would have a 'moral effect'. So far as the argument that the existence of a tunnel would tend to produce panic if ever
Ango-French relations appeared to be strained was concerned, Clarke
maintained that it was 'impossible by any measures of precaution to
prevent alarm on the part of uninstructed persons'. The fact that
Britain's Navy was two and a half times the size of Germany's had not
prevented 'attempts to raise the scare of a German invasion'. He was
sanguine about the 'passing effect' of such attempts, and that, once the
public had become accustomed to the idea of a tunnel, and even more so
once large numbers of persons had actually passed through it, panic
would not be more easily promoted than at present. Moreover, 'panics
based on the existence of the tunnel could arise only in the case of the
anticipation of French hostility and through-railway communication
with France would probably tend to the maintenance and the
strengthening of good relations between the two peoples'.[10] Clarke left it
to others to pronounce upon the economic viability of the project. Its
effect upon the trade and industries of Great Britain was a separate
consideration, and there had been 'no adequate inquiry' into that branch

A. J. Balfour and Sir Henry Campbell-Bannerman,
cartoon by F. Carruthers Gould

of the subject. 'Meanwhile', he concluded, 'unless the reasoning submitted in this Memorandum can be shown to be faulty, the conclusion that a Channel Tunnel would create no new military risks which cannot be obviated by simple measures of precaution seems to be inevitable.'[11]

Drawing heavily on the evidence submitted to the Joint Committee of Parliament of 1883, the Board of Trade's memorandum of August 1906 pointed out that the existing trade of the Channel Ports was mainly an import trade. The main economic effect of a tunnel, therefore, 'would probably be to cheapen and so to increase the volume of importation from France, and perhaps also to some extent from Switzerland and Italy, a large proportion of the imports from those countries already reaching us via France'. It was not thought that the opening of a tunnel route would have much effect on British trade with Belgium, Germany and Holland. Some shipping might be displaced from the main cross-Channel lines, but this was 'a quite insignificant item'. Current passenger numbers between England and France was estimated at 'considerably under 1,000,000'. It was 'a fair assumption' that more than half this total would go by tunnel if a tunnel existed; and that the flow of passengers would be increased overall, given the supposition that the Channel was an actual deterrent to passenger travel. The effect on economic relations of increased facilities for passenger communication between Britain and continental countries, said the Board of Trade, must by no means be lost sight of, but was not one which could be directly estimated.[12]

These distinctly lukewarm conclusions reflected 'some principal points' concerning 'Commercial Aspects' made in a note of 3 August by Sir Hubert Llewellyn Smith of the Board of Trade. Other aspects, however, emerge clearly from another note of the same date, marked 'Confidential':

> The arguments *in favour* of the Channel Tunnel are fairly obvious. The greatest argument, as it seems to me, *against* the Channel Tunnel is the increased danger of popular panic in time of war or in anticipation of war breaking out. This is quite apart from any real military danger. In considering questions affecting the safety of our food supply in war time we have found it convenient to discriminate clearly between what I have called the 'economic rise of price' due to definite and measurable causes, and the 'psychological rise' due to panic.
>
> The latter class of causes though not lending themselves to exact analysis have most undoubtedly to be taken into account.
>
> In the Spanish-American war I believe the dispositions of the American fleet were prejudicially affected by a totally unreasonable fear on the part of the inhabitants of the coast towns that they would be bombarded by the Spanish fleet.

Now if the result of the construction of the Tunnel is to increase the frequency and intensity of popular alarms, it may well tend to require an increase in our military and naval expenditure . . .

I take no side against or for the Tunnel, but the above is in my judgement the most important consideration to be borne in mind *against* the project.[13]

The Channel Tunnel Company deposited its Bill with Parliament on 17 December 1906. On 2 January 1907 Clarke forwarded a copy of his memorandum of June 1906 to the Prime Minister, Sir Henry Campbell-Bannerman, and announced that he was circulating it to the members of the CID. His covering letter reinforced the line he had taken:

The broad conclusions seem inevitable (1) that there is no military danger, and (2) that adequate precautions, amply sufficient to meet the objections which were alleged in 1882-3, can very easily be taken. Under the draft Bill, complete powers are given to the Government to direct any measures for the security of the Tunnel to be taken by the Company.

On the question of the economic advantage to the country, he stressed that there was insufficient data to form an opinion. As, unless there was reason to believe that British industries and interests would benefit, there could be no case for the building of a tunnel, he urged a searching enquiry. He believed that many manufacturers thought Britain would benefit industrially, and that there was also a general idea that she would gain as a distributing centre; authoritative evidence, however, was needed. 'Unless therefore the Government decides on military grounds against the proposed Bill, I think a strong Royal Commission to enquire into the economic question will be necessary.' Clarke ended by noting that since the writing of his memorandum the company had decided to operate the tunnel electrically, and have the power station on the British side of the Channel. This he considered to be 'an additional precaution'.[14] It would, in fact, have satisfied Clarke entirely, as he told Lord Esher; but, as he added, 'it may be politic to lay down other conditions in order to appease "the old women of both sexes" of whom we seem to possess large numbers'.[15] Hence his suggestions at the end of January that sections conferring certain powers upon the Government should be incorporated in the Bill itself instead of being left to be dealt with by Orders in Council. Full and complete provision should be made for 1. the execution, at the cost of the Channel Tunnel Company, of any works of defence or measures of precaution which might be considered necessary for defence purposes; 2. conferring upon the Government powers to close, block or flood the tunnel at any time without becoming liable for the losses thus incurred; 3. conferring upon the Government powers to control the traffic of the tunnel at the Dover end at any time, or to use the tunnel for exclusively national purposes, paying only the ordinary charges for troops or freight which might be forwarded through it. He also pointed out that the passing of such a Bill as was contemplated would require an Anglo-French treaty defining the sections of the tunnel over which each Power would exercise territorial jurisdiction, and incurring immunity from claims for indemnity by the subjects of either Power on any account of any action taken by the government of the other Power.[16]

2. The Wider Debate

By the time the CID met on 28 February 1907 certain other points had been made, both in the press and elsewhere. As the members of the Defence Committee could hardly have overlooked these items, it is worth taking them into consideration here. The Military Correspondent of *The Times* was first off the mark, with two long articles on 2 and 3 January 1907. Colonel Repington's hostility to the tunnel, to dissenting from or setting aside the 'deliberate judgement of the past', was in evidence from the start:

> The Channel Tunnel question . . . is of importance because the construction of a tunnel will in a sense terminate our privileged geographical situation, which is the envy of all foreign statesmen, and has been in the past the primary cause of the greatness of the British Empire. Fascinating though must always be the large and daring operation which the tunnel suggests; captivating though grand generalisations upon the theme of the union of nations must always prove for generous souls; valuable though may appear to be the commercial advantages which the tunnel may conceivably afford us, we must all allow that none of these things can be allowed to weigh in the balance against proof, or even reasonable supposition, that the venture will prove in the remotest degree a menace to our national security by reducing the measure of inaccessibility in time of war which insularity, coupled with the possession of a powerful Navy, implies.

The first article concentrated upon the arguments used against the tunnel in 1882 and 1883. The second article made some new points. One was that 'it is an idea which will be repugnant to national sentiment, and inadmissible from the point of view of national security, that the sole direct line of railway communication between England and the Continent of Europe should run the risk of falling under the control of a cosmopolitan directorate'. It was far better that any such railway should be built as a national enterprise by the two governments and nations most directly concerned, who could then control the whole business from first to last. Another point was this: 'The absence of a tunnel has not prevented the increase of the total annual value of our imports and exports by something like £400,000,000 since the year 1883, and this increase proves, since all trade is seaborne, that it is not the obstacle of the sea which hinders the development of our foreign trade.' Through-railway communication would not necessarily increase trade with France, and whilst tariff walls remained intact foreign merchants would benefit more than British ones – 'Many industries in this country will be heavily hit'. A third point dealt with the utilisation of a tunnel for the purpose of military co-operation in Europe. Repington asserted that 'the benefit thereby derived does not upon examination amount to very much':

> It is difficult to imagine that France and England in alliance will not always control the narrow seas which divide them. On each side of the Channel there are a score of ports connected with the interior by rail and equipped with miles of quays possessing modern plant suitable for the rapid handling and conveyance of military stores and troops. The advantage gained by a tunnel would be a matter of a few hours at the most, and only very extraordinary circumstances would cause the loss or gain of a few hours to influence the fate of a war conducted in common by the 80 million people of France and the British Isles.

The most striking new point followed a comparison between the small size of the British Regular Army and the hosts of the French nation. This discrepancy meant that the French had nothing to fear from an English invasion, and partly accounted for French enthusiasm for the tunnel. There was, however, another element:

> Calais and its immediate neighbourhood are a frontier district, and no natural or artificial obstacles intervene between this district and the Belgian frontier to arrest the march of a hostile army advancing upon France. Nothing exists in Belgium, whether troops or fortresses, sufficient to prevent the rapid advance of a German army from the lower Rhine upon the Pas de Calais. The seizure of Calais, Sangatte, and the French end of the tunnel, in the event of war between Germany and France, is a contingency that must always be faced; and, if we were co-operating with France, the cessation of all traffic by the tunnel would naturally ensue. The greater the transit trade by the submarine railway, and the more numerous the tunnels, the greater the loss to us . . . So long as we trust to the sea for our highway, our foreign trade is safe . . . But if we begin to sterilise the production of mercantile tonnage by opening land routes for trade, we give hostages to the watchful enemy, we allow him to cut the arteries when he

pleases, and we may not hereafter find it easy to replace the carrying trade on
the sea which we may, gradually and little by little, sacrifice to the tunnel traffic.

This gave another dimension to the problem. If the sea was not the only
route by which an invader might invade, then the soldier's view had to be
taken into account. This view was that 'the construction of a tunnel is
only admissible if the Government create a national army of the modern
stamp . . . competent to withstand, and to defeat decisively, the largest
force which can, in the most extreme hypothesis which reason allows,
elude the attentions of our Navy and land upon our shores'. For
Repington the May 1882 conclusion of the Alison Committee held good,
as it never had for Clarke; it remained true 'that "absolute security
cannot be assured in every imaginable contingency"'; and that every
contingency was imaginable.

To Esher, Clarke described Repington's articles as 'feeble, illogical,
and rambling . . . He is, however, consistent in his general policy of
belittling the Navy . . .'[17] Major-General Sir Alfred E. Turner, late
Inspector-General of Auxiliary Forces and a director of the Channel
Tunnel Company, countered some of Repington's arguments with an
article in *Tribune*, summarised in *The Times* on 4 January, and included
under the title 'Military Fears Dispelled' in the Channel Tunnel Company's production *Reports by British and French Engineers and Papers on
National Defence*, published the following month. He pointed out that the
tunnel could be so constructed that the shore facilities at each end would
be open at all times to the fire of British warships. He maintained that
even if the French made a successful invasion, even several tunnels
would not benefit them, whereas in a war with a Power other than France
the tunnel would benefit Britain, as food could then be poured into the
country without being obstructed by enemy warships. As for the suggestion that Germany might successfully invade France, and then turn her
attention to Britain through any tunnels, this 'need not seriously be
considered, as it might surely be presumed that if there was such a war,
or even rumour of such a war, the British people and army would hardly
be lethargic or asleep'. He ended with the appeal

> that a pair of narrow borings connecting the two countries by an underground
> and submarine passage can be regarded in any way as constituting a serious
> factor of warfare appears to be inconsistent with calm and collected judgement,
> and with a knowledge of the true facts of the case. It is hard, indeed, to believe
> that in this century nervousness and vain fears will be allowed to obstruct or
> defeat this great project, or that the 'pale cast of thought' should be permitted
> to prevent 'an enterprise of great pith and moment' such as is the creation of
> the Channel Tunnel.

M. Sartiaux, the General Manager of the Northern Railway of France, in his contribution to the literature of the Channel Tunnel Company, recalled the controversy of the 1880s, and cast doubt as to whether the military question had been the real motive deciding British opinion against the tunnel at that time: 'Was not this opinion rather based on the fear of reducing the importance of the Navy, and . . . on prejudices . . . which would not hold water if those who are imbued with them were to consider them from a practical and not a sentimental aspect?' Sartiaux recalled the earlier opposition led by a section of the British aristocracy and literati, to whom it seemed that if this change took place 'all their traditions, old customs, their insularity, their originality, and even their freedom' would vanish. The military men, he said, had followed the philosophers down this path. Sartiaux did not consider that such self-imposed isolation could be considered advantageous from any point of view: 'Politically, socially, and morally it is evident that the intercourse of nations by frequent inter-communications must be the most powerful means by which they can know, appreciate, and, by the force of example, perfect one another.'[18]

It was the journal *The Nineteenth Century* which in 1882 had led the opposition of the intelligentsia to which Sartiaux referred. In its issue of February 1907 *The Nineteenth Century and After* printed as a special supplement the public protest which it had then engineered, together with a list of the signatories to it. In the same issue the man who in 1882-83 had been responsible for the memorandum 'Hostilities without Declaration of War', now Major-General Sir Frederick Maurice, restated the case he had made twenty-five years previously. He added the Russo-Japanese War and the Boer War to his catalogue, the first to show 'the dangers of trusting to the perpetual vigilance of the defenders of a vital point', the second to show 'the impossibility of taking precautions in the moment of danger'. Now, according to Maurice, were a tunnel built not only would the defence of the kingdom be handed over 'from our supreme navy to our wholly inadequate army', and not only would a force landed on Britain's shores be able to maintain itself there, but the necessary vigilance to be exercised would impose upon the British people the conditions obtaining on the Continent, where 'every detail of daily life is regulated by authority, so far as it may be necessary for purposes of national security'. Vigilance, moreover, would be to no avail: 'Human vigilance has failed nation after nation. Why should we escape?' Beyond that, what was certain was 'that no one except the Cabinet will take the responsibility of all that either flooding or blowing up the Tunnel would entail, and that the very last people who are likely to take that responsibility at a moment when our relations with some foreign Power are strained are, as the experiences of the South African war have shown us, the Ministers themselves'.[19]

Two other public contributions to the debate are worthy of note. Both represented changes of mind. One, however, was much more dramatic than the other. The less dramatic came in the form of a letter from Lord Curzon, the late Viceroy of India, which appeared in *The Times* of 24 January 1907. Curzon wrote:

> When the project was introduced in the House of Commons many years ago, while I was still a member, I was inclined to support it, but after listening to the debate was tempted to abstain. If I were now a member I should vote against the proposal. To the insular position of Great Britain is due a large part of our national strength. It has given us our general invulnerability from invasion, and has strengthened the fibre of the national character. I think that it would be a mistake for a hypothetical and relatively insignificant advantage to jeopardise these gains. With the possible exception of a desert, a sea frontier is the most secure and impregnable in the world. I doubt if any other nation could be found that, having a sea frontier, would propose voluntarily to surrender it. If this be so, I see no reason why we should be either bolder, or more foolish than our fellows.

The statement on 18 February 1907 in the House of Lords by Lansdowne was of an altogether different one. Lansdowne had not only been Foreign Secretary from 1900 until December 1905, but had in 1883 chaired the Joint Committee of Parliament on the Channel Tunnel and written a report to which reference has already been made. Lansdowne protested against the assumption that, because twenty-five years ago he had committed himself to certain strategic views derived from evidence tendered by witnesses, he should be held to the same views in 1907: 'I say frankly that if I had to sit down and write a Report on the question of the Channel Tunnel today, I do not think I should write the same Report that I drafted in 1883.' He denied that his report disposed of the possibility of hostilities without a previous declaration of war, and stated that the memorandum by Maurice did not deserve to be lightly set aside. Lansdowne admitted that when international relations were in no sense strained, and when there was no outstanding difficulty between two great civilised Powers, he could scarcely contemplate that one of them was at all likely to spring suddenly on the other:

> But there may, on the other hand, be periods of international tension when complications may supervene with great rapidity and when it is the duty of any Power that values its own safety to leave no precaution neglected. Therefore I am not at all disposed to neglect the possibility of what is sometimes called a bolt

from the blue, or to think that ample precautions should not be taken to provide for such a contingency.[20]

3. The Admiralty and the War Office

At the meeting of the CID on 28 February 1907 the Admiralty representatives were the First Sea Lord, Sir John Fisher, and the Director of Naval Intelligence, Sir Charles Ottley. They produced a memorandum not previously submitted to, or printed for, the CID, and not subsequently retained amongst its records. This memorandum revealed that the stance of the Admiralty in 1907 was the same as it had been when Admiral Cooper Key expressed his objections to a tunnel in a letter of January 1882 to Lord Northbrook. The Admiralty hit out at the 'private speculators', on whom the onus fell 'to establish an overwhelming case before such a project could receive the sanction of the Government'. They pointed out, as Maurice had done, that the country was free from 'the military burdens which press heavily upon our continental neighbours', and which would accompany the adoption of a land frontier. They dwelt upon the increased expenditure on fixed defences and the additions to the Army Estimates which the construction of a tunnel would entail. They stressed, *à propos* the present relations between England and France, that 'all history goes to prove that international friendships are not based on such secure foundations that they are able to stand the shock of a conflict of international interests or a wound to national pride'. So far as Germany was concerned, they based their case on the Duke of Cambridge's remarks of 1882: 'Any Power . . . which, when at war with France, had taken possession of Belgium would find it possible to seize Calais, and might find it convenient even to punish an alliance of ours with France by a sudden seizure of Dover.' They added, in words that would have appealed to Repington: 'These words, though written nearly twenty-five years ago, have even more weight today in the present position of European politics, than they had in 1882.' Echoing Maurice's article, they doubted whether it was safe to rely on the resources of modern science for means to destroy the tunnel – a step involving the loss of millions of pounds, the property of the shareholders, and the destruction of what would be one of the principal engineering works of the world. They too doubted the resolve of any individual officer and any government to act in time. In short, 'the construction of a tunnel would add to our responsibilities and would swell the Estimates for the defensive forces of this country, while it would introduce, without a doubt, a possible source of danger from raid, invasion, or treachery'. The gains to be derived from improved communications with the Continent for the transit of goods and passengers would not compensate for the abandonment of the advantages of a sea frontier. The balance was 'altogether in favour of non-interference with the natural sea frontier, which has been one of the main factors in the creation and maintenance of the British Empire'.[21]

The War Office's most recent consideration of the Channel Tunnel question had been in 1904. In May 1904 the Ambassador in Paris had forwarded to Lord Lansdowne a copy of a report presented to the Paris Chamber of Commerce by one of its committees. This report was strongly in favour of a Channel Tunnel and its conclusions had been adopted on 11 May. The Ambassador thought it probable that the matter would shortly be brought before the governments concerned. The War Office prepared a précis of the enquiries of former years, and the Director of Military Operations, Major-General Grierson, agreed at the end of July that 'the only strategic change in the condition of the problem, is the decision of the Defence Committee to reduce the strength of the land forces allotted to the defence of the U.K. The decision further strengthens the conclusion that it would be imprudent to risk the advantages of an insular position and sea command by entertaining this proposal . . . '[22]

In 1907 the War Office, like the Admiralty, did not disclose its position in advance. The Director of Military Operations, Major-General Ewart – who together with the Chief of the General Staff, General Sir Neville Lyttelton, and General Sir John French represented the Army at the CID meeting of 28 February 1907 – had had a conversation with Sir George Clarke early in January. Although Ewart agreed that the tunnel would indeed be of great value in a war of alliance with France, he proceeded nevertheless to write a 'frankly hostile paper' on the subject. As he confided to his diary on 8 January:

> I have an insular prejudice against it, not on military grounds for it is easy to exaggerate the danger – but on sentimental grounds. I am prepared to admit that with France friendly or in alliance it might be a Military advantage – but its completion will Europeanise us. I hate Cosmopolitanism. I stick to my insularity.

A few days later he wrote: 'I really do believe that the construction of the tunnel would destroy some of the splendid characteristics of our race and hasten our gradual deterioration by a still larger influx of undesirable aliens'[23]

Ewart's 'frankly hostile paper' was not printed for the CID at the time. It was only formally submitted to the CID with a covering letter on 19 April 1907, and must subsequently have been retrieved. It made one positive point in favour of the tunnel, and three negative ones against it. The positive point was that a tunnel might save one and a half days in the time required for the oversea concentration of the Expeditionary Force, in addition to eliminating uncertainties due to fog and facilitating the maintenance of the Army after concentration. Even this point was qualified: 'it was at the same time pointed out that there was no guarantee that the existing situation would continue or that the continental end of the tunnel would remain permanently in the hands of a Power friendly to this country'. The effect of the relative increase in British naval power since 1883 was considered to be clearly adverse: 'since, invasion by sea being ruled out, the tunnel would introduce a risk otherwise non-existent, while the possibility of raids being admitted increased the risk of Dover being captured'. The other adverse arguments were: 'the moral effect on British public opinion, which would see in the tunnel an enhanced risk of invasion and, having little confidence in the Territorials, would react unfavourably on the employment of the Expeditionary Force'; and the possibility of Dover being ceded to the enemy as one of the conditions of peace after an unsuccessful war. On the whole, Ewart saw no reason to depart from the opinions of the Duke of Cambridge, Lord Wolseley and Admiral Cooper Key.[24]

4. A 'Puerile' and 'Sentimental' Decision

According to the official minutes of the meeting of the CID, no discussion whatsoever took place. Sir Henry Campbell-Bannerman, who had voted for a Channel Tunnel on the last occasion when a Bill was before Parliament, on 5 June 1890, flatly stated that general policy with reference to the tunnel should be based on the decisions as to its naval and military aspects, thus setting aside whatever the Board of Trade might say; and that he understood that both the Admiralty and the General Staff were opposed to the building of a tunnel. The conclusion of the meeting was recorded as: 'The Committee note that the Admiralty and the General Staff are opposed to the construction of the Tunnel.'[25] Thus was reached, apparently, a decision which Clarke had described in advance as 'puerile'.[26]

It is possible that there really was no discussion on this occasion. Clarke had stated in July 1906 that he could take no part in CID

discussions, and had to confine himself to recording the recommendations made.[27] On the other hand, he did speak from time to time, as for
example at the 88th meeting. Given the personalities of the protagonists
and the strength of the views committed to paper; given also Haldane's
recollection of March 1914 that in 1907 the General Staff 'had not
objected to the tunnel on the ground that it would be difficult to defend,
but that, taking into consideration the possibility of surprises and raids,
the protection of the Dover outlet would be an expensive undertaking',[28]
– a recollection which does not square precisely with Ewart's memorandum – it is also possible that something was said, and that the official
record conceals the sort of confrontation that took place on 3 December
1908, at the first meeting of the CID sub-committee to consider the
military needs of the Empire, which the minutes of that meeting
successfully concealed, and the dimensions of which are revealed only by
other material.[29] Either way, the outcome must be added to the catalogue of setbacks suffered by Clarke as Secretary of the CID.[30] This may
well be one reason why Clarke did not draw attention to it in his
memoirs.

A week before this meeting of the Committee of Imperial Defence,
the Cabinet had considered the Channel Tunnel Bill. Campbell-Bannerman reported to the King, who was opposed to the project, on 20
February, that 'it was resolved that the Government should decline to
support it, and should allow the House to express its opinion freely,
which it is anticipated will be strongly hostile to the measure'.[31] The
Committee of Imperial Defence meeting altered the Cabinet's approach
to the extent of causing it to drop the idea that members of the
Government should vote as they pleased. As Lloyd George, who was
then President of the Board of Trade and who disagreed with his
advisers there, later recalled: 'But the military advisers were against it,
and then the Government by a very considerable majority . . . decided
that we could not fly in the face of military and naval opinion, and run
the risk of establishing what might be a means of access to this country on
the part of a great hostile European army.'[32]

On 21 March 1907 the decision taken was given to the House of
Commons by the Prime Minister and to the House of Lords by Lord
Crewe. Parliament was told:

> H.M. Government fully recognise the deep concern felt in this matter, and have
> no other desire than to take the House fully into their confidence . . . Briefly, I
> may say that our view of the public interest leads us to be opposed to this project
> of a tunnel. Even supposing the military dangers involved were to be amply

guarded against, there would exist throughout the country a feeling of insecurity which might lead to a constant demand for increased expenditure, naval and military, and a continual risk of unrest and possible alarm, which, however unfounded, would be most injurious in its effect, whether political or commercial. On the other hand, there has not been disclosed any such prospect of advantage to the trade and industries of the country as would compensate for those evils. As to the personal convenience of passengers and the transit of light articles, it seems well that further consideration should be given to other means of conveyance, such as are used in the ferries across great channels of the sea in other parts of the world.[33] These considerations lead us, while rejoicing in anything that facilitates the communication with our neighbours, to view this scheme with disfavour.[34]

A.J. Balfour, the Leader of the Opposition, expressed his 'great satisfaction' at this announcement. Lord Lansdowne repeated his retraction of his 1883 stance on the professedly 'sentimental' grounds that 'if the chances of its being used against us were only as one in a hundred, or one in a thousand, I do not think that the people of this country would tolerate an operation which would oblige us to run that hundreth or that thousanth chance', and that if to the apprehensions which would arise if Britain were engaged in war with a great Power, or if such a war was imminent, were added those which the presence of a tunnel would create, 'we should make the position, already grave and anxious enough, doubly grave and doubly anxious'.[36] These two declarations gave to the Government's decision an all-party quality. Lord Rosebery withdrew his motion for papers to be presented to Parliament. The Prime Minister then told the House of Commons that as the decision had been arrived at on general grounds of policy involving more than purely military or naval considerations (which was certainly not the way in which he had handled the matter at the CID, although true) it was 'not desirable that individual opinions as regards special aspects of the question should be made public'.[36]

Chapter 3

The Committee of Imperial Defence, 1913-14

1. Sir John French v. The War Office

There the matter rested until the spring of 1913. Although the Chairman of the South Eastern and Chatham Railway, Cosmo Bonsor, had raised the whole issue again by writing to the Foreign Secretary in October 1912; and although Sir Arthur Conan Doyle had sent direct to the Secretary of the CID an extract from a forthcoming article in December of that year,[1] it was not until Arthur Fell, chairman of the all party committee of MPs in favour of the construction of a Channel Tunnel, asked certain parliamentary questions in April 1913, that there were further developments. On 9 and 14 April he was told by the Prime Minister that the question had not been examined by the CID since February 1907. On 24 April Asquith replied to his request that the matter be considered by the CID in such a way as to give the impression that it was 'under consideration by the Departments concerned'.[2] Asquith's reply caused the Foreign Secretary to ask for the views of the Admiralty and the Army Council. The Admiralty, now under Winston Churchill, who in March 1913 had noted that he was in favour of the venture (the note was made on a letter from Fisher in which the latter penned the blatant lie that he, Fisher, had 'ever been a firm believer in the Channel Tunnel') replied on 10 June to the effect that they were of the opinion that the matter should be referred to the CID, before which they were prepared to lay their views in full. Grey had to ask the Secretary of the Army Council for an answer on 25 June, and again on 19 July, and again on 5 August 1913.[3] On the last of these dates the Prime Minister had received a deputation of eighty-seven MPs, led by Arthur Fell, who pressed the case for a tunnel, and had told them that a review of the strategic aspects was 'in the course of prosecution at the moment' by the CID.[4]

The Army's reluctance to comply with the Foreign Secretary's requests and to get the Prime Minister off the hook is accounted for by a minute by the Director of Military Operations, General Sir Henry Wilson, dated 15 May 1913:

> in view of the fact that so lately as last January or February the Secretary of State [Colonel J.E.B. Seely] said he would not consider the problem I have not added any considered opinion on the advisability or otherwise of the scheme. In fact I do not see how we can give such an opinion until the FO in the first instance informs us what the policy of HM's Government is.
>
> If our troops are not to be employed on the Continent of Europe then the project has a very different military aspect to what it would have if they were to be employed.
>
> Again, the value of an Entente is probably quite different to that of an Alliance.
>
> Any military opinion, on so large and complex a subject, must be based, if it is to be of any practical value, on the Policy of the country as determined by HM's Government, and therefore until this Policy is defined we are not, I am afraid, in a position to help the Foreign Office.[5]

After Asquith's statement to the parliamentary delegation, however 'indefinite' it might have appeared to *The Times*,[6] and however difficult the German Ambassador found it to find in it any reference to any kind of agreement between Britain and France,[7] obstruction was more difficult. In September 1913 Seely asked Field-Marshal Sir William Nicholson for figures on the amount of foodstuffs and the number of troops that could be conveyed through a tunnel in twenty-four hours, and Nicholson obtained them forthwith.[8] On 3 October Hankey, the Secretary of the CID, who had been pestered of late by communications from adherents of the scheme, reminded the Foreign Office, Admiralty, War Office and Board of Trade, with Asquith's encouragement, of the Prime Minister's statement of 5 August, and notified these departments that the question would shortly be coming before the CID.[9]

The Foreign Office immediately put the onus on the Service Departments. Assistant Under-Secretary Sir Eyre Crowe was directed by the Foreign Secretary 'to state that the manner in which the existence of a tunnel would affect the foreign relations of this country is a question which in his opinion depends so predominantly on the naval and military considerations involved that he does not think he could usefully make a statement of the Foreign Office point of view before the naval and military aspects have been thoroughly elucidated'.[10] It was the Chief of the Imperial General Staff, General Sir John French, who took up the matter in a memorandum of October 1913 for the Secretary of State for War.

French departed dramatically from the line hitherto taken by the Army. He took it that there were reasonable grounds for assuming that a tunnel would lead to great national economic advancement, weighed against this the military objections made in the past, and found them wanting. If it was the British Government's intention to continue the present policy of friendship with France, and to send an Expeditionary Force across the Channel in the event of war between France and Germany, he considered that the proposed tunnel, 'so far from weakening our present position, will prove an asset of considerable military value':

Granted that we intend to render actual assistance to France by the despatch of our Expeditionary Force to the Continent, a Channel Tunnel would:

(i) Expedite its concentration in France or on the Belgian frontier.

(ii) Obviate the danger which must admittedly attend the transportation of so large a force, in view of the advent of submarines and aircraft.

(iii) Free the Navy from the duty of furnishing escorts not only for the transports conveying the force, but also for those carrying supplies, reinforcements etc., thus enabling it to devote its attention to its legitimate role.

(iv) Ensure the arrival on the Continent of all supplies etc. despatched from England during the campaign, the safe transit of which, if on transports, could not be ensured.

(v) Render the transfer of troops between the two countries a rapid and easy operation, and, by so close a connection between the allied armies, would establish the best means to enable the allied Powers to act combined on 'interior lines'.

Food supply from the Continent would also be improved, and cruisers thereby freed to safeguard other trade routes.

French was not deflected even by the possibility that, at some stage in the future, France might become an unfriendly Power:

The idea of a surprise attack by a large body of troops cannot be seriously entertained; for it is inconceivable that preparations of any magnitude could be made without our knowledge.

The danger, therefore, would lie in a sudden attempt by a small force only, aided probably by local agents, to secure our end of the tunnel; and surely we cannot admit that we are unable to cope with such a contingency.

Even if a small force was successful, the difficulties then facing it would be such that the balance of advantage would be overwhelmingly with the British – so much so 'that even in the event of a war with France, or of any other Power obtaining control of the French end of the tunnel, the possibility of the tunnel being utilised for invasion does not constitute so grave a threat as our predecessors would lead us to believe'. French concluded, therefore, 'that the military objections to the project are on the whole of insufficient weight to justify us in placing an embargo on a scheme which may possibly prove of vast economic advantage to the nation at large'.[11]

In another note for Seely, French went even further. Impressed as he clearly was by the development of submarines, mines and various forms of aircraft, he wrote: 'after mature thought I venture to go so far as to submit that our sea defence, even now, has practically vanished and that when we oppose the construction of the Channel Tunnel on the ground that our insular position would be imperilled we are simply engaged in a futile attempt to shut the stable door after the horse has gone'. There was little to lose by the construction of a tunnel, and much to gain, not only in economic terms, but in the sense that, 'Unless we are prepared to adopt Continental methods and keep on foot a large conscript army, it is absolutely essential to us that a friendly or allied Power should hold the other side of the Channel.'[12]

Colonel Seely was not prepared to go so far as his CIGS. According to the running commentary on these developments which General Wilson kept on the docket of the file, Seely took no action on French's memorandum. He did not produce it when the CID finally came round to discussing this matter, not in the autumn of 1913 but only in March 1914. Nor did he give the substance of Wilson's minute of 15 May 1913, which was a call for the Government and the Foreign Office to declare their position, a call with which Seely had given Wilson the impression, at the time, that he agreed.[13]

It was Seely's responsibility that the 125th meeting of the CID had before it no contribution on paper from the War Office. What the members of the CID did have, thanks to Hankey, was a brief history of the scheme from 1867 to 1907, a résumé of the decision of 1907, and a reprint of Wolseley's memorandum of 16 June 1882.[14] From the Board of Trade they had a substantial memorandum effectively duplicating the scepticism displayed by that department in 1906 as to any positive effect on British foreign trade, and considering that it was improbable that the tunnel could be utilised for the purpose of bringing into the country any large supplies of food and raw materials in time of war.[15] From the

THE POSITION OF THE CHANNEL TUNNEL QUESTION IN MAY, 1914.

STATEMENT ON BEHALF OF THE HOUSE OF COMMONS CHANNEL TUNNEL COMMITTEE

BY

ARTHUR FELL, M.P.

CHAIRMAN

LONDON

HUGH REES, LTD.

5, REGENT STREET, S.W.

1914

The Position of the Channel Tunnel Question in May 1914,
pamphlet by Arthur Fell

Admiralty, they had the following paragraph, sent by the Chief of Naval Staff, Admiral Henry Jackson, on 27 February:

> The Admiralty consider it indispensable that a Channel Tunnel should be capable of being flooded or otherwise effectively cut at any time by the Navy through the gunfire or other action of warships without military assistance, even though both ends of the tunnel are in the hands of the enemy. It is for the promoters of the scheme and their engineers to satisfy this vital condition. If they are able to do so, the project offers various important strategic advantages, including a greater assurance of our food supply. If they cannot do so, the Admiralty would be compelled to oppose the scheme.[16]

Discussion on 3 March revolved around the Admiralty's condition. The First Lord, Winston Churchill, stated that this proviso had been made, not through doubt of the ability of the Army to guard the tunnel exit or through any desire to relieve the War Office of this responsibility, but because the Admiralty 'did not wish to break in on the principle that the Navy was in all circumstances able to prevent the invasion of this country by a considerable organised force'. Churchill was clearly reluctant to condemn the project and, even after eliciting from Admiral Fisher that the Admiralty had in 1907 furnished a memorandum 'entirely condemning' it, stated that, 'If it could be proved by the promoters that, even were France in possession of both ends, the tunnel could, nevertheless, be breached by warships, then it would be very difficult to oppose its construction'. Seely took a harder line. Having attempted to justify the War Office's silence on the grounds of lack of detailed information, he stated categorically: 'If France were to be postulated as hostile, or even luke-warm, the General Staff would be opposed to the project . . . Only if it could be assumed that the two countries were on such intimate terms, that in the event of war they could be regarded as one nation, would there be a sound reason for making the tunnel.'

Before the Prime Minister adjourned the discussion by calling for a statement of views of the War Office at the next meeting, and the production by the Admiralty either of the 1907 memorandum or, if they dissented from their predecessors' views, a further memorandum, Field-Marshal Nicholson, French's predecessor as CIGS, made a very sound point. He said:

> the Admiralty's proposals seemed to imply that no other nations possessed any war vessels. The means suggested for destroying the tunnel could equally be taken advantage of by a maritime Power with a view of preventing this country from drawing supplies from the continent or of utilising the tunnel for other proposed purposes.[17]

2. 'A Somewhat Paradoxical Situation'

According to his diary, the DMO, General Wilson, told the CID on 3 March 1914: 'if we are going to take part in European wars, the more tunnels we have the better, if not, then the fewer we have the better'.[18] According to Hankey's minutes of the meeting, Wilson made no contribution at all. To meet the wishes of the Prime Minister for a statement of the views of the War Office, Wilson wrote a memorandum on the Channel Tunnel. In this he ruled out the possibility of a 'bolt from the blue': 'the seizure of the Dover defences in a time of profound peace, by a trainload of troops in disguise is too fantastic to be seriously considered'. He poured cold water on the idea that Dover was more vulnerable to attack, the CID in its reconsideration of the invasion problem having admitted that 70,000 men (as opposed to 5,000 in 1907) might be landed: 'although the navy may not be able to prevent the landing of 5,000 or 7,000 men *at every point on 1,000 miles of coastline* it is surely possible to secure one definite locality that is known to be of vital importance!' Considering the value of a tunnel for operations on the Continent in support of France, he supported the point made on 3 March by Nicholson. As for such purposes the tunnel had to be absolutely secure, this 'rules out devices, such as that recently proposed, by which the shore ends of the tunnel connections could be destroyed by the guns or torpedoes of the fleet'. For, if that were the case, 'it would be possible for a hostile fleet also to destroy the connection and thus to upset the plans of concentration that depend on it'. His concluding paragraph is worth quoting in full:

> Summing up the conclusions arrived at in this paper it may be said that there is cause for enquiry only on the assumption that it is proposed to employ the Expeditionary Force on the Continent. Given certain conditions of efficiency and reliability for military purposes, together with adequate safeguards against its use by an enemy it may then be said that from the purely military point of view the advantages offered would outweigh the risks entailed. It is however impossible to ignore the fact that the existence of a tunnel would tend to drive us more and more into the Continental orbit and force us to take sides in Continental quarrels whether we wished to or not.
>
> The final decision therefore resolves itself into one of National policy. If this country is in a position and can in the future maintain a position of complete independence with regard to the various groups on the Continent and is prepared, if need be, to make head against a hostile combination of Naval Powers, then the construction of a Channel Tunnel is to be deprecated. But,

should circumstances compel us to abandon such an attitude and to range ourselves definitely on the side of France then the existence of a tunnel would contribute materially to the chance of success of our arms.[19]

Wilson was still attempting to draw the Government into an explicit commitment to France. If successful, this would have provided additional support for the call he had made the previous year for a standing army of at least 500,000, which, he claimed, would be the best guarantee for the preservation of European peace.[20]

Such restraint as Wilson displayed in March 1914 was an acknowledgement that his views were not shared by those in his immediate vicinity. As it was, he had to change the conclusion of this memorandum of March, at the insistence of Seely. By 8 April he had drafted another ending:

The construction of a Tunnel will add something to the cost and much to the anxiety of the military and naval authorities . . . These disadvantages, serious as they are, may be outweighed by the fact of the increased facilities gained by the transport of our troops and stores to the Continent of Europe if HMG has such an operation in view. In short, from a purely military point of view, if our troops were to become engaged in a European war fighting alongside the French the more tunnels we possess the better, if on the other hand no such operations are in contemplation then we want no tunnels at all.

As Col. Seely said at the 125th CID, 3 March 1914: 'Only if it could be assumed that the two countries were on such intimate terms, that in the event of war they could be regarded as one nation, would there be a sound reason for making the tunnel.[21]

Seely resigned at the end of March over his handling of the Curragh affair, and Asquith appointed himself Secretary of State for War two weeks later. The CIGS, Sir John French, also resigned, and was replaced by General Sir Charles Douglas on 3 April. Wilson submitted both his memoranda to Douglas, who wished him to recast the second one. Wilson did this immediately by adding, after the quotation from Seely:

On the other hand, even if we assume that these conditions now prevail there is no course of certainty as to how long they may continue to prevail. The question is, therefore, ought we to saddle ourselves permanently with the increased military responsibilities and anxieties involved by the construction of tunnel merely for the sake of the advantage to be derived from one set of conditions alone, which, in the nature of things, is liable to undergo a complete change at any moment? In the opinion of the General Staff the answer is in the negative.[22]

1 An English print of about 1801 showing Napoleon invading by
a secret tunnel (*Eurotunnel*)

2 Henry Horeau's plan for a tube suspended beneath floating towers anchored
to the sea bed (*Eurotunnel*)

3 Thomé de Gamond (*Eurotunnel*)   4 Lord Richard Grosvenor (*Eurotunnel*)

5 Field-Marshal Sir Garnet Wolseley   6 Field-Marshal H.R.H.
the Duke of Cambridge

7 Borings at Abbot's Cliff in St Margaret's Bay (from a distance).
Engraving about 1880

8 Borings at Abbot's Cliff in St Margaret's Bay. Engraving about 1880

9 Sir Edward Watkin defeating French invaders by flooding the tunnel.
Penny Illustrated Paper (1882)

10 Sir George Clarke
(Lord Sydenham of Combe)

11 Winston Churchill and Lord Fisher outside the offices of the Committee of
Imperial Defence (*Press Association*)

12 H. H. Asquith

13 Field-Marshal Sir John French

14 Sir Arthur Fell

15 Marshal Foch and General Henry Wilson

16 Maurice Hankey and David Lloyd George

Wilson's cumulative conclusions of April survived. That of March was dropped. The former, and the paragraphs dealing anxiously with 'a hostile France' and the references to Wolseley's 'strong case' of 1881 and the Alison Committee's point about 'the uncertainty which always exists in dealing with physical agencies, to the fallibility of human nature, and to the possibility of a long period of peace engendering carelessness', represented the views of Seely and of the new CIGS and were responsible for the distinctly negative tenor of the General Staff memorandum printed on 1 May and submitted to the CID meeting on 14 May.[23]

The Admiralty, meanwhile, had found their memorandum of 1907 and reprinted it, with a note to the effect that their brief statement of March 1914 embodied the result of their full reconsideration of the subject, and they had nothing to add to that.[24] These were the only additional documents before the 126th CID on 14 May 1914, though the former First Sea Lord, Fisher, recently active on the Royal Commission on Fuel and Engines, who was unable to attend, sent a short note to Asquith in which he said that he had tried to go back on the Admiralty memorandum of 1907 but could not – 68A (the number given to it by Hankey in 1914) was, in his view, 'impregnable'.[25]

On 14 May 1914 the Admiralty played into the hands of the General Staff. Churchill, who was really in favour of the tunnel, declared that he was wholly opposed to it if it was made indestructible from the sea. Challenged by Seely (who though no longer Secretary of State for War remained on the CID) and by Nicholson, who repeated that the conditions postulated by the Admiralty could never be really assured, he said that 'the principle underlying the conditions laid down by the Admiralty was the preservation of our insularity'. By this what he really meant was 'the preservation of the Admiralty's traditional role', which is what he had more nearly said at the meeting on 3 March. Asquith summarised matters well when he said that 'a somewhat paradoxical situation had been arrived at. Colonel Seely was in favour of the tunnel only if it could not be destroyed; the First Lord was in favour of it only if it could be destroyed . . . The General Staff were against the tunnel, but the two Field-Marshals present were apparently in favour of it'. One of these Field-Marshals, French, had at the outset distanced himself from the General Staff view, saying that he was personally in favour of the scheme: 'It was yearly becoming less of a military danger, and from the point of view of improving communications with the other side the sooner we could agree to its construction the better.' He elaborated on this, producing an opinion described by the Foreign Secretary, rather

inadequately but damning all the same, as 'novel'. What French said was
that

> he was in favour of it because, in his opinion, it would improve our strategical
> position. This was quite apart from whether the French were friendly or
> hostile, and immaterial whether the tunnel were destructible or not. He held
> that it was necessary for us to hold the opposite side of the Channel, either by
> ourselves or with an ally. It would be a grave danger to us if an enemy held
> Calais. That was why he wanted to see the tunnel built.

The other Field-Marshal, Nicholson, was more subdued than this,
merely saying there was much to be said in favour of a tunnel if the
Admiralty were unable to guarantee the food supply. Sir Edward Grey,
still shocked by the 'novelty' of French's contribution, suggested that the
papers were not sufficiently complete, and the meeting was adjourned
for a week so that Nicholson and French might make good the
deficiency.[26]

Nicholson found this easier to do than did French. His memorandum
was completed by 19 May. Nicholson was impressed by what had
emerged from the 122nd meeting of the CID on 6 February 1913,
namely that the Navy might now not be in a position to safeguard the
supply of food and raw materials. From this point of view, a Channel
Tunnel might help to compensate. Even so, Nicholson preferred the
establishment in the country of a reserve of wheat, flour and other
foodstuffs. As for its utility in the despatch and maintenance of an
Expeditionary Force in support of France against Germany, Nicholson
agreed with the General Staff 'in doubting whether the contingency is
sufficiently probable, and our entente with France sufficiently permanent, to justify the construction of a tunnel for this reason alone.[27]

As French's paper was still not ready, the question was dropped from
the agenda of the meeting on 21 May, and postponed until 14 July.[28] In
the interim Churchill tried his hand at a solution to the particular
engineering difficulties he had set the promoters. He suggested bringing the tunnel to the surface of the sea a quarter of a mile from the shore,
taking the railway tracks from there on a bridge into which would be
built a drawbridge section, and then running the railway along the coast
for half a mile. He went on.

> As long as we are effectively superior at sea and can command the debouches of
> the tunnel and cut the communications by naval gunfire, there is no reason why
> we should not have all the advantages of a certain immunity from attack
> through the tunnel when France is our enemy, and of a trustworthy line of

communication easily maintained to the Continent when we are at war with another Power and France is our friend.

Churchill believed he had disposed successfully of the possibility of treachery, and said 'it would be interesting to hear of any combination of circumstances not covered by the above-named precautions'.[29]

At this point the Secretary of the CID, Hankey, intervened.

Maurice Pascal Alers Hankey plays a large part in this story of the Channel Tunnel. It would not be going too far to say that he became, as he grew more powerful, the 'demon king' of the affair, orchestrating as he did much of the opposition to it. Born in Biarritz of an Australian mother, he had entered the Royal Marines in 1895, and passed out first with the sword of honour from the Royal Naval College. He served in the Mediterranean from 1899 to 1902, and then in the Naval Intelligence Department of the Admiralty from 1902 to 1907. In 1908 he was appointed an assistant secretary in the CID. When he became Secretary of the CID in 1912 he was only thirty-five years of age. He had become a devotee of Admiral Lord Fisher, and remained one throughout his life. In the aftermath of the Agadir crisis of 1911, during which war was most definitely in sight between Britain and France on the one hand and Germany on the other, he was heavily engaged in combatting the 'continental' strategy of the General Staff and in trying to substitute for it a strategy which would place the Army under the instructions of, and at the disposal of, the Navy. During the Great War, which was not fought as he wanted, he became successively secretary of the War Council, the Dardanelles Committee and the War Committee. When the War Cabinet Secretariat was established by Lloyd George, Hankey was put in charge of it, and was responsible for designing and developing its organisation and its ethos. He remained Secretary to the Cabinet until 1938, combining that position of influence and responsibility with the secretaryship of the revived CID and, from 1923, with the clerkship of the Privy Council. He was created first Baron Hankey in 1939, returned to public life to join Neville Chamberlain's War Cabinet as Minister without Portfolio, was made Chancellor of the Duchy of Lancaster by Churchill in May 1940, then Paymaster-General from 1941 until March 1942, when Churchill finally dismissed him for talking too much.

In a note of 8 May 1914 he had drawn attention to the fact that the following conclusion of the Sub-Committee of 1908 on Oversea Attack had been reaffirmed by the Sub-Committee which had reported in April 1914: 'The Committee consider that the possibility of a surprise attack being made upon this country during normal diplomatic relations is not sufficiently remote to be ignored. They agree with Mr Balfour that if the German Government believed that the adoption of such a plan made the difference between failure and success, it is conceivable that they might resort to it.'[30] In a draft memorandum of 1 July 1914 Hankey proceeded to hoist the Admiralty with their own petard:

> The case against the Channel Tunnel has always been based mainly on the argument that the Dover end might be seized by a *coup de main* as the first act of a sudden outbreak of war. The CID has recently re-affirmed its previous conclusion that this danger was not so remote to be ignored, and throughout the recent inquiry into the question of Oversea Attack the Admiralty, and more particularly the First Lord have reiterated their opinion that the outset of a war was the most probable moment for a raid. In fact it was at the insistence of the Naval Members that the recommendation (so embarrassing to the Army) was inserted that it must be assumed that a raiding attack may be made immediately on the outbreak of war.

If France attacked, wrote Hankey, she would use submarines, mines and aircraft to keep the British Navy at a distance. Days might elapse before the tunnel was rendered inoperative, and in this time the invaders might affect a lodgement: 'Meanwhile a great panic would have set in; the naval and probably the military plans would have been dislocated; some ships might have been sunk; and forces of both branches of the Service would have been drawn towards Dover, unmasking other parts of the coast.' If Germany attacked, in order to prevent the British Expeditionary Force using the tunnel, 'even if the war were preceded by a period of strained relations it would take a day or two to mobilise our defences, and during this time the tunnel approaches would be vulnerable'. To Hankey the tunnel would always be a hostage to fortune, 'always a weak spot, and feints might be successful in diverting forces thither away from their proper role'. Churchill's plan he considered unreliable – it 'neither safeguards us against the danger of the Tunnel in the event of a hostile France, nor secures the sole advantage which we should obtain from it in a war with Germany'.[31]

Hankey's views coincided with those of the Prime Minister, who on 14 May had seen no reason to depart from the Admiralty's 1907 position, even though the Admiralty itself had done so. In the final version of the memorandum, 'Prepared by direction of the Prime Minister' and printed on 7 July, Hankey rubbed even more salt in to the Admiralty's self-inflicted wounds by quoting paragraph 36 of the Report of the Sub-Committee on Oversea Attack, which said:

With regard to sudden naval attack, the Admiralty consider the following assumption justified:

'That simultaneous attacks at different points upon ships lying at anchor or upon forts, under peace conditions, can be made at any time by foreign warships without noticeable preparation of any kind, and that serious injury might thereby be inflicted on the British naval forces. Whether this contingency is to be taken into account by the Admiralty in times of profound peace is a question which must be decided by the Government. The Admiralty must, however, point out that the strain of "War in Peace", which the necessary precautions, in themselves only partially effective, would impose, could not be kept up for any length of time. In short, there is no defence against such an act of treachery, unprecedented in the history of civilised nations.'[32]

At the beginning of July the former Secretary of State for War also fired shots across Churchill's bows. Contrary to what he had been told in March 1914 by his DMO and in October 1913 by his CIGS, Seely maintained that the possession by the enemy of both ends of a tunnel in working order for even twenty-four hours would enable him to transport an army much larger than 70,000 men. In general terms, Seely contended that a tunnel connecting a very weak military state with very strong military neighbours must be an added risk to the weaker state. More specifically, the Admiralty's condition that the tunnel must be easily destructible from the sea was fatal to all plans for using it to supplement food supply and to send the Expeditionary Force to the Continent.[33]

Field Marshal French was still having difficulty in expressing himself. On 1 July he wrote to Hankey: 'I will try to let you have paper on Channel Tunnel in a day or two. I find it most difficult to express my ideas without leaving an impression of exaggeration. I have a very clear conception of what is in my mind but on paper it looks far-fetched and Utopian . . . '[34] French's memorandum finally appeared on 9 July. French was not concerned to refute objections to the tunnel. He considered all these to have been conclusively refuted in an address given by Sir George Clarke, now Lord Sydenham, to the House of Commons Channel Tunnel Committee on 29 June.(Sydenham effectively reproduced here his arguments of June 1906; his address was issued as a pamphlet.[35]) Going well beyond the position he had taken up in October 1913 and May 1914, French revealed his fear of invasion as a result of recent developments in aircraft and submarines. So spectacular had these inventions proved, and so much had they affected and would they affect the command of the sea, that French anticipated command of the

Straits of Dover being settled 'by success in a trial of strength between forces composed of submarines plus aircraft'. Envisaging the defeat of France by Germany and the concentration on the east Channel coast opposite Dover of three-quarters of the submarine and aircraft strength possessed by all the great European powers, his recommendation was visionary in the extreme. For he held

> that the only reliable defence against a powerful attack by hostile aircraft and submarines in vastly superior numbers, is to possess a strong bridge-head on the French coast with an effective means of passing and re-passing across the Straits, which would only be secured by the projected Channel Tunnel.

With the Channel tunnel a complete and indestructible line of communication between the two countries, even if disaster befell the Franco-British armies, France would have an effective *point d'appui*, would be able to hold the neighbouring terrain, deny the use of her ports to hostile submarines, and could not then be 'so overwhelmed as to necessitate . . . sacrifices most disastrous to this country'. Should France be unfriendly, for 'experience proves that alliances and ententes are not everlasting', French admitted that the tunnel would have to be rendered 'temporarily ineffective'. For the moment, noting the consistent French support for a tunnel, he set the following high fence for the Foreign Office to ride at:

> it would seem to be not altogether outside the bounds of possibility to secure agreements, which in certain contingencies would give this country the right to hold the French side of the Tunnel. Of course, this is a matter which has to be judged by diplomatists; but, speaking personally, I should not despair in the present state of feeling of arriving at an arrangement by which we could permanently do so.[36]

The 128th meeting of the CID began, not surprisingly, by taking up French's memorandum. The Prime Minister pointed out the different attitudes on the part of French and of the Admiralty towards the destructibility of the tunnel. Nicholson disagreed with French. He considered 'that a bridge-head in our hands on the far side of the Channel would be dangerous unless we had an adequate military force to hold it. *Ex hypothesi* there would be no such adequate military force'. (Seely added later that the matter of military strength might be summed up 'by saying that we should consider conscription first and the tunnel afterwards'.) Lord Kitchener, who had spent some time with Hankey earlier in the month inveighing against the scheme, said that 'it would put us in the position of a continental nation with a land frontier, and we should be faced with all the disadvantages which land frontiers entailed'. If the tunnel were built, he doubted 'whether this country would ever feel sufficiently confident to send the Expeditionary Force abroad'. The meeting then developed into a contest between Churchill and Asquith. The latter made it clear that he considered Seely's paper 'a formidable reply' to Churchill's, that he considered the four short sentences of the Admiralty's latest paper did not represent a reasoned statement showing that the Admiralty no longer held its views of 1907, and that no one had been able to refute Campbell-Bannerman's dictum concerning the 'feeling of insecurity' that would exist throughout the country even supposing the military dangers to be amply provided against. Asquith, who had voted with Campbell-Bannerman in favour of the tunnel on 5 June 1890, administered the *coup de grâce* by stating that the discussion had shown no sufficient ground for reversing the decision of the Government in 1907. Lord Crewe seconded this. French, Churchill and Battenberg, the First Sea Lord, formally recorded their dissent.[37]

3. Conclusion

In 1907 the main proponent of the Channel Tunnel, apart from the company itself, was the Secretary of the CID, Sir George Clarke; the Service Departments were unanimous in their opposition to the scheme; and Prime Minister Campbell-Bannerman insisted that the project be considered solely from the naval and military point of view, without allowing any wider-ranging enquiry, such as Clarke had wanted, to develop. In 1914 the Channel Tunnel had higher-ranking support, in the form of the First Lord of the Admiralty and the CIGS, but the Service Departments were split. (Even if French had remained CIGS there would have been incompatibility between his and Churchill's conditions as to the destructibility of the tunnel.) The inconsistency of the Admiralty's position relative to one CID enquiry with its position relative to another was most effectively demonstrated by Clarke's successor, Hankey. In the absence of a strong positive lead from either the Board of Trade or the Foreign Office, there was no case for authorising the careful and extensive enquiry which Esher – who opposed the scheme but did not attend CID meetings because of his disgust at the Government's Irish policy – believed would be required to alter the decision of 1907.[38]

The part of Campbell-Bannerman's public statement of March 1907 which Asquith found most persuasive involved 'a feeling of insecurity, which might lead to a constant demand for increased expenditure, naval and military, and a continual risk of unrest and possible alarm'. The parts of the 1907 Admiralty memorandum which most appealed to him mentioned divided responsibility, increased danger, diminished security and interference with the natural sea frontier.[39] One wonders whether these possibilities sufficiently account for the decisions of 1907 and 1914. Behind the continental bridgehead envisaged by Sir John French two spectres lurked. One was that the adoption of conscription, one of the great taboos of British politics, might have to be reconsidered. This was picked up by the author of the 1907 Admiralty memorandum, Lord Fisher, and given as his reason for returning to the fold which he had at one stage left: 'at one time I was rather hot on the Channel Tunnel, but I discovered this was an artful dodge towards Conscription, so I bolted'.[40] There was something in this. Artfulness was General Sir Henry Wilson's *forte*. The other spectre was that the pretence that a choice persisted between entanglement and non-entanglement in continental wars and the sending or withholding of the Expeditionary Force might have to be abandoned. Fisher, who believed that 'As the people of this country will never permit an English soldier to fight on the Continent of Europe in a Franco-German war, there will later on be a hell of a row with France as to *Perfide Albion*', also picked this up, saying to another correspondent that he had dropped the Channel Tunnel 'because I see I should play into the hands of the Major-Generals who are constantly going to and from our War Office to Nancy as regards our sending an Army to Flanders!'[41] One had to remember, as the Secretary of State for India, echoing the Admiralty, wrote in 1907, 'that in the great high latitudes of policy all is fluid, elastic, mutable; the friend of today, the foe tomorrow; the ally and confederate against the enemy, suddenly *his* confederate against you; Russia or France or Germany or America, one sort of Power this year, quite another sort and in deeply changed relations to you, the year after!'[42]

These were powerful incentives towards doing nothing, towards leaving the situation unchanged. Behind them, again, lurked other traits. The Channel Tunnel proposal came to grief in the decade immediately preceding the First World War as a result of both too much imagination and too little. From too much complacency about the present, and too little self-confidence to try to shape the future, the Liberal Governments of Campbell-Bannerman and Asquith consigned the British people to more of their traditional separate development.

CHANNEL TUNNEL VISIONS

PART II

1914–1945

Chapter 4

The First World War, 1914-18

1. From the Outbreak of War to the Fall of Asquith

In November 1913, at the monthly luncheon of the Federation of French Manufacturers and Merchants held at the Hotel Continental in Paris, M. Albert Sartiaux, chief engineer of Nord du France Railway Company, had congratulated the *Daily Chronicle* on its positive coverage of the Channel Tunnel issue: 'This important journal', he said, 'has taken the initiative of a referendum among leading people in England. I find on the average that out of every three people consulted two were in favour of the Tunnel and one was opposed to it'.[1] Although the *Daily Chronicle* continued to give its support, and was far from alone, amongst the organs of the British press, in doing so, this was, as we know, to no avail. The CID, at least, had adopted a view akin to that of *The Times*, which had stated that the tunnel would take from Britons their feeling of insularity, a 'feeling of insularity' so important that its loss would outweigh even a conclusive and demonstrable advantage in regard to food supply or the movement of troops in time of war,[2] a view castigated by the *Daily Chronicle* in the following terms:

> What is, then, this feeling of insularity . . .? If it means the mere feeling of oversea isolation, surely that has been made impossible by aviation no less than it would be by a tunnel; indeed more so, since you can close the Tunnel when you cannot close the air . . . But if *The Times* means something more substantial; if it means that extra national segregation is a good thing, that the small number of travellers between Britain and the Continent is a good thing, that our national virtues can only be preserved by cloistering them (and many old fashioned people undoubtedly take these views) then we can only say that we differ entirely, and believe that the best sense of the nation will differ likewise.[3]

On the outbreak of war, in August 1914, the promoters of the Channel Tunnel scheme suspended their activities temporarily. In March 1915, however, Arthur Fell, Chairman of the House of Commons Channel Tunnel Committee, issued a statement that on the termination of the war the supporters of the tunnel would press the matter forward without delay. There was at this point very little press interest in the tunnel, although in the following July both the *Globe* and the *Universe* deplored the fact that it had not been built before the war.[4] In April 1916, however, the *Yorkshire Post* announced that the course of the war, and in particular the damage being done to British shipping, had caused it to drop its pre-war opposition to the scheme, and to become an advocate of it:

> there can be no question that, in present conditions, the provision of a railway route between this country and France would add enormously to our means of supplying our troops, thus relieving a considerable tonnage of our merchant shipping, and would enable neutral and our own ships to unload at any port in France, Italy, Spain, or Portugal, the cargoes being run by rail directly to this country.

The *Yorkshire Post* went on, typically, to fail to see 'why German prisoners of war should not have been employed on the work of constructing the Tunnel'.[5] This was followed by two articles by Walter Behrens, ex-President of the British Chamber of Commerce in Paris, on what he called 'The *Entente Cordiale* Line'. He suggested that opposition to the tunnel could be broken down were a committee established to make propaganda for the scheme, and offered to serve on this committee himself.[6] Two weeks later, the *Observer* took up the cause, with an article entitled 'The War and the Channel Tunnel: A Lost Opportunity'.[7]

Further impetus was given when the press reported the evidence given on 24 May by Sir Lionel Earle, Secretary of the Office of Works, before the Select Committee of the House of Lords, in connection with the South Eastern and Chatham Railway Company's Bill for the strengthening of the Charing Cross railway bridge over the Thames. Sir Lionel stated that the end of the war would see an enormous increase in traffic on this railway, ultimately to the Continent, and that a Channel Tunnel was probable. He went on:

> Surely, if the site of Charing Cross is inadequate at the present moment, how much more so will it be from this large increase of traffic if the Channel Tunnel comes in the future, as I think it probably will. My own idea would be that, if it

were possible, to delay (strengthening the existing bridge) for further consideration. I have always had a hope that it might – that it would make a most
magnificent memorial if a fine bridge could be built at that spot somewhere –
one of the most important spots in London – to the memory of those who have
fallen. I have always been led to believe that the site of Charing Cross – a site of
four acres – is so valuable that it would practically re-instate a new station on the
other side of the river, where the site would be less expensive.[8]

The promoters of the Channel Tunnel immediately responded by
issuing a statement that they had always regarded the construction of an
international station on the south side of the Thames, opposite the
existing terminus of Charing Cross, as an essential complement of their
scheme. If Charing Cross Station were moved to the south of the river,
both the promoters of the Channel Tunnel and the Managing Committee of the South Eastern and Chatham Railway hoped that advantage
would be taken 'to build a monumental bridge, approached by a new
public thoroughfare giving direct access to the Western districts of the
metropolis'.[9] On 1 June W. Turner Perkins, the literary Secretary of the
Channel Tunnel Company, sought an interview with Hankey.[10]
Although unsuccessful in this, morale was sustained when, on 10 June,
the *Yorkshire Post* chipped in again and allowed itself, untypically, to raise
the prospect of state assistance to the scheme:

> having regard to the fact that England and France had between them contri-
> buted some £8,000,000 per day to carry on the war . . . the supporters of the
> Channel Tunnel have not the least hesitation in affirming that, if the suggested
> railway is henceforth to be looked upon as a monument of civilisation which will
> indissolubly link the destinies of the two countries, the respective Governments
> may readily provide either the money necessary for the work, or, at least, offer
> the assistance demanded by way of guarantees on the capital required.[11]

The next thing to improve morale was the Economic Conference of the
Allied Governments held in Paris between 14 and 17 June 1916. It was
widely believed that the resolutions arrived at by this conference had a
distinct and direct bearing on the Channel Tunnel scheme. In this
climate, Arthur Fell gave formal notice of a motion he wished to move in
the House of Commons:

> That in the opinion of this House the progress of the war has demonstrated the
> great advantages which would have accrued to this country and to the Allied
> Powers had a railway tunnel beneath the Channel been constructed and in
> operation, and that the time has arrived for H.M. Government to support the
> proposal, so that the final plans may be prepared and powers obtained to

proceed with the work as soon as the war is over and the necessary labour is available.[12]

This opened the floodgates of favourable opinion. Sir Arthur Conan Doyle was the first into print, writing that national folly could not rise higher than it had in 'allowing ourselves to be frightened off from doing what was clearly to our advantage by the most absurd bogies, such as that we would be invaded through a rabbit burrow in the ground twenty-six miles long'.[13] The *Daily Chronicle* took up the cudgels again in earnest, with an article on 'The Channel Tunnel in War Time: The Purposes Which it Would Have Served': 'Posterity will marvel how we managed to carry on our gigantic share in the greatest Continental war in history without the Tunnel. It would have saved the State millions of pounds and not a few lives.'[14] Fell delivered the same message in the *Daily Graphic* on 10 July: 'A Channel Tunnel: How it Would Have Helped to Win the War'; on 14 July he reported to the House of Commons Channel Tunnel Committee, now 140 strong, on his recent visit to Paris, where perhaps the most important person he had seen was M. Clementel, the French Minister of Commerce, who had told them that the carrying out of the arrangements made at the Allies' recent conference in Paris depended to an extent upon the construction of the Channel Tunnel, and that the Italian and Belgian Governments, equally with the French, were eager to see the scheme completed as soon as possible.[15]

Throughout the following fortnight the press was full of pro-Tunnel material. Engineering aspects were addressed in the *Daily Telegraph* on 17 July. On 19 July H.W. Wilson, the military correspondent of the *Daily Mail*, pointing to the development of long-range artillery, aircraft and submarines, concluded that the experience of war had 'entirely vindicated' the views of Lord Sydenham (the title Sir George Clarke had taken) and was convinced that 'the Tunnel is coming – of that there can be no doubt'. The *Financial London Mail*, on 22 July, agreed, and saw the tunnel as a way of permanently sealing the *Entente Cordiale*. The *New Statesman* of the same date agreed and mocked the remarks of *The Times*' military correspondent, who had stated soon after the outbreak of war that the war was the death-blow to the idea of a Channel Tunnel. The *Practical Engineer* of 27 July stated that 'the war has disposed of many shibboleths, of none more surely than that strange one of "splendid isolation" as a kind of national policy', and went on to speak of the 'golden possibilities' of the Channel Tunnel. The *Daily Chronicle* of 27 July carried an interview with the French economist and former Minister of Public Works Yves Guyot, and on this same day the *Evening*

THE CHANNEL TUNNEL

MILITARY ASPECT OF THE QUESTION

IMPORTANT ADDRESS

BY

Rt. Hon. LORD SYDENHAM OF COMBE,

G.C.S.I.

Formerly Secretary of the Committee of Imperial Defence.

HOUSE OF COMMONS: GRAND COMMITTEE ROOM No. 10

Monday, 29th June, 1914

The Channel Tunnel: 'Military Aspect of the Question',
pamphlet by Lord Sydenham, July 1914

Standard commenced a three-part series of articles by Arthur Fell. C. Lewis Hind, in the *Daily Chronicle*, went beyond an earlier position, which had been that a new bridge over the Thames at Charing Cross be designated a National Memorial, and waxed lyrical about an Imperial Memorial, one component of which would be the Channel Tunnel:

> Into the Imperial Memorial comes naturally the making of the Channel Tunnel – that symbol of our faith and confidence in our great Ally. In the years to come Charing Cross Station – the new Charing Cross on the Surrey side – will be the London terminus of an immense Continental traffic – Charing Cross to Baghdad, Petrograd to Charing Cross – and Empire Bridge will be the great highway along which all must pass into Imperial London. Station and bridge are one with the Channel Tunnel, the chapel and the statues, and each must be worthy of this great adventure of peace – this Imperial Memorial.[16]

On the evening of 28 July 1916, Fell presided at a dinner given in the members' Dining Room of the House of Commons to afford those attending an opportunity of meeting representatives from France and other Allies who favoured the construction of a Channel Tunnel. He spoke at length, and introduced M. Guyot, who declared, 'In France the Channel Tunnel is not a question. All sections consider that it is a matter of absolute necessity', Sir Francis Fox, who had been involved in the building of the Simplon Tunnel and the Mersey Tunnel, and who recalled, to laughter, the tremendous objections raised by Lord Palmerston to the Suez Canal 'as it would ruin our Indian Empire', and others.[17] The success of this meeting, and the widespread press coverage which continued,[18] caused Arthur Fell not to wait for parliamentary time to be found to discuss his motion. On behalf of his committee he wrote to the Prime Minister on 10 August. Fell reminded Asquith that he had told the deputation which he had received three years earlier that the question was being considered by the relevant Government Departments, and that the opinion of the Government had still not been made public. Raising the issue again, as something to be taken up as soon as the war ended, Fell made several points:

> It will provide a large amount of work for labour, both on the work itself and in the making of the machinery and plant . . . It will improve the means of communication between this country and our Allies on the continent out of all measure, and enable the Paris resolution to be carried out by providing a rapid means of communication with France and also with Belgium and Italy, countries which will need every help to enable them to divert their trade profitably from Germany to this country. It will so strengthen the military position of the Allies for a possible further war that the commencement of the tunnel will

render such a war less likely, and the mere fact of its construction being determined on will have a favourable effect on the conditions of peace which the Allies may be in a position to enforce.

The course of the war, Fell maintained, had proved the correctness of the statements made by the promoters of the scheme; his committee had grown from 100 to 160 members from all four parties in the House of Commons, and had so much support from both the outside public and representatives of the Allied Powers that it was appropriate to ask the Government 'to consider the subject from the experience gained in the war and the new conditions which now prevail', and to give the matter its most urgent attention. Fell ended by saying that he proposed, at the end of the summer recess, to ask Asquith to receive a deputation to which the decision of the Government would be announced.[19]

Fell's letter was formally communicated only on 28 August to the War Office, Board of Trade and Admiralty. The newly-appointed Director of Military Operations, General Sir Frederick Maurice, was already discussing it with his old ally against the scheme, Repington of *The Times*, on 16 August, and giving vent to the same cautious views as expressed by his predecessor, General Robertson, in an audience with the same military correspondent on 4 August. Robertson, Maurice and Repington were all agreed that the main thing was 'not to let this scheme proceed until we are sure of our National Army'. Only if the conscription of war-time became a permanent feature of British life would they change their position.[20] This was the substantive point made by the Army Council in its formal reply to Hankey of 2 September. After quoting the views expressed by the General Staff in May 1914, the Army Council said that 'they do not feel that the above conclusions can be suitably reviewed until they are informed as to what is to be the military policy of H.M.'s Government after the war'.[21] The article which Repington began on 25 August and finished on 7 September argued the same case at greater length.[22] At the Board of Trade, one official took the line that 'the war has shown how useless a Tunnel would have been for the purpose of bringing in to the U.K. supplies from oversea and indeed from the adjacent countries'; more hostility manifested itself in the not entirely consistent thought that 'the Germans might conceivably have made Calais one of their principal objectives if only for the purpose of destroying what would have been a useful means of communication and supply for the Allied forces in Flanders'.[23] In its formal reply the Board of Trade called the attention of the CID to the considerations set out in its memorandum of 1914, claiming that it was based on recent statistics. The reply went on:

> The Board are aware that para. 2 of section (C) of the Recommendations of the Economic Conference of the Allies, which was held in Paris in June 1916, provides that, 'in order to permit the interchange of their products, the Allies undertake to adopt measures for facilitating their mutual trade relations both by the establishment of direct and rapid land and sea transport services at low rates and by extension and improvement of postal, telegraphic, and other communications'.
>
> They are, however, disposed to doubt whether such increase of traffic in particular directions as might result from the adoption of systematic steps to cultivate trade between this country, Belgium, France, and Italy could be sufficient to outweigh the grave disadvantages to which an all-rail route would in any case be subject, or could seriously affect the financial aspects of the scheme referred to . . .

Finally, the Board of Trade invoked the prospect of financial embarrassment and the necessity to conserve the resources of Allied countries 'for essential purposes' and advised against large expenditure on a Channel Tunnel 'unless supported by weighty considerations of a non-economic character'.[24]

By 12 October, on which day in reply to another parliamentary question from Fell Asquith said that he would be pleased to receive a deputation, although no date was set,[25] the Admiralty had still made no reply. On 16 August Repington had advised Maurice to get on terms with the Admiralty on the subject, 'as united opinion was a great strength'. That opinion would be united however, was put in doubt when on 20 August Balfour, the First Lord of Admiralty, gave Repington the impression 'that the Admirals were so upset by the German submarines, that they would be very glad of the tunnel'.[26] By 21 October the Admiralty had sufficiently recovered its poise as to dub the reopening of the question as 'premature' – so much so that they thought it unnecessary 'to express any considered opinion upon the carrying out of such an undertaking'.[27]

Asquith's reception of Fells' deputation had now been arranged for 26 October. By way of preparation, Hankey produced two memoranda. The larger, and more neutral, of these dealt with the history of the scheme over recent decades. Hankey allowed his summary of 'pros' to outnumber 'cons' by six to four; in summarising the latest Departmental views, however, he underlined the words of the Army Council: 'until they were informed as to what is to be the military policy of HM's Government after the war'.[28] In his shorter memorandum Hankey reminded Asquith that if the decision of 1914 was released then the fact that there had been dissentient voices from Churchill, Battenberg, and French would also have to be disclosed. He then marshalled arguments against the points and claims made in Fell's letter of 10 August, listing these as the Labour Argument, the Paris Resolutions Argument, the Military Argument, the Popularity Argument. He ended this version by writing:

> In view of the unanimous opinion expressed separately and independently by the Admiralty, the War Office, and the Board of Trade, it is submitted that the Deputation should be informed that the time is not ripe for the reconsideration of the Channel Tunnel project, but that HM's Government will be prepared to study the question at some future date when the circumstances are more favourable.[29]

Asquith was much kinder to the deputation than Hankey had hoped. He began by giving the CID's decision of July 1914, and emphasised that it was arrived at 'not unanimously but by a majority'. He then accepted the point made by the deputation that the experience gained by the war was 'a new factor of enormous and indeed immeasurable importance'. He seems to have been impressed by what he had been told of French opinion in favour of the scheme, and by the opinion of British soldiers in France and Flanders, represented on the deputation by Major Courthope. Considering 'all this experience and that state of opinion', Asquith had no doubt that it was both desirable and necessary that the question should be reconsidered. Despite the pressure of war work, he was of the opinion that 'this matter in all its aspects, particularly in the light of the new experience which we have gained from the War, should be reviewed by the War Committee, or by the Committee of Imperial Defence . . . and, without prepossession or prejudice, that they should be invited and indeed required to express their judgement upon it'. He promised to see that time was found.[30] The six weeks that remained of Asquith's premiership, however, was not enough for the promised investigation to get under way, despite the additional pressure exerted by the adoption of the following resolution by the Presidents of the French Chambers of Commerce on 11 November: 'That measures be taken by the English and French Governments, with the object of collaborating in the construction of the New International Line under the Channel, and that this should be done before the end of the War, in view of the pressing economic needs which will have to be satisfied, when the War ceases, for the benefit of the two countries.'

2. From the Advent of Lloyd George to the Armistice

The War Cabinet meeting of 1 February 1917, with Lloyd George in the chair, had before it Hankey's memorandum of 23 October 1916. This was because, as Hankey (now Cabinet Secretary) put it in an additional note, it was anticipated that the new Prime Minister would in the near future be asked in Parliament to state what steps had been taken to give effect to the engagement entered upon by his predecessor. Hankey's note considerably altered, and diluted, that engagement. According to Hankey, Asquith 'promised that, subject to the paramount obligations of making provision for the successful prosecution of the war, time would be found, and opportunity given for a full reconsideration of the question'.[31] Asquith's stance had been much more positive than this: he had not made reconsideration 'subject' to the war, but had said that *despite* the war and its demands, time would be found for reconsideration. Prompted by Hankey's slanting of the recent past, however, the War Cabinet decided, 'That the opening of the question at the present juncture was premature; that its official reconsideration should be postponed until after the conclusion of peace; and that, if necessity should arise, a statement to this effect should be made in both Houses of Parliament'.[32] The necessity for such a statement did arise when in April Mr Lynch, MP, asked the Prime Minister about submitting the question to a small committee composed of British and French experts. The Chancellor of the Exchequer, Bonar Law, replied that the question had been carefully considered, 'but it has not been found practicable to proceed further with the matter during the continuance of the war'.[33]

The new Government's decision to set the matter aside was not accepted by Fell. On 27 June he sent Lloyd George a request signed by 110 MPs for a debate upon another motion that he had devised which, if passed, would have committed the Government to the making of plans and to the implementation of them as soon as the war ended. Fell pointed out that the House of Commons had never debated the issue since his Channel Tunnel Committee had been formed, and that there were nearly one hundred members of that Committee who had not been able to sign the request submitted.[34] When Lloyd George brought this before the Cabinet on 17 July it was decided to consult the naval and military authorities and the Board of Trade before answering.[35]

Sir William Robertson, now Chief of the Imperial General Staff, replied almost immediately. He developed at some length an argument based on the uncertainties of the post-war situation:

> It is evident that our military policy after the war must depend on the general policy of HM's Government, and that this again must depend on the nature of the peace settlement, upon the political and military conditions in Europe which will result from it, and upon the strength of the British Army and Navy. For instance, if the present system of alliances continues after the present war and if Germany continues to threaten the balance of power in Europe, railway communication with the Continent, as providing a safer and more rapid route for the transport of troops and material, might be of considerable military advantage; but the security of this line of communication would depend on many factors which it is impossible to forecast, such as the complete withdrawal of Germany from Belgium, the strength and efficiency of the French and Belgian Armies, and the prospect of arresting a German offensive before it could reach the Channel ports. On the other hand, if it seems probable that new combinations of Powers will result from the peace settlement, and that in a future war France may be neutral or even hostile, a Channel Tunnel might involve grave military disadvantages.
>
> Moreover the question cannot be decided without reference to the size and organisation of the British Army in the future, on the degree of support which it will be able to render to a Continental Ally, and on the numbers which will be available for home defence.

The political and military conditions of the future being totally unknown, an opinion as to desirability or otherwise on military grounds could be based only on conjecture, and would be quite valueless. Robertson was happy to note that Fell did not envisage any work being done, or money spent, during the war. He advised that it was premature to attempt to come to a decision.[36]

Although some naval persons had, earlier in the year, been so lacking in confidence about overcoming the submarine menace that they had privately said that the tunnel should be built, the official Admiralty view on this occasion was a reiteration of that produced in October 1916: 'official consideration of the Channel Tunnel should await the termination of the war'.[37]   The views of the Service Department were leaked to Arthur Fell before the Cabinet met to consider them. Anticipating a negative answer to yet another parliamentary question asking for Government support for a Bill to link up the South Eastern and Chatham Railway with the Chemin de Fer du Nord, Fell made a last-ditch attempt to rescue the situation. He wrote to Lloyd George on 13 August:

On the broad international question [the anticipated decision] must have a depressing influence on our own people and on France, Italy and Belgium . . . It will be received with great satisfaction in Germany. It points to the fact that the Peace to be obtained will not be of long duration, and that after it is declared we shall not be able to devote our energies to trade and commerce but shall still be trammelled by a so-called strategic and military policy. The great enterprises which are being considered . . . are still to be dependent on the Government Departments, and under these conditions, little will certainly be done.

His committee's hopes for a great increase of trade with France, Italy and Switzerland would be dashed or postponed; the Government was losing the chance to put new heart into the Allies, and rendering peace itself more distant. He inveighed against the cast of mind of the Service Departments:

The strategic difficulty raised is, perhaps, still more disheartening. Why the Admiralty was consulted, we fail to understand. If it were a Channel ferry or bridge, one could appreciate it.
 The question is – what has the Admiralty to do with tubes under the sea situate [sic] below any possible attack by mines or explosives?
 The War Office is rightly asked how the tunnel mouths in England should be defended and where they should emerge, but the policy involved in their construction is not for the WO officials but for the Government to decide. The officials change but they do not change their system. The Channel Tunnel 'dossier' is handed on from the Duke of Cambridge and Lord Wolseley down to the present holders and they all support the system and the old theories. Aeroplanes and submarines or the starving of this country have no effect on their theories.

This was somewhat unfair, the views of service personnel having been less monolithic than this over the years, but Fell's comments were well calculated to appeal to Lloyd George. Fell went on to dispose of what he presumed to be the War Office view that peace with Germany would only last ten years by saying that the tunnel could be built in that time and would have incalculable benefits in another German war – hence German opposition to the project. As for other countries, 'If the War Office suggest that we should run the risk of invasion by France through the tunnel at some future time, this Committee declines to consider this suggestion or discuss it'. The question should be viewed in a wider perspective:

If, however, a long Peace is to follow, then the tunnel is a matter of commerce and trade and not of strategy and that is how this Committee regards it. If Peace is to endure for fifty years, there will be half-a-dozen tunnels long before then pouring wealth and commerce in and out of this country and no one at the War Office would have the hardihood to prophesy what will be the means of attack and defence at that date.[38]

Fell would have been even more devastated had he known the attitude of some officials in the Board of Trade, which on this occasion did not even deign formally to reply to the Prime Minister's enquiry. One official wrote that 'our main trade interests must be imperial and extra-European'; to those might be added trade with Russia; the money that would have to be spent on the tunnel 'could be spent better on the modernisation of the ports of London and Liverpool'. In short, 'The interests of the U.K. will on the conclusion of peace more urgently demand increased facilities for the vital ocean trades than for the specialised and smaller Continental trades especially if close scrutiny of the National Finances continues to be necessary'.[39]

At its meeting on 15 August the War Cabinet reaffirmed their decision of February.[40] Fell was clearly stung by the Lloyd George Government's betrayal of what he regarded as Asquith's pledge, and by his failure even to have the matter debated in Parliament. In the autumn he produced another pamphlet, *The British Government and the Channel Tunnel*, which began with a proclamation issued by Le Monde Industriel et Commercial of Paris in September 1917:

> The tunnel under the Channel, if it could be brought into play in a year, would be a crushing blow to the German submarine warfare, would reduce the length of the war, would render victory more rapid and more complete, and would assure the indissoluble union of France and Great Britain.

Taking as his theme that the Channel Tunnel had become the outward test of British friendship with France, he nevertheless did address the War Office position which in his letter of 13 August to Lloyd George he had deemed inadmissable. If France and Belgium were to join with Germany in attacking Britain, he said, the tunnel would on the outbreak of hostilities be closed: 'It would be a jointly-owned property, and, beyond blocking it securely, neither country would be likely utterly to destroy it.'[41] The year's press coverage of the Channel Tunnel drew to a close with an item in *The Times*' 'Through German Eyes' column on 19 December which suggested that, whilst Fell might have a valid point as regards the danger a tunnel would constitute to Germany, the War Office had an equally valid and contradictory one in that, realising the above, the Germans would prolong the war with a view to depriving France of her northern coast and the British of a bridgehead.[42]

Even the award of a knighthood was not enough to deflect the Chairman of the Channel Tunnel Committee of the House of Commons. As Sir Arthur Fell, he returned to the fray in 1918 with another motion:

> That in the opinion of this House the construction of the Channel Tunnel should be undertaken at the earliest possible moment after Peace, to cement the friendship of the Allies in Western Europe, to improve their means of communication, and to promote their mutual commerce; that a statement by the Government of this country that they will join with the French Government in supporting the proposal will give greater confidence to the Allies during the war, and strengthen their position in the negotiations for Peace, and that the time has arrived to make such a statement.[43]

As before, parliamentary time was not put aside for this.

Fell's activities in 1918 included the giving of a paper called 'London and the Tunnel' to the London Society in June, and addressing an International Parliamentary Commercial Conference held at the House of Lords in July on 'The Tunnel in its Commercial Aspects'. These, together with a lecture on the history, benefits and prospects of the tunnel given to British soldiers in Paris by Baron Emile d'Erlanger, the Chairman of the Channel Tunnel Company, were published in October as a ninety-page pamphlet.[44] In September the French Ministry of Public Works appointed a committee to consider the question of the Channel Tunnel. In October Sir Francis Dent, a director of the South Eastern and Chatham Railway Company, was called to give evidence before the recently appointed House of Commons Select Committee on Transport. As the Board of Trade recognised in the following year, he delivered an opinion regarding the technical and commercial success of the Channel Tunnel which was highly favourable:

> My own calculation about the Channel Tunnel is shortly this: We think it will cost varying sums, and I will take the very highest, £25,000,000. Our traffic before the war in 1913 was 800,000 passengers a year. That traffic grows every ten years by something like one third, so that in 1923, and the Tunnel could not be finished by then, because it would take eight years at least to build, under normal conditions that traffic would be considerably over one million passengers. Taking an average of ten shillings per passenger, which is about what it works out to, that is over half a million pounds. The actual working of the Channel Tunnel would be extraordinarily cheap; it is a through load and a full load with a natural decline for acceleration and a natural incline for deceleration, and, not having to consider property conditions, the curves would be extremely easy, so that you could run through at high speed. I do not think the cost of working that Tunnel electrically would come out to more than 20 per

cent; that would leave about £450,000 in 1923 as profit on passenger traffic alone.

So convinced was he that there would be an enormous increase in the volume of traffic, chiefly with London, through the tunnel that he thought it would pay his company to spend a million pounds on altering the loading gauge on their main line to agree with the continental gauge.[45]

The war ended on 11 November 1918. Exactly a week later Lloyd George received a memorandum on the transport situation from the First Lord of the Admiralty, Sir Eric Geddes, whom the Prime Minister had suggested might leave the Admiralty for the Ministry of Transport. Geddes ranged widely over the whole scene, making the point that the present dislocation of economic life on the Continent gave Britain 'an absolutely priceless opportunity of expanding British commercial interests in those countries'. Among the 'minor points which should not be forgotten' he brought up the matter of cross-Channel traffic: 'We have got the various train ferries State-owned, and we have, as you know, down at Shoreham the nucleus of those remarkable Towers which might go so far to rendering easy a tunnel to the Continent, should that policy be decided upon . . .'[46] All was not yet lost. Great oaks might yet grow from the small acorns of the abandoned workings of earlier decades.

Chapter 5

The Paris Peace Conference, 1919

1. Euphoria at Fontainebleau

On 28 February 1919 the British War Cabinet was discussing the proposals put forward by Foch, the Commander-in-Chief of the French Armies, for the delimination of the frontier of Germany, the main one of which was that the Rhine, the only natural barrier, be utilised for this purpose. Winston Churchill, who had been Secretary of State for War and Air for only one month, said that Foch's proposals 'might prove to be wise, subject to America bearing her share'. Recognising that it would be difficult, at one and the same time, to treat Germany 'humanely' and to be as 'sympathetic' to the French as possible, he suggested 'that France might feel a greater sense of security if we would meet her wishes in regard to the construction of the Channel Tunnel'.[1] The minutes of the meeting do not record the reception given to Churchill's suggestion – in all probability because they were being kept by Hankey, a determined and thoroughgoing opponent of the scheme. That it did not fall on deaf ears, however, is clear from what occurred a few days later. Asked by Horatio Bottomly M.P. on 10 March if, in order to find employment for discharged soldiers, he would approach the French Government with a view to beginning immediately the construction of the Channel Tunnel, Bonar Law replied that he was in communication with the Prime Minister, who had returned to Paris, on the subject.[2] The parliamentary-correspondent of *The Times* reported: 'The fact is that the British Government have for the first time decided in favour of the construction of the Channel Tunnel in principle, and have issued instructions in this sense to Sir H. Llewellyn Smith and a Board of Trade delegation who are now in Paris examining the question'; and *The Times*' leader of 11 March was devoted to the Channel Tunnel, stating that 'On the whole our experience of the war has not strengthened [the military arguments against the tunnel]' and that 'The solid argument against the tunnel is psychological rather than military'. It posed the question: 'What matters more – that we should have the power to intervene rapidly on the Continent of Europe or that we should pile up insurances against anyone on the Continent interfering here? Are we to regard ourselves as a Continental Power primarily or as an island?'[3] On 11 March, according to *The Times*' parliamentary correspondent, talk in the Lobby was dominated by the Channel Tunnel issue. As he put it: 'It seems that it is by almost imperceptible stages that the British Government have reached the position of approving the construction of the Channel Tunnel in principle. The former opposition has faded away during the war; nothing more is heard of the strongly adverse military opinion; and it is stated on good authority that the last objector in the War Cabinet has been converted.'[4]

This was not mere speculation. On the day that report was published Lloyd George was already moving to translate principle into practice. At a meeting of the secret Committee of Three in Paris he suggested to the other members, French Premier Clemenceau and President Wilson's adviser Colonel House, that a Channel Tunnel be built so that British troops could be put into France in the space of forty-eight hours.[5]

Repington, who had moved from *The Times* to the *Morning Post* a year before, was now more on the defensive than he had ever been, and this manifested itself in the tone of a two-part article published on 12 and 13 March. He had to admit that the situation, 'except on the sentimental side', had greatly changed: 'Submarines and aircraft have introduced disturbing elements into military appreciations. Our islands are full of trained soldiers, and a war fought for over four years shoulder to shoulder with our French friends precludes us from imagining, despite all the lessons of history, that our two peoples can be anything less than friends for ever.' His main point was made in a relatively subdued way: 'if our Army at home bears in future a more reasonable proportion to the Armies of the Continent, and the old naval objections are no longer entertained, then the military argument against the Tunnel loses much of its weight . . .'[6] His second article, called 'The Sentimental Factor', was rather more cutting. Positing that 'the real question is how, and in what manner, the project will affect our trade, and whether we are prepared to sacrifice our insularity for gain', he concluded: 'We shall probably lose, but this is only conjecture.' The important thing was 'not to rush in upon the crest of a wave of Celtic enthusiasm' until everything had been fully weighed. He ended with quite a long section which brought out what, for him, was the basic 'sentimental' factor:

> There is also the Continental side of this question involved in the loss of our insularity and the easy arrival of shoals of aliens on our shores. Thanks to our insularity, the population of these islands has now for many centuries remained distinct, and with its own special, marked, and valuable characteristics. When we cross the Channel or the North Sea we land in a different world . . . By breaking down the barrier of the silver streak we shall in course of time alter the character of our people and begin to internationalise them. Just when we are tardily taking measures to have among us as few aliens as possible, we start a project which will eventually enable them to return in battalions. That does not seem a very consistent or a very wise course to adopt.
>
> We shall have, as it is, a considerable infusion of Latin blood owing to the large number of marriages contracted by our men in France . . . The Anglo-Saxon stock is perhaps brightened up, and its womenfolk, at all events, improved in looks, by a Latin alliance once in every half-dozen centuries or so, but enough is as good as a feast, and we can have too much Latin. The Latin races have great qualities of their own, but they are different from ours, and things which alter the character of a stock usually cause it to deteriorate. Our insularity is a heaven-sent benefit, and although when the Tunnels are opened, there will be feasting and speech-making galore and indescribable enthusiasm, many then living will feel that it is a very bad day and that we shall have rashly sacrificed our precious insularity for dubious commercial gain.[7]

Such was the inbred idea of the 'splendid isolation' which reports from Paris continued to confirm that the French, for their part, were only too enthusiastic to end.[8]

Further parliamentary questions kept the issue to the fore, and on 13 March 1919 Fell sent postcards to as many Members of Parliament as he could asking them to state whether they were in favour of or opposed to the scheme. By 17 March 256 replies had been received. Of these, 246 were in favour and only six against; the other four had not yet decided. These figures of Fell's 'plebiscite' were published on 18 March, and in an obviously co-ordinated move Baron d'Erlanger contacted Churchill and offered to place the Channel Tunnel Company's plans before a commission of experts appointed by the War Minister.[9] On the same day L.S. Amery, who was Parliamentary Under-Secretary for the Colonies, wrote to Churchill claiming that the cost of a tunnel would be £50,000,000, which sum might better be devoted to communications within the U.K. or to aviation. He hoped Churchill would use his influence 'to get the Channel Tunnel put well into the second class as among the things which it may be desirable to carry out twenty or thirty years hence, but which ought not to take away money from more deserving enterprises'.[10] Amery had picked the wrong man. He heard from General Creedy at the War Office on 20 March that Churchill was 'weak and in favour of' the Channel Tunnel and was trying to make arrangements to bring together the promoters and the General Staff.[11] Similarly the French informed themselves on 22 March that the British Admiralty had no naval objections to the Tunnel.[12]

During the week-end of 22-23 March, Lloyd George retired from the fray of the Peace Conference in Paris to the comparative quiet of Fontainebleau to discuss peace terms with his closest advisers. Present throughout were the Chief of the Imperial General Staff, Field Marshal Sir Henry Wilson, the Cabinet Secretary, Hankey, and Lloyd George's Private Secretary, Phillip Kerr. Others came and went. On the 22nd Lloyd George picked Hankey to represent the views of an 'insular Briton'.[13] The choice could not have been more apt. Hankey was to die happy in this respect. On this occasion, however, he was bested by Henry Wilson, who was picked to present the French point of view the following day. When the two performances were over, Wilson listed Lloyd George's views of the peace terms in twelve 'salient' points. Only if these are given in full can the full impact of Point 12, to which no one, to the best of my knowledge, has hitherto drawn attention, be appreciated:

1 Deprive Germany of nearly all of her Navy.

2 Reduce her Army to small dimensions and impose Voluntary Principle.

3 Before agreeing to any description of a League of Nations come to a clear understanding that America will not compete with us on the sea but will leave us in command.

4 Refuse to put too crushing terms on Germany either in money or in cession of territory or other things.

5 Allow Germany raw material in order that she may recover.

6 Put her in a position to stop Bolshevism spreading into her country.

7 Put France in Syria, America into Constantinople and Armenia and Italy into the Caucasus.

8 Keep S.W. Africa, German East Africa, Palestine, Mosul and Mesopotamia and the Pacific Islands for the British Empire.

9 Draw the Empire close by every possible means.

10 Hand over the newly created States to the League of Nations to knock them on the head!

'Charing Cross to Bagdad',
Daily Chronicle, special supplement, 1917

11 International Labour Bureau.

12 Refuse France any more than the Saar Valley but make Great Britain and America promise immediate support if Germany attempts to invade France. Build Channel Tunnel to help in this guarantee.[14]

The building of the Channel Tunnel was, then, the necessary and indeed essential complement of an Anglo-American guarantee of support for France against future German aggression. It was an integral feature of Lloyd George's vision of the future, all the more so when his attitude to the League of Nations is taken into account, for as Wilson's diary goes on to record, 'Lloyd George told me specifically that he was only in favour of a League of Nations when it was reduced in its activities to absolutely insignificant and innocuous proportions'.[15] Wilson was 'delighted' with Lloyd George's list of objectives.[16] Hankey was not. He could not ignore, however, the Celtic enthusiasm prevailing at Fontainebleau, and recorded it in a memorandum of 23 March on 'British Empire Interests: Outline of Peace Terms'. He listed only three points, the last one being:

> Joint guarantee by the British Empire and the United States to come to the immediate assistance of France with their whole strength in the event of German aggression ... The British Government to initiate building of a Channel Tunnel if the French will cooperate.[17]

Given that, on the same day, 23 March 1919, the committee appointed in September 1918 by the French Ministry of Public Works finished its enquiry and brought out a report entirely favourable to the building of a tunnel, no difficulty in securing the co-operation of the French was to be expected. Prospects for a Channel Tunnel had never been better. They were further enhanced when, in answer to another question from Bottomley as to whether, in the event of the British and French Governments coming to an understanding in regard to the construction of the tunnel, it would be necessary to delay the commencement of operations pending the ratification of the scheme by the President of the United States, Bonar Law answered, 'No, Sir'.[18]

Lloyd George took his and Sir Henry Wilson's enthusiasm for the tunnel back to the Peace Conference in Paris. It manifested itself at a meeting of the Council of Four (Lloyd George, President Wilson, Clemenceau, Orlando) on the afternoon of 31 March. Marshal Foch read two memoranda to the Council of Four on this occasion. The first gave his reasons for a French occupation of the Rhineland; the second was designed to show, on the assumption that Britain would not have departed from the Voluntary Principle, that any other solution of the German problem would be both less certain and more costly. Foch maintained that in any future war Britain would be unable to produce, at the outset, a larger force than in 1914: 'moreover, this insufficient help can only be a late one, on account of distance, on account of the crossing of the Channel, and because, even if there is a submarine tunnel – anyhow subject to possible destruction – a single line (even if it be double-railed) cannot give a greater rapidity of transportation than that which we knew in 1914'. In the questioning which followed, an exchange took place between Lloyd George and General Wilson:

Lloyd George	I would like to ask General Wilson a question. Marshal Foch seems to believe that the Channel tunnel would not assure us of more rapid transportation than in 1914.
Wilson	I believe that Marsh Foch sees the tunnel as an alternative to transport by sea. Obviously everything would be changed if one were added to the other.
Lloyd George	It seems to be that in that case you could double the speed of the transports?
Wilson	That depends upon the state of the French railways and their congestion at the time of a mobilisation.[19]

At this point the military figures present were asked to withdraw. After they had done so General Tasker H. Bliss of the United States Army told General Wilson that it was 'scandalous that the President did not make it clear that neither he nor the Senate nor the people of the United States would form an Alliance with France'. Wilson commented in his diary: 'I had not realised this and it does away with Lloyd George's proposal that England and America should automatically go to war with the Boche if they crossed the Rhine.'[20] It went without saying that this also had serious repercussions so far as the building of a Channel Tunnel was concerned, though as Bonar Law had indicated earlier in the month it was by no means the be-all and end-all of the matter.

When on 9 April the French Chargé d'Affaires in London handed the report commissioned by the French Ministry of Public Works to the Foreign Office, he stated that the French Government had adopted the conclusions arrived at. He conveyed his Government's strong desire that a start should be made on the tunnel project and that an understanding should be arrived at with the British Government so that the scheme might be carried through.[21] The French wish to know the views of the British Government regarding what the former described as a great and interesting enterprise began a long process during which many Departments of State had to put their cards on the table.

2. Drawing Breath

On 22 April the Army Council suggested to the Admiralty that the question of the Channel Tunnel be considered by the Home Ports Defence Committee or an alternative body; Churchill on the following day warned D'Erlanger that any investigation would take a considerable time.[22] On 29 April the Admiralty agreed with the Army Council's suggestion. The Secretary to the War Office wrote formally to the Secretary of the Home Ports Defence Committee on 9 May suggesting that 'in anticipation of sanction to the construction being given by the Government', the HPDC should examine the question of the security of the exit of a tunnel and lay down the essential conditions for the information of any firm which might desire to carry out the work. The Air Ministry followed suit on 13 May.[25] At the Board of Trade a summary of the French report was made by E.J. Elliot, who found it 'curious' that the French should say 'that British isolation has already been sufficiently threatened by the development of aviation for there to be no longer any validity in any desire to maintain it'. He did admit, however, that there were many reasons why the subject should be considered 'more or less *de novo*', including 'the considerable advances which have been made in recent years in the construction of tunnels, and the much nearer prospect not only of working the Tunnel itself by electric traction, but of applying this system to the railways at both ends'. He continued: 'Indeed, it seems that the decisions which may be taken with regard to the electrification of the main line railways, as foreshadowed by Sir Eric Geddes, will have an important bearing on the Channel Tunnel question; similarly there are considerable indications that on the Continent railway electrification will be proceeded with very actively in the near future.'[24] H.F Carlill minuted Elliot's summary as follows:

On the commercial aspect full memoranda have been prepared by the Board of Trade in the past, and that of January 1914 is attached. To a considerable extent these memoranda must now be regarded as out of date, since it seems clear that the conditions of trade will have been profoundly altered as a result of the War. Trade with France, Switzerland and Italy will presumably be very much increased as compared with Germany; and it is not unlikely that the transport policy of the Continental Powers, as embodied, for example, in the proposals for an Inter-Allied through railway route from London to the Near East, will result in diverting various streams of traffic through France . . .

Apart from quasi-political considerations, which are not, however, without a real practical effect on transport, our previous arguments on the question have, I think, been too conservative even on the economic side . . .

The sea-change in attitude as compared with the views expressed before and during the war, continued:

On the financial question it should be observed that Sir Francis Dent estimates that the passenger traffic alone will be sufficient by the time the Tunnel could be constructed to provide a net revenue of £450,000, and that with M. Fougerolle's new method of construction the French Committee hope to bring the cost down to £5,240,000 at most . . . No doubt this question must be re-examined fully, but even if the tunnel itself did not pay much the indirect advantages might still make it worth while to construct it.[25]

Early in May Lloyd George had told the British Empire Delegation at the Peace Conference that the French wanted a British guarantee, since the Germans might be at Paris before the machinery of the League of Nations could get under way to stop an aggression such as that of August 1914, and that he was confident that Britain would agree to such a guarantee: 'Twice within living memory the soil of France had been violated and devastated by this wild beast, and each time the havoc had been wrought within a few weeks of the declaration of war.'[26] On 17 May Lloyd George sent out a note from the Villa Majestic, Paris, asking that the subject of the Channel Tunnel be discussed at an early meeting of the British Empire Delegation.[27] This item was put on the agenda of the British Empire Delegation for 29 May, and the Board of Trade sent out to Sir H. Llewellyn Smith all their papers. The meeting was postponed to the 31st, when the item was taken off the agenda, and no discussion took place.[28] It was not to return to the fold of the British Empire Delegation, which met again on 10 June 1919, but which after that did not meet for a full twelve months, until 18 June 1920.

On 17 May 1919 Turner Perkins of the Channel Tunnel Company had written to General Creedy at the War Office: he wanted Churchill to be told that Lord Sydenham (formerly Sir George Clarke), Vice-Admiral Sir T. Jerram, and Sir C. Sykes MP, had accepted seats on the board of directors of the company. The object was to have directors who commanded the confidence of the Admiralty, the War Office, and the whole of the Allied Powers.[29] A month later the General Staff produced some 'Notes on the Proposals for the Construction of a Channel Tunnel'. From their military standpoint any scheme had to satisfy two main conditions, '(a) Immediate means for putting it out of service must be provided (b) the tunnel itself, its approaches, and any machinery or installations vital to its use must be protected from surprise attack, from bombardment and from bombing either from aircraft or submarines'. The idea of an exposed viaduct at the British end, an idea espoused by Churchill before the war, was dismissed on the ground that its bombardability would make it possible for an enemy to destroy and so deprive Britain of its use during wartime. Instead, a 'dip' which could be flooded at a moment's notice was suggested:

> But this alone would not guarantee security against the use of the Tunnel by a raiding force as a 'bolt from the blue', an extremely improbable contingency, but one which would have to be guarded against, in order to satisfy public opinion . . .
>
> It is suggested that some such precaution as the following should be adopted: the weight of the train on entering a certain section should operate a strong gate, closing the Tunnel against further progress. The mechanism for putting this gate out of action, or for opening it after it has closed, should be installed in a defended post some distance inland.
>
> There should be a British examining post at the French end of the Tunnel which would telegraph in code when each train left. In times of peace on receipt of the code the gate could be opened so that passage of the train should not be delayed, but any surprise attempt to push through a train could be automatically frustrated, as the doors would shut against it if the code message clearing the train had not been received.

This was most ingenious, not to say 'novel', but even this was not considered to be enough, and one version of these 'Notes' went on:

> But the human element cannot be eliminated however good the mechanical means for securing safety may be. In this, and in the difficulty in selecting the psychological moment for operating them, lies the great danger. If the Tunnel is privately owned this difficulty will be increased, and it is therefore urged that it should be built and controlled by Government.
>
> To cover the inevitable element of risk from a surprise attack, it is essential that there should be not only an enclosed work commanding the tunnel opening, but also a force in the vicinity capable of strong and immediate counter-attack. This means the redistribution of a portion of the Regular Army and consequent expense on barracks. Further as long as there is the slightest

danger of an attack from across the Channel, a portion of the Regular Army must be retained in the country as a precautionary measure. This has obvious disadvantages from the point of view of reinforcing our Eastern possessions.

The second part of the 'Notes' addressed the question of 'Protection of the Tunnel against Attempts to Destroy it'. One of the dangers of basing plans and calculations for the transportation of the British Expeditionary Force to the Continent on the capacity of the tunnel was stated to be that 'should the latter be put out of action by the enemy, we should be in a much worse position than if it had never been constructed, for we should not have the same amount of cross-Channel shipping to replace it, as would exist were the Tunnel never commenced'. It was to be expected that an enemy would attempt to destroy or block the tunnel before war was formally declared: 'Charges of explosives might be sent disguised as luggage or goods, with a clockwork mechanism to fire it during the passage through the Tunnel . . .' The only safeguard would be 'a careful scrutiny of all packages and personal luggage before loading them on to the trains, and such scrutiny appears . . . an essential military precaution during any period of strained relations'. Junctions and sidings would be large and hard to conceal. Measures of protection envisaged here were: duplication; keeping them 'as far inland as is consistent with the economic aspect of the enterprise'; as a protection against aerial bombardment by night 'to install a system of false lights or other camouflage devices'. Power stations and other relevant installations should be placed underground, and if possible duplicated, and 'to prevent destruction by agents or hostile detachments it will be necessary to surround these places with an unclimbable fence and to keep permanent guards there'. There must also be guards at the tunnel mouth, 'and the entrances should be so constructed that it is impossible to approach them except by coming along the railway line for a considerable distance, as a set approach of this nature will add greatly to the difficulties of carrying out a surprise attack'. Finally, the possibility that the tunnel could be damaged by torpedoes fired from submarines resting on the bed of the Channel, or by explosive charges placed in holes bored by submarines resting on the bed of the Channel, was raised:

Absolute protection against deliberate boring can only be obtained by keeping the Tunnel at such a depth as to make it impossible to get within shattering distance of it with a charge. What the depth should be for this purpose would have to be decided after consultation with experts, and it would then have to be considered whether the geological formation would permit of the Tunnel being carried through at this depth. Probably however reasonable security could be obtained by mining the water above the Tunnel, and by aeroplane patrols to locate any submarine lying in the bottom . . .[30]

The ominous feature of these 'Notes' was the extent to which some of the attitudes displayed were redolent of what Sir George Clarke had described as the 'old-womanish' cast of mind of the later nineteenth and earlier twentieth centuries. If there was any single thing that could not be left to chance, someone was determined to find it.

Progress was somewhat slow during the summer. The Board of Trade read in *The Times* of 1 August that the French Minister of Public Works, M. Claveille, had asked the French Ambassador to make representations to the British Government with a view to the appointment of a Franco-British Commission to draw up an agreement for the construction of the tunnel. The Board of Trade had received nothing from the Foreign Office on this by 8 August and issued a mild reproof: 'We should be very glad if when the further French representations are received they could be sent along to us.'[31] The Board of Trade was itself intending to discuss the Channel Tunnel question at a meeting on 5 August, but the discussion was deferred until after the holidays. There was some confusion as to which committees should be contacted, both the Committee of Imperial Defence and the Overseas Defence Committee being mentioned, but not the Home Ports Defence Committee.[32] Even so, Carlill managed to interview Mr Tempest, the engineer of the South Eastern and Chatham Managing Committee, and Elliot took another, and rather critical, look at the Board of Trade memorandum of January 1914. Noting that the latter had properly made the point that imports to the U.K. exceeded exports and that therefore a Channel Tunnel would favour French importers more than British exporters, Elliot wrote:

> The problem of increasing the proportion of British exports to imports is one which is not likely to be made essentially more difficult by the provision of further transport facilities, and will have to be solved in quite other directions. In any case the increase in imports can hardly be unaccompanied by a corresponding increase in exports, and the example of the Trelleborg-Sassnitz Ferry and its effect on trade between Sweden and Germany tends to show that the Channel Tunnel is likely to result in a great increase of trade between England and the Continent, of which the memorandum appears to take very little account, treating the subject rather as a static than a dynamic problem.

Moreover, 'Although the 1914 memorandum concludes that the Scheme must stand or fall by the passenger traffic the advantageous position . . . if the Scheme does so stand was ignored'.[33] On 21 August

Carlill saw Sir P. Nash of the Ministry of Transport, who told him that thought was being given to the remodelling of some main railway lines, at least as far as London, so that French waggons could run on them. Nash thought that the Ministry of Transport would look into the engineering and waggon questions, and the Board of Trade into traffic statistics, and that ultimately the whole subject might be examined by a committee of the two departments. He also thought 'we ought certainly to tell the French Government that we approved the project in principle, and experiments should be encouraged'.[34]

On 16 August the French renewed their pressure for an understanding between the two Governments. This was passed on to the Board of Trade on 25 August. Elliot suggested that the Foreign Office acknowledge the French communication in sympathetic fashion, and explain that the consideration being given must be somewhat prolonged owing to the number of aspects of the highest importance from which the project had to be viewed.[35] On 19 September the Board of Trade took the bull by the horns and wrote to the War Office: 'It is clear that the question should first be considered from the point of view of defence and the Board of Trade accordingly desire me to ask that Mr Secretary Churchill will be so good as to arrange for the early consideration of the question by the Overseas Defence Committee with a view to reaching a definite decision.' Opportunity was taken to remind the War Office both of Foch's positive view of the scheme and of the claim in the French report of March that the British War Office and Admiralty were also in favour of it.[36] Acknowledging this on 28 September, the War Office replied that the Overseas Defence Committee was considering the matter.[37]

One other development that took place in the summer of 1919 is worth mentioning at this point. On 15 August the War Cabinet discussed the estimates of the Service Departments. The conclusion was reached that the Admiralty, War Office and Air Ministry should work out their estimates on, as the minutes recorded, certain 'bases'. The first of these was that

> It should be assumed, for framing revised Estimates, that the British Empire will not be engaged in any great war during the next ten years, and that no Expeditionary Force is required for this purpose.[38]

This, as it stood, was a not inauspicious development so far as the fortunes of the Channel Tunnel were concerned. The ten-year rule was not mentioned explicitly in the debate and discussions on the Channel Tunnel that were to take place later. The reader would do well to bear in mind, however, when dealing with the remarks of Field Marshal Sir Henry Wilson and Sir Maurice Hankey, that both these individuals were present at the meeting at which the rule was promulgated.

Chapter 6

Hankey-Pankey

1. The Cabinet Secretary and the Home Ports Defence Committee

In the end, the committee that undertook to look into the question of a Channel Tunnel was not the Overseas Defence Committee but the Home Ports Defence Committee. This was a significant development in the fortunes of the Channel Tunnel project, and by no means a positive one. For the chairman of the HPDC was Sir Maurice Hankey, and Sir Maurice Hankey was an out-and-out opponent of the scheme. As Secretary to the Cabinet as well as chairman of numerous government bodies, he had unrivalled access to Ministers. On this particular issue he played a role which still remains to be evaluated.[1]

It was, then, to the HPDC that, on 16 October 1919, the Admiralty sent its views of the conditions necessary to ensure the safety of the proposed tunnel. These were:

(a) That the entrance of the British side should be so situated and constructed as to render its destruction by bombardment from the sea or from the land on the opposite side of the Straits extremely improbable.

(b) That the Tunnel should be so far below the bed of the sea as to render it immune from danger by explosion by charges placed on the bed of the sea. Anti-submarine measures will prevent the possibility of an enemy submarine making a successful attempt to bore in to the tunnel.[2]

Before the HPDC could get to grips with the matter there was another development. The French Government had made an approach to the new Foreign Secretary, Lord Curzon, immediately upon his appointment of 29 October, pressing for a Franco-British Commission. This seemed to them, in contradistinction to the hoops the British insisted on putting themselves through, the best way of examining, 'au point de vue technique', the diverse questions involved. In this context Lloyd George suddenly announced, at the Cabinet of 5 November, that he wished to receive a deputation from Fell's House of Commons committee and that, before receiving it, he wanted to discuss the matter at the next Cabinet, in a week's time.[3] Hankey, clearly miffed at the 'very short notice', which was, in fact, no notice at all, circulated to the Cabinet his memorandum of October 1916, which he claimed contained 'a dispassionate summary of the pros and cons'.[4] He also wrote a note which dealt with political and military considerations. Under 'Political Considerations' he wrote:

> If the world had settled down to the Millenium under the auspices of the League of Nations and War had been banished for ever, there would be no danger to this country in the construction of the Channel Tunnel. Such is not the case. On the contrary five years at war have left the World in a tumult and ferment. The desire for revenge is still firmly implanted in some of the Enemy States. The chaos in Russia is such that no one can foresee what will emerge from it. Even before the War the political changes that took place within a decade or two could not be foreseen. In present conditions the future is even more difficult to fathom . . .
>
> If the Channel Tunnel is built, and if it is a danger, it is a danger for all time. No British Government could afford to agree lightly on its construction unless it is sure either that Peace is assured for an indefinite period or that there is no danger in the Channel Tunnel.

Under 'Military Considerations' he insisted that the danger, which was that an enemy might succeed in getting possession of both ends of the tunnel at once, was 'far greater under modern conditions than in the past', because of the speed of modern vessels and the ability rapidly to concentrate artillery. If by a raid an enemy secured the bridgehead of the Channel Tunnel, 'the raid becomes the prelude to invasion', and even if the tunnel itself had been destroyed 'the enemy would almost certainly find means to pump out and repair' it. Because the British people objected even more strongly than before the war to compulsory military service Britain would be unable to retrieve the situation. And even if Britain had the troops and the guns, 'we should be so nervous of an attack in our "Achilles heel" that we should be compelled to lock up forces in Eastern Kent . . . that might urgently be required elsewhere'. This plea from Hankey that the risks be very carefully weighed was given to the Prime Minister and to one other person – A.J. Balfour, now Lord President of the Council, whom Hankey regarded as an ally.[5]

This note of Hankey's did have an impact on Balfour. It had none on Lloyd George. What happened is best described in Hankey's diary:

Rather a scandalous circumstance in connection with the Channel Tunnel. A parliamentary deputation had been promised an interview on the subject. There was no time for a full discussion on the subject, but, as it was on the Agenda, the PM brought it up at the fag end of an exhausting and exceptionally long Cabinet meeting on Ireland, just as everyone was getting up to go to the Guildhall to the lunch to Poincaré. Although this question has at least 14 times been turned down by Parliament, and has been rejected 6 times by Committees after prolonged inquiry, including the Committee of Imperial Defence in 1907 and 1914, the PM thought fit, without any discussion, and without hearing the views of a single expert, to take opinions. To my surprise the Cabinet were on the whole almost unanimously in favour, Balfour alone saying that his opinion was shaken by a letter I had written to him. This, and a few rather hedging utterances by other Ministers about agreeing, provided there was no risk to national safety, enabled me to record a very feeble support in the official conclusion.[6]

The conclusion devised by Hankey read: 'Subject to there being no danger to the security of the country, a point on which the view was expressed that further technical enquiry was necessary, the general trend of opinion in the Cabinet was in favour of not opposing the construction of the Channel Tunnel.'[7]

Hankey was so upset that he wrote immediately to Lloyd George. 'It is no part of my duty, as Secretary to the Cabinet', he wrote, 'to comment on, much less to question or criticise, any decision of the Cabinet', and proceeded to do both, complaining petulantly that the summary he had circulated had clearly not been read.[8] He also did some lobbying for his own cause, and here again his diary is the best source:

The PM and Bonar Law both thought they had received complete agreement, but I saw them both before the Deputation on the following day [12 November] and convinced them that it would be unsafe to agree without much fuller inquiry into the project. Balfour, Sir E. Geddes [Minister of Transport] and Dr Addison [Minister of Health] all came to me to say they hoped I had not recorded a decision in favour of the Channel Tunnel.[9]

As Hankey rightly put it, when revealing yet more of his own attitude:

What power lies in the draughtsman's hands! I could easily, had I been a Channel Tunnel man, have rushed the situation, recorded a decision, and induced the PM to tell the fact to the Deputation. In fact he told me afterwards that I only had induced him not to do so. As matters stand I may be able to block the whole thing, though at the moment I seem to stand almost alone in my opposition.[10]

The verbatim record of what Lloyd George told Fell's deputation on 12 November should be read in the light of the diary entry and in the knowledge of Hankey's interventions and activities. It was, in fact, a much more fair and balanced presentation than Hankey himself would have provided. The Prime Minister revealed that the Cabinet had recently discussed the matter, and that the tone and content of the discussion contrasted markedly with that displayed in the past: 'Ministers when discussing it who, on looking at all the records of the past are found to have had a rooted hostility to the whole enterprise, have now changed their general attitude, and are prepared to support this scheme, subject to a further examination by our military and naval advisers.' Military and naval advice was necessary – and here was the contribution to the balance made by Hankey – to consider the dangers of a surprise attack: 'We must not take risks, and I think that all the members of the deputation will agree that if there is a real risk of an enemy capturing the bridgehead and converting this country from an island into merely a sort of part of the continent of Europe . . . that is a thing which we could not for a moment face'. With a view to preserving the 'providential advantage' of the fact that Britain was an island the problem had to be examined very carefully from the military engineering and the naval and air point of view. The difficulty was not a political one, but purely a military and naval one, and if the military advice was favourable, 'the Ministry will certainly be prepared to support the scheme on general grounds'. When Fell showed his disappointment that the military authorities had not yet formed an opinion Lloyd George tried to mollify him with the words, 'I am not suggesting that the soldiers advising us are against it. I do not think they are'.[11] On the same day he asked the Army Council to submit a memorandum on the expediency or otherwise of a Channel Tunnel in the light of present conditions and possible future developments.[12]

Between 10 and 12 November Hankey had begun to recover the ground he had lost at Fontainebleau on 22 and 23 March. Much remained to be done, however, as he himself was the first to recognise. Everything would depend on the nature of the 'expert' advice solicited and given, and Hankey knew both that the Admiralty was not opposed to the scheme, and that at the War Office the Minister, Churchill, was actively in favour of it, whilst the CIGS, Henry Wilson, had been, and might be again if certain conditions of his were met.

The initial disposition of the War Office to please the Prime Minister is to be found in the first paragraph of fourteen pages of 'Rough Notes' prepared as a basis for discussion within the Home Ports Defence

HOME PORTS DEFENCE COMMITTEE.

Minutes of the Thirty-third Meeting held at 2, Whitehall Gardens, S.W., on Friday, November 21st, 1919, at 3·30 P.M.

Present :

Lieut.-Colonel Sir M. P. A. HANKEY, G.C.B. (*in the Chair*).

Captain B. ST. G. COLLARD, D.S.O., R.N., Deputy Director of Operations Division, Admiralty.

Captain F. LARKEN, C.M.G., R.N., Director of Local Defence Division, Admiralty.

Captain B. E. DOMVILE, C.M.G., R.N., Deputy Director of Plans Division, Admiralty.

Wing-Commander J. A. CHAMIER, C.M.G., D.S.O., O.B.E., Directorate of Operations and Intelligence, Air Ministry.

Major-General Sir P. P. DE B. RADCLIFFE, K.C.M.G., C.B., D.S.O., Director of Military Operations, War Office.

Lieut.-Colonel P. K. LEWES, D.S.O., Assistant Director of Artillery, War Office.

Colonel E. P. BROOKER, C.B., C.M.G., Assistant Director of Fortifications and Works, War Office.

Major-General C. F. ROMER, C.B., C.M.G., Chief of the General Staff, Forces in Great Britain.

Mr. S. ARMITAGE-SMITH, C.B., Treasury.

The following were also present :

Rear-Admiral Sir C. DE BARTOLOMÉ, K.C.M.G., C.B., Director-General of Development, Ministry of Transport.

Brigadier-General S. H. WILSON, C.B., C.M.G., *Secretary.*
Lieut.-Colonel L. STORR, C.B., *Assistant Secretary.*
Mr. P. WICKS, *Assistant Secretary.*

Note.—*Minutes of Meetings prior to Thirty-third held on the 21st November, 1919, were recorded in a Minute Book and were not printed. The Minute Book is kept by the Secretary to the Committee, 2, Whitehall Gardens.*

Minutes of last Meeting.

1. The Minutes of the 32nd Meeting were confirmed.

Coast and harbour defences of the United Kingdom.

2. The Committee had under consideration a letter from the War Office dated the 1st November, 1919, in connection with the policy to be adopted in the immediate future as regards the manning and maintenance of coast and harbour defences of the United Kingdom (Paper H.P.D.C./1).

The Chairman, referring to the War Office letter, from which he quoted extracts, pointed out that the Army Council did not propose to effect, in the immediate future, any alterations in the existing coast and harbour defences of the United Kingdom, but to apply the available resources to research and to the digestion of the experiences gained during the war. The Army Council requested that they might be informed whether these proposals had the approval of the Committee.

Extracts from minutes of 33rd meeting of
Home Ports Defence Committee, 21 November 1919

Committee by its Secretary, Brigadier-General S.H. Wilson, between 12 and 18 November. It recalled the War Office letter of 9 May, and read: 'The War Office in anticipation of approval being given for the construction of a Channel Tunnel, have referred to the HPDC the question of laying down the conditions necessary from a Naval, Military, and Air point of view to ensure the security of the exit of a tunnel.'[13] Paragraph 6, however, went on to pick up the more ominous reservations made by the General Staff in June:

> The military members have, however, now urged on the Committee the importance of bearing in mind that once a tunnel is constructed it will become a leading factor in all military plans for war, that in all cases in which France is our Ally, the assured maintenance of the tunnel will relieve the Navy of much convoy work, and that consequently the arrangements for its efficient protection against attempts to destroy it may be even more important than the arrangements for denying its use to a hostile Power. Further, it is argued that should the tunnel be put out of action by an enemy, the British Forces would be in a much worse position than if it had never been constructed since there would not be the same amount of cross-channel shipping available to replace it as would be the case if it had never been made.[15]

On 21 November Hankey, who had confided in his diary on the 16th, 'I will stop at nothing to prevent what I believe to be a danger to the country', chaired the 33rd meeting of the Home Ports Defence Committee. He was not displeased with what transpired, writing on 23rd November: 'I did my best, on the one hand to show that our measures would involve such outlay that no one would ever build the tunnel, and on the other hand to show that, as safeguards, they are futile. In this I met with some success and I am now hoping to kill the tunnel in spite of the bias in favour of it.'[16]

Hankey had begun by raising the question of the rolling-stock which would have to be used in the tunnel, saying he understood that French rolling-stock would not get through the tunnels on the English railways. He also referred to the question of siting the power station for the tunnel on the English side of the Channel. The point of his initiative was to move the committee as a whole towards thinking in terms of invasion and therefore of security: 'If English rolling-stock only could be used in the tunnel it might . . . be possible in this way to afford an additional measure of security against the tunnel being used for invasion purposes.'[17] Another example of Hankey's technique was his asking Rear-Admiral Sir C. de Bartolomé, the Director-General of Development from the Ministry of Transport, who was present although not a member of the committee, whether, if the enemy seized the English end of the tunnel after it had been flooded, it could rapidly be pumped out. This produced some interesting opinions from de Bartolomé, who said the Ministry of Transport held rather strong views on the question of flooding, which might be done in two ways:

(a) The tunnel might be flooded at leisure after the declaration of war, which would be a very simple matter involving only the opening of an ordinary hydrant.
(b) Provision might be made for instantaneous flooding in the event of a 'bolt from the blue' i.e. some means might be provided for letting in the sea.

In the latter case he did not see how it would be possible to prevent the whole of the tunnel being flooded except by a very complicated system of hydrostatic valves. If this type of flooding were provided for and the public were aware that arrangements were in existence by which at the will of perhaps one man the sea might be let into the tunnel, it was the view of the Ministry of Transport that strong pressure would be brought to bear upon the Government to see that no undue risk was taken of the tunnel being flooded accidentally. The machinery would also have to be tested almost every day for fear of treachery, and to ensure its efficiency, and it would also have to be made quite 'foolproof'. Such tests would naturally dislocate traffic, and constant opening and closing of valves would render an accident possible. In the circumstances the Ministry of Transport would prefer to rule out the 'dip' and simply have an arrangement for blowing in the end of the tunnel if necessary.

This argument about the necessity of reassuring the public impressed the committee, despite the fact that the War Office had made it a condition that there should be a 'dip' in the level of the tunnel, capable of being flooded.[18]

The Director of Military Operations, General Radcliffe, had already raised another complication in connection with guns firing on the exit of the tunnel:

from the point of view of keeping the tunnel open as a means of communication with France, some precautions would have to be taken to prevent the enemy from shelling the English exit . . . and in this connection it was agreed that provision must be made for the distant future when probably great improvements would take place in the manufacture of lethal weapons, it being pointed out that should an enemy ever reached Ostend, the British exit of the tunnel might be well within effective range, since even during the late war there is evidence that the German 15 inch guns could attain a range of between 50,000 and 60,000 yards, and even this range might be increased.[19]

Wing-Commander Chamier, of the Directorate of Operations and Intelligence at the Air Ministry, said that an air attack was the most likely form that a 'bolt from the blue' would take, and that the Air Ministry's view was that 'the air defences of London would have to be mobilised the moment relations with a foreign country might become strained'.[20]

Despite the difficulties to which attention was drawn at this meeting Hankey was not absolutely satisfied. In summing up he left the committee in no doubt as to the tone its conclusions would take. As the minutes relate:

> *The Chairman*, in summing up the discussion, asked if it was the view of the Committee that they were expected to express any opinion as to the adequacy of any precautions they might suggest to meet every possible contingency. He thought that unless the Committee in their report specifically safeguarded themselves in this respect it might be assumed that they were of opinion that the precautions suggested would ensure security against every possible contingency. It appeared to him that the whole crux of the question was that nothing could really provide satisfactorily against a 'bolt from the blue' if such form of attack were regarded as possible. In his opinion the position has retrograded in this respect since 1914, when Mr Churchill had contemplated a lighthouse which would form a ventilating shaft for the tunnel and could be destroyed by warships, thus admitting the sea into the tunnel. This was no longer possible in view of the War Office argument that it was even more important to arrange for keeping the tunnel open as a means of communication than providing for its destruction . . . It was necessary to remember that alliances were short-lived, and it was only twenty-years previously that England had been on the verge of war with France. He proposed to add a paragraph to this effect to the Secretary's memorandum which would be redrafted as the result of this discussion and resubmitted for consideration to the Committee.[21]

This peroration brought further support from the Director of Military Operations, who said 'that there could be no doubt that once the tunnel was built there would be tremendous opposition to any suggestion for its destruction in certain eventualities, and if a war with France at any time in the future were regarded as possible it was certainly a question as to whether the tunnel should be built at all or not.'[22]

Hankey, who by this time had discovered that Field Marshal Haig was, like himself, 'violently opposed' to the scheme,[23] drafted his conclusions on 22 November. He stated that 'the Committee feel bound to draw attention to the fact that their proposals (for safeguarding the country against the use of the Tunnel by an enemy) are less reassuring than those assumed to be practicable in previous enquiries', whilst on the other hand 'the old objections urged by Lord Wolseley and others remain precisely where they were . . . ' He wanted to conclude:

Reviewing the question in the light of the above considerations, the Committee, therefore, do not challenge the following statement made at the conclusion of the Report of the War Office of 1882:

'That even the most comprehensive and complete arrangements which can be devised could not be relied upon in every contingency.'

The HPDC desire to lay stress on the fact that their proposals are based on the fundamental condition that Dover is safeguarded against a raid by the Power in occupation of the Continental side of the Channel. This question has been profoundly modified by technical developments in naval, military and aerial warfare during the last few years and involves considerations of high policy which are beyond the present reference of the HPDC.[24]

The Home Ports Defence Committee reconvened on 16 December to discuss alternative drafts of its report.[25] Between the meetings Hankey had taken the chance, as he put it, 'to do a good deal of subtle propaganda against the Tunnel. Although our reference was limited . . . it gave me as Chairman the opportunity to set forth many of my objections, and to educate the Admiralty War Staff and the War Office General Staff on the subject'.[26] What transpired at the second meeting is best captured by a later entry in the Hankey diary: 'I required a good deal of dexterity in handling the Committee, but eventually they accepted a very satisfactory report, which was by no means favourable to the Tunnel. In fact I got the General Staff man, General Kirke, to draft the most damning paragraph.'[27] Brigadier-General W.M.St G. Kirke was the Deputy Director of Military Operations, taking Radcliffe's place on the committee. What the *most* damning paragraph was is hard to say, for there were, from Hankey's point of view, many damning paragraphs. Part of paragraph 10 might be the one Hankey was referring to. It read:

The Committee purposely refer to the forms of attack considered *possible*, although it is usual only to provide defences to meet such forms of attack as are regarded as *probable*; but in a case such as this where national independence might be at stake it is considered that all *possible* attacks must be taken into account.[28]

2. A Sort of 'Wolseley Up-to-Date'

The Home Ports Defence Committee had done Hankey's work, but the matter did not end there. Knowing that the final decision would be taken by the Cabinet, and being aware that Ministers who had wavered once in his direction might waver again in the opposite direction, Hankey spent the rest of the month preparing yet another memorandum, which he described as 'a sort of "Wolseley up to date" '. He held this in reserve, intending to release it when it would have most impact.[29]

In the course of January 1920 the Report of the Home Ports Defence Committee was released to departments. On 21 January it was circulated for information to the Cabinet.[30] The Admiralty were first to respond, telling Hankey on 24 January to inform the Cabinet that subject to the conditions for security enumerated in the report being adopted, they had no objections to the scheme.[31] Hankey decided that the moment was ripe for the release of his 'formidable' memorandum of the Christmas period. He dated it 28 January 1920 and circulated it to the Cabinet. In a covering note he revealed that he had always been troubled at the narrowness of the terms of reference given to his Home Ports Defence Committee. Addressing the Cabinet as if he were one of their number, he wrote:

> I feel . . . that I should be failing in my duty if I allowed it to be thought that the safeguards recommended, even though the best that the Committee can devise, provide security to the country from the dangers of the tunnel. As a matter of fact, the safeguards now recommended are materially less effective than those proposed in 1914, as, owing to modern developments of submarines and aerial warfare, the idea of exposing a portion of the railway line to fire from the sea has had to be dropped. I agree with Lord Wolseley that if the Channel Tunnel is constructed there will be no real security without compulsory military service, and I do not believe that the country will face this in the future any more than in the past. In any case, it is too heavy a price for the country to pay for the inconsiderable benefits of the tunnel. Without a large army, however, I consider that the safety of the country will be compromised if the tunnel is constructed. These views are based on wider grounds than could be dealt with under the limited reference to the Home Ports Defence Committee, and I therefore venture to circulate a comprehensive memorandum on the whole subject.[32]

In his introduction he maintained, as had the report of the committee, that the tunnel would cost between £30 and £50 million to build – an estimate far in excess of those in the hands of the Board of Trade.[33] He also used arguments which he had not yet used in his Committee or on Lloyd George and Balfour. One of these would have appealed greatly to Repington: 'There arises also the question of whether it is desirable, in present economical and political conditions on the Continent, to open up this country to an immense influx of foreigners. This is largely a matter of home and labour policy. At the same time, the desirability, in the interests of our transatlantic shipping supremacy, of providing direct railway communication to the Continent from our ports of embarkation and disembarkation deserves consideration, so that the Ministry of Shipping is not unaffected.'[34] Part I of the memorandum, 'Advantages claimed for the Channel Tunnel', occupied paragraphs 3 to 8 inclusive; Part II, 'Disadvantages of the Channel Tunnel', occupied paragraphs 9 to 44 inclusive. In paragraph 15 he went so far as to say:

> In spite of the highly reassuring result of the recent French elections, it would be impossible to predict with any certainty that in a more or less distant future Bolshevism will not spread to France itself. Yet no responsible person would wish to have the Channel Tunnel if a Bolshevik Power occupied its Continental end.

Warming to his theme, he continued:

> Apart from Bolshevism, however, there is another disquieting symptom in Europe, namely, the weakening of control of the Central Government. In Italy the Central Government has only the feeblest control over the Army and Navy; the same applies in Germany, and probably in most of the countries of Central and Eastern Europe. This, again, is a symptom that, in the difficult economic days that are to come, may well spread. Should we ever come into a state of strained relations with the Power on the other side of the Channel, a d'Annunzio or a Von der Goltz might be found who, in the hope of laying England open to invasion, would undertake the hazard of a raid on Dover even in time of normal relations (and it may be that normal relations may some day become far more disturbed than they were before the war) . . .[35]

His deduction was that the economic and political state of Europe was so unsettled, the future so uncertain and beset by doubts, that this was a bad moment to run any risks. He was convinced that there were risks. He produced a number of examples of behaviour during the recent war which were sufficient to show him 'that an attack on the British end of the Channel Tunnel might in all probability be made as a first act of hostilities, either with or without a declaration of war'.[36] His examination of whether preparations would be equal to dealing with such an emergency convinced him they would not be:

> The fact is that both the human and mechanical factors are occasionally apt to fail in an emergency. In the case of a surprise attack . . . the risks would be increased. A telephone works badly; or a telephone operator takes in a message wrongly; or the apparatus for flooding or blowing up the tunnel . . . jams or refuses to function in some way, or is out of order, and the man who can mend

it cannot be found; the responsible officer is still on leave and cannot get back owing to a strike, and his substitute is sick[37] . . .

Hankey's imagination piled contingency upon contingency, scenario upon scenario. He pointed out that the possibility of a raid had always been regarded as such by the Committee of Imperial Defence before the war, and that a large force had been retained in the country throughout the war to guard against it. He went on to raise the stakes still higher:

35 It may be remarked that the existence of a Channel Tunnel would provide an incentive to a raid such as no enemy has ever had before. This incentive would be all the greater if the enemy possessed a great army raised by compulsory service, as France does, while Great Britain only had a small army raised on the voluntary principle, such as is now intended.

36 It does not require very much imagination to conceive a situation in which the normal risks of a raid on the British end of the Channel Tunnel might become especially dangerous. Supposing, for example, trouble had broken out in India, Persia, Mesopotamia, Palestine, Egypt, or elsewhere, which had drawn overseas the whole of our Regular Army. We should then be dependent on Territorial Forces, who might or might not have been mobilised. Looking to a distant future this risk ought not to be dismissed, for it is only twenty years ago that this situation actually arose during the South African War, when the country was almost denuded of trained troops.

37 With this actual experience before us it is easy to understand Lord Wolseley's belief that the Channel Tunnel ought not to be made unless we had an army on the Continental scale, and conversely that we must 'when joined on to the Continent, sooner or later, if we wish to remain an independent people, become like the Continental nations – a Military Power'.

Wolseley had been reincarnated as Hankey: 'not only do all Lord Wolseley's objections still hold good, but in many cases they are much stronger now than they were when he wrote them'.[38] Hankey ended:

On balance . . . it is submitted that the objections immeasurably outweigh the advantages, and the carefully-considered decisions on the subject of the Government's predecessors are justified. It is difficult to discover any new factor in the situation which renders the construction of the Channel Tunnel more desirable or less undesirable than in the past. The advantages are not greater. The risks are not less. The safeguards are actually weaker. The moment for reversing previous decisions is . . . from many points of view extraordinarily ill-timed.[39]

S.y.S

Is it wise to compare with the Channel Tunnel promotion before the Cabinet has agreed to the principle of a Tunnel?

H W
7.1.20

Sec.
C.I.G.S

I see no reason why we should not interrogate them fully on this aspect. Indeed I think it is essential if we are to advise. I will if necessary provide myself.

Another method is the ventilating shaft in the Channel.

This is accessible only by sea & even if both ends of the tunnel are in enemy occupation it can be demolished & the water let in.

On the other hand of course the tunnel wd be less safe for our use.

But no use to our enemy:
All these class of points must be searchingly examined

WSC
8.1.

Exchanges between the CIGS,
Field Marshall Sir Henry Wilson (HW), and the
Secretary of State for War, Winston Churchill (WSC),
in January 1920

Chapter 7

Departmental Decisions

1. The Air Ministry

Hankey had chosen his moment well, for on 31 January the Air Council sent in their reply to the Report of the Home Ports Defence Committee. The Air Staff, which had always taken the prospect of a Channel tunnel in their stride, simply referred to their most recent statement of this view; they were 'of opinion that the aerial interests of this country would not be affected either favourably or otherwise by the construction of the Channel Tunnel', and after reconsideration of the questions desired to confirm that opinion.[1] Hankey was at this stage in a minority.

2. The Admiralty

This minority was real, although behind the façade of the reply already received from the Admiralty Hankey would have found some crumbs of comfort. The Admiralty had discussed the matter towards the end of November 1919. Admiral Sir Osmond de Beauvoir Brock, the Deputy Chief of the Naval Staff, calling for the general question of the advisability or otherwise of a Channel Tunnel to be brought before the Board of Admiralty, minuted on 20 November: 'I have an instinctive dislike of this project, based I confess on sentimental grounds. It is difficult to advance strong arguments against it'. Plans Division of the Admiralty produced a memorandum which, after listing objections made in the past, concluded:

> Modern developments of war and the changed European situation both tend to reduce the value of the Channel as our sea frontier. Dover is already within the range of modern heavy guns from Calais; our shores can be reached by air as

well as by sea; while we have already taken upon ourselves, in our own interests, the obligation of defending France and Belgium from Germany. The Channel no longer counts for what it did as a natural means of defence, and we have to reckon with the fact that some of the advantages of our insular position have gone for ever.

The Deputy Director of Planning endorsed this, writing, 'Although the Board of Admiralty may feel reluctant, on grounds of sentiment, to give their approval to the tunnel, there is little doubt that, from a naval point of view, the advantages outweigh any objections that can be urged against it under modern conditions of warfare so far as they can be foreseen.' This was the view that prevailed at the meeting of the Board of Admiralty on 11 December 1919. It concluded: 'The feeling of the Board was generally adverse to the scheme, but it was considered that from a naval point of view there were no substantial reasons which could be urged against it.'[2]

3. Mr Balfour

The balance was restored to some extent by the indispensable A.J. Balfour, the elder statesman who as Prime Minister had made the Committee of Imperial Defence into a viable concern, who subsequently had been First Lord of the Admiralty, then Foreign Secretary, and to whom still clung something of the aura of his uncle, Lord Salisbury (who himself had once joked, *à propos* the Channel Tunnel, 'Ce que nous craignons, ce ne sont pas les têtes de colonnes de l'armée française, mais les trains de plaisir du dimanche').[3] Balfour had been flattered by Hankey, who had singled him out for special treatment on 10-11 November 1919. His maxims of 1905 about making, when discussing the problem of invasion, 'a series of assumptions unfavourable to this country', had been quoted approvingly by the Committee of Imperial Defence in its Report on Invasion of 1914, and had been cited yet again in the recent Report of the Home Ports Defence Committee.[4] For Balfour, it was 'of the first importance that the country should be secure from invasion; it is almost as important that if it is secure, it should think itself so. For only thus can we avoid the perpetual agitation and the recurrent alarms which are inevitable if our existence as a nation is in doubt'. For his argument, it was sufficient that contingencies, such as 'some accident happening to a complicated machine, or a nervous official losing his head', were 'remotely possible'. He did add, however, that 'what is not only possible, but relatively easy, would be the destruction of the tunnel by sabotage, at a moment when military operations based upon its use were being carried out on the other side of the Channel'. He was more afraid of the dangers that were unknown and incalculable than of those which were known and were calculable:

> All that has happened in the last five years in the way of military and naval development – submarines, aircraft, and long-range guns – have tended without exception to render the Channel Tunnel a more dangerous experiment. These have all made it more difficult for us to be sure that it will be open when we want it to be open, and closed when we want it to be closed.
>
> And have we the least ground for thinking that the process is going to be reversed? And if it is not, if after the economic and sound habits of the world have adjusted themselves to this new mode of access to the Continent we find that it is fatal to our safety, what are we going to do? Destroy the tunnel in times of profound peace? Impossible. Wait till its dangers have been proved by a disastrous war? Still more impossible. The riddle will be insoluble.

Balfour, the greatest survivor in British politics at the time, was not one 'to sing amongst the uncertainties' until it was absolutely necessary. In the meantime he preferred the solid safety barrier of the sea:

> It may of course be said that the unknown dangers which I fear, may possibly be of a kind which will put an end to our position as an island Power, and make the command of the sea useless as a means of defence. It may be so; but let us wait till it is so, and so long as the ocean remains our friend do not let us deliberately destroy its power to help us.[5]

4. The War Office: Wilson *v.* Churchill

On 4 February Hankey had pressed the War Office to send in its paper on the Channel Tunnel, saying that the Cabinet had to take an early decision. Four days later Churchill ordered a General Staff paper to be forwarded, together with an additional memorandum from himself, and on the same day the Channel Tunnel question was placed on the list of Questions Awaiting Consideration by the Cabinet.[6] In fact, two memoranda were sent forward. Both were by Field Marshal Sir Henry Wilson, the CIGS, and both had been requested in November by his fellow enthusiast of the Fontainebleau weekend, the Prime Minister.[7] The first, dated 16 December 1919, was called 'Notes on the Military Advantages and Disadvantages of the Channel Tunnel'. The second, dated 23 December 1919, was called 'The Probable Effect which the Channel Tunnel would have had on the Recent War'.

Henry Wilson's memoranda revealed that he was an enthusiast for the Channel Tunnel only if it was accompanied by something for which he was, and long had been, even more enthusiastic – a British Army based on compulsory military service. A Channel Tunnel had military advantages if it was a matter of deploying twenty British divisions behind the Meuse in thirty to forty days; if it was a matter of deploying the mere six infantry and one cavalry divisions of 1914 the time gained would be minimal. The size of the British Army was important because a tunnel in being would profoundly modify German strategy in any future campaign, just as, had the tunnel existed in 1914, it 'would have acted as a magnet drawing the enemy in the direction which would have proved most fatal to the Allies'. Indeed, 'With a force of only six divisions, under the conditions given and under the opening moves of the campaign of 1914 as they actually took place, it is not too much to say that the existence of the Tunnel in that year would have lost us the campaign'. Moreover the French would have a difficult problem in having to cover both the centre and south of France and the Channel Tunnel exits, which would become a more decisive objective than Paris had been. Wilson's distrust of the French only reinforced his main point:

> From past experience it would appear unwise to rely on the French entirely, and we must therefore be ready to despatch a force capable of securing the area of deployment well in advance of the exits from the Tunnel, and this emphasises the point already stated that the *Tunnel is not only useless, but a positive danger unless there is a military force of sufficient size ready to use it.*

  (i) Assuming France to be friendly, the Tunnel is highly desirable on economic grounds as affecting the development and maintenance of military forces in war.
 (ii) If our policy is irrevocably bound to the defence of France and Belgium it is essential on military grounds.
(iii) Such a policy entails the maintenance of military forces on a scale commensurate with that of our potential enemies, both as regards numbers and degree of readiness. It further requires a firm determination on the part of the Government to mobilise at the same time as our Allies and enemies.
 (iv) The Tunnel contains an element of danger, however perfect the security arrangements, owing to the personal factor. These dangers increase by so much as our standard of military preparedness falls, whilst the military advantages of the Tunnel correspondingly decrease.
  (v) Unless we are prepared to intervene on the Continent on a continental scale the military advantages of the Tunnel do not outweigh the military disadvantages; that is to say that for an offensive war on the Continent we want the Tunnel, but for a defensive war in England we do not . . .

Sec G. HgL.
 _____
 15/1/20
CIGS

(1) In the forefront is the need and value of the Tunnel for peace purposes. Even if the Tunnel were automatically destroyed on the first outbreak of war the enormous peace advantages wd ~~been~~ ~~bad~~ ~~point~~. justify its construction.

(2) The second question is whether the military risks of the Tunnel having captured by an enemy are such as to make us forego the above advantages.

(3) The third, much smaller, question is whether we ed weaken sure of keeping the tunnel open because of its military advantage in time of war.

2 & 3 are mixed up together in these papers & means of certainly closing the Tunnel where we want to, are excited because they will make it ~~easy & ~~ easier for the enemy to close it when we dont want to. This is not fair to the project.

I still consider that yr memo. does not draw sufficient distinction between temporary & permanent destruction. ML 15.1

Exchanges between the CIGS,
Field-Marshal Sir Henry Wilson (HW), and the
Secretary of State for War, Winston Churchill (WSC),
in January 1920

Wilson's second memorandum ended by saying that it would be unwise to suppose that the Channel Tunnel would prove anything but an anxiety at the commencement of any future campaign 'unless our military forces are commensurate with the magnitude of the task in view. If, however, our forces are proportionate to our responsibilities, the Channel Tunnel would have an important economic and military value'.[8]

When these memoranda were submitted to Churchill he entirely missed the point they made, merely saying, 'Public opinion will not tolerate the slightest risk as regards the security of these Islands, and our strategy cannot afford to neglect the fear of invasion, however ill-founded it may be', and that absolute reliance could not be placed on mechanical means, owing to the personal factor. Churchill's reaction, however, was that of someone who still saw himself as First Lord of the Admiralty, rather than as Secretary of State for War:

> One or more short depressions in the tunnel could be made, the flooding of which would effectively close the tunnel without at the same time doing anything which would be irrevocable. Or, again, it would be possible to bring the tunnel up either on an artificial island in the sea, whence it would go by a bridge to the shore, or at some point where it would be constantly commanded from the sea. In either of these cases our command of the sea, which must be postulated, would enable us to interrupt by naval artillery the use of the tunnel and smash the railway altogether, even if both ends were in the hands of the enemy . . .

Churchill wanted Wilson to study this aspect further, and to confer with the promoters of the scheme.[9] Wilson doubted the wisdom of doing this 'before the Cabinet has agreed to the principle of a tunnel'. When Churchill insisted, Wilson pointed out that this aspect had been 'searchingly examined' by the Home Ports Defence Committee, and sent Churchill a copy of their Report.[10] Churchill's response brought out what, for him, was the fundamental reason for supporting the scheme: 'In the forefront is the need and value of the Tunnel for peace purposes. Even if the Tunnel was automatically destroyed on the first outbreak of war the economic peace advantages would justify its construction.'[11] This had to be balanced against the military risks of the tunnel being captured by an enemy, and Churchill considered that Wilson had not sufficiently distinguished between temporary and permanent destruction.

At this point the Director of Military Operations, Radcliffe, volunteered his own view:

It may be difficult for HM's Government to say definitely either today or at some future date whether they wish to employ British troops on the Continent or not. The existence of the tunnel would enhance the possibility of successful intervention and would thereby tend to facilitate the decision as to whether we should intervene or not, as it is obvious that the latter would be materially influenced by the chances of success or otherwise. The tunnel would therefore constitute a political as well as a military weapon of the first importance in the hands of the Government. The vital question is 'can this weapon be effectively used against us?' I have no hesitation in saying 'No' provided we retain command of the sea . . . Taking into account that the point of departure itself would be under fire from the fleet it may confidently be said that invasion in such circumstances is not a feasible operation of war.

In the light of the above considerations and assuming that our existence as a nation presupposes the maintenance of our command of the sea, I do not consider that the risks involved outweigh the military, political and economic advantages to be derived from the construction of the channel tunnel.[12]

The point of Wilson's that Radcliffe did not take up here was, of course, the necessity for conscription. Wilson delayed answering Churchill for a whole fortnight, and then claimed both that it was not clear what the Secretary of State meant, and that what he himself had written was quite clear. Churchill countered by asking for a single-word verdict, 'Yes' or 'No'. Wilson replied:

I am so sorry that my conclusions are not clear and yet on reading them over they seem to me to admit of no doubt. They amount to this:

If France is our friend
If our policy is the defence of France and Belgium
If we are prepared to engage in a Continental war on a continental scale

Then with all the necessary mechanical and other precautions I am wholly in favour of the Tunnel; but

If France is unfriendly
If it is not our policy to defend France and Belgium
If we are only prepared to intervene on a small scale

Then I am wholly opposed to the Tunnel.[13]

This was a repetition by Wilson of his pre-war ploy, but Churchill, of course, could not give any definite answers on these points. He admitted that the disposition of France and the policy of Britain might change as the years passed. He then asked Wilson once again whether on the whole he voted for or against. For Wilson it was all or nothing. Half a loaf was not better than none. So he replied: 'Then if a consistent and well-defined foreign policy of friendship for France, of determination to defend France and Belgium from German aggression and if a plan for fighting on the Continent on a continental scale is impossible then I am opposed to the Tunnel.'[14]

Churchill was in a dilemma. Although the Director of Military Operations supported him, the Chief of the Imperial General Staff did not. He decided to forward Wilson's papers to the Cabinet with a cover note of his own, and they went into circulation on 14 February. Churchill's cover note read as follows:

> The General Staff argument treats this question as if the project were dependent upon its military advantages. This is, of course, not so. The positive case for the Tunnel stands wholly upon its commercial advantages. The question for the General Staff is whether we must deny ourselves these advantages because of military dangers.
>
> However, the commercial advantages are now found to be reinforced by military advantages of an important character. These military advantages are carefully balanced against the military disadvantages by the General Staff. It will be seen that an attempt to carry out an invasion of England through the Tunnel is not seriously apprehended, and that the means, mechanical and otherwise, of destroying the Tunnel or putting it out of action or closing the débouches from it afford ample security. The military objections are more directed to the danger of losing the use of the Tunnel through the very ready means which may be devised for destroying it.
>
> In these circumstances it would appear that, if the commercial advantages are sufficient in themselves, the War Office would not be justified in vetoing the project on military grounds.[15]

5. The Treasury

Churchill's handling of the matter was clumsy, but the best he could do in the circumstances, given the status of the source of the internal opposition with which he had to deal. It did not advance the cause of the Channel Tunnel, however, and was in fact more in the nature of an 'own goal'. Coupling his note with Wilson's memoranda only advertised the lack of unanimity at the War Office, and gave his Cabinet colleagues the opportunity to be more impressed by, and to react more strongly against, the composite case made by the CIGS, than to embrace Churchill's short statement. Certainly this was so in the case of Austen Chamberlain, the Chancellor of the Exchequer, whose own memorandum of 26 February began, 'A careful study of the memoranda of the CIGS dated 16 and 23 December 1919, has produced upon my mind a very different impression from that which it has apparently left upon the mind of the Secretary of State for War'.

In Chamberlain's view 'nothing short of a treaty of defensive alliance with France, and probably with Belgium also', would have met one of Wilson's hypotheses, namely that had the tunnel existed before the war 'our obligation to France would have been of a more definite nature and one which would have exerted a stabilising effect on the attitude of Belgium'. For Chamberlain, the advantages of a stabilising effect were outweighed by the disadvantages of treaties of defensive alliance, which constituted altogether too much in the nature of obligations. He recognised that Wilson's words about 'forces proportionate to our responsibilities' and England exerting 'her whole strength from the earliest moment', entailed the re-establishment of conscription and the maintenance of the British Army on the pre-war continental model. He was appalled at the suggestion that the tunnel be owned and constructed by the Government, and even more so that the justification for this was that the existence of the tunnel entailed such dangers that it might have to be destroyed at any moment, something that private interests might not be inclined to do. That alternative sea bases and means of transport would have to be maintained to take the place of the tunnel if destroyed Chamberalin saw as probably involving future subsidies to ports and cross-Channel shipping. Of the idea that French strategical plans would have to be so recast as to secure French cooperation in the defence of the tunnel he wrote, 'This apparently involves French acceptance of the view that the tunnel is more important than either Paris or Alsace-Lorraine'. It was all too much, especially as the Home Ports Defence Committee had stressed the necessity for 'an extended naval defence and land defences, the garrisoning at all times of a mobile force in the vicinity, and the provision of an efficient air defence and anti-aircraft defence', whilst adding that the tunnel must be so far beneath the sea-bed that it could not be destroyed by explosives placed there. Chamberlain concluded a very powerful demolition job of his own:

> These requirements when thus placed together make the tunnel so completely master of both our military and political future that they seem to me conclusive against its construction. It is scarcely too much to say that, if we accept them all, England would exist for the defence of the tunnel rather than the tunnel for the defence of England.[16]

It is not without interest that Chamberlain made hardly any use of the arguments provided by Treasury officials. He had no time for the sentiment expressed by one official, that 'in the event of another Continental war, it might quite well happen that the Tunnel would provide rapid and safe access, and would be an adequate answer to a submarine threat'. On the other hand, as the same official pointed out, the tunnel would not enable any reduction in peace time expenditure; the only effective protection against sabotage was careful scrutiny on both sides, which would adversely affect the transportation of goods; and 'the capital commitments of the future (Housing, Electricity) added to the capital expenditure postponed during the war on for example public health services are so heavy that a demand of £50,000,000 for anything which is not absolutely essential should certainly be resisted': these were arguments that the Chancellor did not employ.[17]

6. The Ministry of Transport

Ministry of Transport officials had worked out their reply to the Cabinet enquiry of 15 November 1919 by the end of the year, well before the views of the War Office were circulated. They noted that the Channel Tunnel Company's pre-war estimate of £16,000,000, which included the cost of approach lines, marshalling yards, junction with the South Eastern and Chatham Railway, and other things, had now been increased to £35,000,000 for the tunnel itself, exclusive of the above items. They believed that £60,000,000 would be a more realistic figure, and this was apart from the meeting of naval and military requirements. They also noted that, in order to derive full benefit from the tunnel, the Berne Loading Gauge should be adopted throughout the country so that continental stock could run in the UK. It was their understanding that the cost of doing this, however, would be prohibitive. Nevertheless, they concluded that the construction of the tunnel was expedient, 'considered solely from the point of view of the development of traffic and business relations between this country and the Continent'. At this point Admiral de Bartolomé, fresh from his contribution to the Home Ports Defence Committee, tried to introduce a harder and more hostile line. He wanted it to be said that if it was proposed to provide means for destroying the tunnel at a moment's notice, as opposed to merely flooding it then 'it is considered that knowledge of this might produce such misgiving on the part of the travelling public that pressure would be brought to bear with a view either to the removal of these means of destruction, or to ensure their not functioning whilst a train was in the tunnel'. He added that it was 'also for serious consideration whether it is wise to embark on a project costing many millions which might be destroyed in a moment by some accidental functioning of the destroying apparatus or by the action of evilly disposed persons'.[18]

The Minister of Transport, Sir Eric Geddes, did not approve of de Bartolomé's work, and refused to send the memorandum as revised by him to the Cabinet. Instead he wrote a letter of his own, which was much more favourable towards the project:

> As to the expediency from an international point of view, apart from naval and military considerations, either of offence or defence, I should think that it would be a valuable asset, both from a political and from a commercial standpoint, and, if the naval and military considerations do not condemn the scheme utterly, I would hold the opinion that the project should go on if from a financial point of view it could be undertaken.

If it was intended to invest Government money up to half of the cost, Geddes thought that it was possible, provided that the naval and military requirements did not add materially to the cost and did not depopularise the tunnel because of the prejudice which arrangements for its drastic and immediate destruction might cause, that the tunnel might pay its way with an all-round 5½ per cent interest on the capital invested.

7. The Ministry of Health

On a strictly numerical basis, more Cabinet Ministers were at this stage in favour of the tunnel than were against it. Dr Christopher Addison, the Minister of Health, evened things up with a short note of 4 March, writing:

> At the commencement of our discussions on this subject, I confess I was prejudiced in favour of sanctioning the Channel Tunnel project, but I must say that, after having read the report of the military and naval authorities [i.e. the HPDC Report] I think that the matter is attended with real risk, and that we might in consequence find ourselves hereafter involved in the adoption of compulsory military service, or in running serious risks in the absence of its adoption. On the whole, therefore, I do not think that a case has been made out for justifying the sanctioning of the proposal.[20]

8. The Board of Trade

The Board of Trade, like the War Office, the Treasury and the Ministry of Transport, was not all of one mind, and spent three weeks thrashing out its position. The first effort was made by E.J. Elliot, who on 27 February forwarded a memorandum with that from Balfour attached, under the following covering note: 'It seems that there is a danger lest the real merits and positive advantages of the Scheme for peace pur- poses should never be considered owing to the fears created by military possibilities.' He wondered if his superiors would think it 'open to us to put forward any observations on the most general aspects of the Scheme as a part of human progress or whether we could advance any criticism of Mr Balfour's memorandum e.g. the question of extinction of the race of cross-Channel s[team] s[hips] invites further examination'.[21] Elliot's memorandum did not refrain from taking the lead he suggested. It began:

> The Secretary of State for War, *mirabile dictu*, is the one Minister who appears to view the case for the Channel Tunnel from what is to the Board of Trade obviously the right aspect viz: that the primary and essential consideration is the economic advantage likely to accrue in time of peace by its construction. British policy is surely committed to the maintenance of peace and even if the League of Nation fails to prevent another world-wide war or a European War of the first order everything points to that not arising for a century. Any such war arising within say a generation is again likely to be so catastrophic in its economic effects that the possible destruction of the Channel Tunnel will be merely incidental and its seizure is a remote eventuality which it appears can be met by the precautions recommended by the Military advisers of H.M.'s Govern- ment. The cost of those precautions would appear to consist chiefly in that of the maintenance of a mobile garrison force near Dover which should not be much greater than that of maintaining it anywhere else and it does not appear that the defence of the Channel Tunnel *per se* will involve an actual addition to our armed permanent forces.

It was, then, not everyone who maintained, or leapt to the conclusion, that full-scale compulsory service was required. Intermediate positions could be occupied by those who did not have the vested interests that Hankey and Wilson, for different reasons, had. Elliot continued:

> The general economic function and effect of a Channel Tunnel in being will be to join the railway system of Britain intimately to the Continental railway system for passenger and mail services and for traffic in goods of a perishable or valuable nature.
>
> The Tunnel has to be regarded as an item in the general economic fabric of Europe and among the necessary elements of the reconstructed Europe are primarily a general drawing closer of our relation with Europe and a necessity that British Enterprise, Capital and Experience should be ready to supply the needs of an extended but exhausted France. France will require the help of a more industrialised neighbour to develop her great resources and England should supply the need not Germany or the United States of America; quick and ready personal intercourse is therefore essential.

Elliot welcomed the Ministry of Transport's opinion that the tunnel might pay its way with an all-round 5½ per cent interest on the capital invested, and thought it 'not improbable that special engineering processes may reduce the cost to not more than £40 millions'. He offered as a conclusion that 'the Board of Trade are of opinion that the Government should approve in principle the construction of the Tunnel as likely to accelerate the development of British trade and to improve the position of the UK in the general transport system of the World, all due precautions being of course taken'.[22]

Elliot's effort was not at all well-received. Carlill drafted another one. He was concerned with the military objections to the tunnel only in so far as they had a bearing on its commercial utility, and admitted that two did have such a bearing: '(1) that it may become necessary to destroy the tunnel, in which case the money spent on it would largely have been wasted (2) that the existence of the tunnel will lead to the extinction of the cross-Channel shipping on which we might have to depend in an emergency'. He found it difficult to believe that it would not be possible to make the tunnel impassable without destroying it. Moreover, he too thought British commercial relations with the Continent would be closer than before the war, and that 'the facilities offered by the tunnel will help British capital and enterprise to extend their operations on the Continent'. He ended by saying: 'On the whole it seems to me that the advantages of a tunnel largely outweigh its possible disadvantages, and that the Government would be justified in supporting the promoters and aiding their investigations'.[23]

At a meeting of the Board of Trade Council on 16 March the Permanent Under Secretary, Sir S. Chapman, made it clear that even this latest memorandum was not on the right lines. He thought that 'in view of the world-wide shortage of capital the enterprise ought not to be encouraged'. He was backed by Fountain, who said the export of British goods would not be materially benefited, and that so far as goods traffic was concerned a ferry would give all the advantages of a tunnel and be much cheaper. It was agreed that Carlill's memorandum be redrafted and that the conclusion should 'on the whole be adverse to the construction of the tunnel in view of the scarcity and high price of capital at the present moment'.[24] The redrafted memorandum was much more hostile to the scheme, and the shorter version of it presented by Sir A.C. Geddes to the Cabinet was more hostile still:

In the opinion of the Board of Trade it would be madness to recommend the locking-up of a very large sum (which might amount to as much as £60m) in an enterprise of this character, which could not possibly yield any return – or any adequate return – for many years to come, at a time when there is a world-wide shortage of capital involving insufficient supplies for industrial and other economic purposes, and consequently a high rate of interest. Confronted by the immediate necessity of restoring war damage, France cannot possibly find any appreciable funds; this country is already beginning to realise that she will have the utmost difficulty in maintaining at an efficient level her industrial equipment; and, even in America, where the strain is least, it is reported that the need for capital, in consequence of its diversion to war purposes during the war, is likely to be in excess of what is available. It appears to the Board of Trade that, on economic grounds alone, the scheme of the Channel Tunnel should not be entertained for a moment at the present juncture.[25]

Geddes thus disagreed with his brother Eric, the Minister for Transport, and tipped the numerical balance of ministers against the scheme.

9. The Foreign Office

By this stage, the only major Department of State which had not announced its views was the Foreign Office. The Foreign Office had hitherto taken the view that there was no need for it to make a special departmental study of the question. In late 1913, when the Committee of Imperial Defence had suggested that the problem should be examined from the point of view of the Foreign Office, the Committee of Imperial Defence had been told that the manner in which the existence of a tunnel would affect British foreign relations depended so predominantly on the naval and military considerations involved that no useful statement of the Foreign Office point of view could be made before the naval and military aspects had been thoroughly elucidated. In March 1920, apparently unaware that the naval and military aspects had been investigated and reported on, Assistant Under Secretary of State Sir Eyre Crowe was inclined to adhere to the line previously taken by the Foreign Office. Crowe nevertheless did attempt to cover a certain amount of the ground. He wrote:

For practical purposes the question can – and perhaps should – be put more precisely by specifying, as the decisive factor for the purpose of this particular enquiry, our relations with France at a time when England may be at war, or threatened with hostilities. France may be in alliance with England; she may be an enemy; she may be neutral. It is for the naval and military authorities to weigh all the considerations material to the problem of the tunnel, as affecting the position of this country in any one of the three alternatives. The Foreign

Office is only called on to say in which of the alternative positions it is to be expected that we shall find France now and hereafter.

To the question so put, no categorical answer can safely be made; and the first point to emphasise, is this inevitable uncertainty. An opinion may perhaps be hazarded with some degree of assurance that, in the near future, France will not, single-handed, go to war with England. It would not be prudent for any student of history to go further than this. It is at least conceivable that England may find herself involved in hostilities whilst France remains neutral; and should the political condition of the world, which is far from stable at present, bring about, at any time, a situation in which England was confronted by a formidable alliance of hostile Powers, it is impossible to forecast on which side France would be found. Her hostility cannot be excluded.

He concluded that 'The answer therefore to the naval and military advisers in the hypothetical case here discussed, is that in calculating the nature and degree of the dangers which may threaten the safety of the tunnel, and against which prevention must be made, they would not be justified in neglecting the possibility of a neutral, or even an unfriendly, if not hostile, France'.[26]

A week later the Foreign Office heard from its Ambassador in Paris that the French Finance Minister, M. Marsal, wished officially to inform the Foreign Secretary that the French Government was prepared to make an immediate start from the French side of the Channel as soon as it heard that the British Government was willing to allow the work to proceed.[27] At this French prompting, the Channel Tunnel question was placed on the Cabinet agenda for 7 April, and the Permanent Under Secretary at the Foreign Office, Lord Hardinge, sent Crowe's memorandum to Curzon. Curzon considered it 'of too qualified and balancing a character to be of much use to the Cabinet in arriving at a decision'. He thought the Cabinet would want from the Foreign Office what it had received from other departments, a final Yes or No, and that the Foreign Office should not throw the responsibility back to the naval and military authorities. Curzon indicated the line he wanted to be taken: 'I have a clear idea of which answer I would give, viewing the instability of the Continental outlook, and remembering the teachings of history'.[28] Hardinge was given the job of drafting something based on the Foreign Office experience and traditions which Curzon claimed not to possess. Hardinge finished this piece of work on 25 April. Like Crowe, he thought the question resolved itself into that of the relations in the near and distant future between England and France. Then, drawing on the experience and traditions of the Foreign Office, he produced a thoroughly negative picture of future Anglo-French relations:

It must be remembered that until a century ago France was England's historic and natural enemy, and that real friendship between the inhabitants of the two countries has always been very difficult owing to differences of language, mentality and national character. These differences are not likely to decrease. The slightest incident may arouse the resentment or jealousy of the French and fan the latent embers of suspicion into a flame. Nor can Great Britain place any reliance upon public opinion in France being well-balanced and reasonable.

He recalled incidents from 1893 (over Siam), 1898 (over Egypt), and the hostility of France to Britain during the Boer War, and went on:

These incidents of comparatively recent date show clearly that it would be unwise to place reliance in the future on the friendship of France. It is almost certain that we shall have conflicts with France in the future as we have had in the past. Even now, while we are still Allies in the field and while our representatives are meeting in amicable conference, even while the French Government is already receiving favours from us and is daily importuning us for more, nothing could well be more provocative or hostile than the French press, always – as we know – in the closest relations with the French Foreign Office and with French statesmen.

Nothing can alter the fundamental fact that we are not liked in France, and never will be, except for the advantages which the French people may be able to extract from us.[29]

It was as if the War had never been, as if the *entente cordiale* of the last seventeen years had been and still was some kind of mental aberration. Hardinge's 'lessons of history' were not those taught by recent history; he attached more importance to the events of twenty years, or of one hundred and twenty years, previously. Even Hardinge's diatribe, however, did not satisfy Curzon, who strengthened the anti-French element in the concluding paragraph before sending it to the Cabinet on 1 May. The amended conclusion read:

The Foreign Office conclusion is that our relations with France never have been, are not, and probably never will be, sufficiently stable and friendly to justify the construction of a Channel tunnel, and the loss of security which our insular position, even in spite of the wonderful scientific and mechanical developments of recent years, still continues to bestow.[30]

Within a few months, Hardinge was awarded a position he had always coveted – that of British Ambassador to Paris. Such are the ways of the Foreign Office.[31]

10. The Reasons Why Not

Lord Hardinge credited himself, in his memoirs, with having given the Channel Tunnel scheme 'a knock-out blow'.[32] This is a considerable exaggeration. Although it is fair to say that a positive Foreign Office view would have made the strictly numerical 'score' four all, instead of three for and five against, the matter was not taken off the Cabinet agenda of 19 May, where it had been placed,[35] simply on account of the memorandum forwarded by Curzon. The Foreign Office was so much in eclipse at this time that, when Hankey drew up for the Prime Minister on 10 June (which itself suggests that the issue was still alive at that date) a summary of the views returned, he omitted to mention that expressed by the Foreign Office.[34] (In passing, it must be added that Hankey did not neglect this opportunity to distort the record yet again. Instead of summarising only the views expressed by Ministers, he included a summary of those expressed by the CIGS. He also added a half-page summary of the conditions to be satisfied from a naval, military, and air point of view to ensure the security of the exit of a tunnel, as recommended by the Home Ports Defence Committee, whose Report had been concurred in by the Admiralty, Air Ministry and Army Council.)[35]

The reason why the Channel Tunnel question was not discussed on 19 May and was relegated on 15 August to the Cabinet's List of Questions for Later Consideration[36] was that the requisite degree of unanimity had evaporated and was no longer present. Well before the Foreign Office, which he despised, pronounced, Lloyd George must have known that he could not carry the Cabinet with him, and that he must attach his Celtic enthusiasm to something else. Lloyd George therefore had to disappoint his former friend Robert Donald, the erstwhile editor of the *Daily Chronicle*, the newspaper which had throughout led the press campaign for the Channel Tunnel, who published in the July 1920 issue of the *Contemporary Review* an article called 'The Channel Tunnel and Anglo-French Relations' which expressed pro-French views which were at the opposite pole of perception to those quoted above from Hardinge and Curzon.[37]

In the one very brief treatment of the fate of the Channel Tunnel question at the end of the First World War that has hitherto been attempted, the author placed most weight on what was called 'the revival of traditional British attitudes to foreign policy within decision-making circles', and, in order to do so with plausibility, went rather beyond the time-frame within which the decision on this specific question was taken.[38] In a recent work by the same author, the only mention made of the Channel Tunnel is contained in the sentence, 'The resistance, in 1919 and 1920, to plans to build a Channel Tunnel, was symbolic of a wish to distance herself from the continent'.[39]

As we have seen, however, the reasons why no decision was taken to give the approval of the British Government to the project of a Channel Tunnel are to be found as much in the process of decision-making as in particular substantive points. The process was, to start with, a very long and drawn out one, and consultation was much wider and fuller than had been the case either in 1906-7 or 1913-14. Much happened between the spring of 1919 and the summer of 1920. Serious and sustained consideration of the issue had to await the return of the British Delegation from Versailles. The summer holidays, and some confusion over which body to refer the matter to, then supervened. The seed of doubt planted by Hankey on 10 and 11 November 1919 overcame the relative optimism of the time of the promulgation of the ten-year rule, and grew, under the treatment given to the matter by the Home Ports Defence Committee, into a climate of fear regarding the military possibilities. This was increased by Hankey's incarnation of Wolseley, who though dead he would not allow to fade away, in the memorandum circulated as from 28 January 1920.

Not all Ministers and officials succumbed to this climate of fear, but not enough of them had the vision, generosity of spirit, optimism or determination to create a new and better world manifested by, for example, Elliot of the Board of Trade and Churchill at the War Office. The latter's campaign was severely undermined by the fact that he was clearly at odds with the most senior and charismatic figure in the British Army, Field-Marshal Sir Henry Wilson, between whose insistence on linking the Channel Tunnel with full-scale compulsory military service and what he was told by the American General Bliss on 31 March 1919 there is a direct connection. The defection of the United States of America from the taking on of responsibilities for the peace of Europe and the defence of France invoked the prospect of Great Britain going once more, but this time single-handed because without the Russia on whom pre-war reliance had always been placed,[40] to the rescue of France. And how could she do this without adopting conscription – and given the expense and unpopularity of conscription how could any government, never mind a coalition, that announced its intention to introduce it hope to survive, especially at a time of grave economic dislocation, civil strife and mutinies among servicemen still not fully returned from abroad?[41] As early as 22 April 1919 Lloyd George had said at the Council of Four, 'You know how impatiently England is waiting for the abolition of compulsory military service'; the United States Senate rejected the Versailles Treaty and, in effect, their guarantee to France, first on 19 November 1919 and again on 19 March 1920.[42]

As the process proceeded euphoria was replaced by self-doubt, confidence by fear, trust by suspicion, extroversion by introspection. Prudence and caution took over. Horizons narrowed. In considerations of the expense, the complexity and the uncertainty, the vision and ambition of from Charing Cross to Baghdad expired as the realisation hit home that Great Britain had already bitten off more than she could chew,[43] and was in no internal condition to try to realise this particular enthusiasm. In some individuals, the substantive difficulties satisfied and fed more basic racialistic and insular urges, which the vocabulary of tradition and realpolitik existed in part to conceal and encode.

THE CHANNEL TUNNEL

Its Position in October, 1921.

STRATEGIC VALUE OF THE CHANNEL TUNNEL:

Remarkable Testimony by Marshal Foch.

UNEMPLOYMENT AT HOME:

How the Tunnel would afford Immediate Relief.

By Sir ARTHUR FELL, M.P.,

Chairman, House of Commons Channel Tunnel Committee.

The Channel Tunnel,
pamphlet by Sir Arthur Fell, October 1921

Chapter 8

Between the Wars

1. 'Flooding Out', 1924

Neither the Channel Tunnel Company, nor the House of Commons Channel Tunnel Committee, nor the French, easily reconciled themselves to the absence of a decision in favour of a tunnel from the British Government. In March 1921, at the Cercle Interallié in Paris and in the presence of Arthur Fell, Marshal Foch said, 'Had there been a tunnel under the Channel before the war, it might have prevented the War'. Foch gave Fell permission to publish this and an earlier statement that 'Had the British and French been in possession of the Channel Tunnel in 1914, the War would have been shortened by at least two years'. Fell incorporated these statements in a pamphlet which he published in October 1921. In July 1921 the International Chamber of Commerce, meeting in London, approved the Channel Tunnel Scheme. In February 1922 the French Government attempted to use this as a lever, and renewed their request of October 1919 for a joint Anglo-French commission to examine the question. Curzon sent the French request to the Committee of Imperial Defence, hoping for their agreement with the answer he proposed to give. This was that 'in view of the present financial situation in this country, HM's Government are not at present prepared to consider the question of participating in a joint commission of enquiry'. Curzon's wish was granted at a meeting of the Standing Defence Sub-Committee on 14 March 1922, one member having spoken to the Chancellor of the Exchequer, Sir Robert Horne, who 'strongly supported the Foreign Office view and was of opinion that for financial reasons an enquiry at the present time was highly inexpedient', and Hankey having reminded his colleagues of the views expressed officially by the Board of Trade in March 1920.[1] In the following month a French

move, employing the French Channel Tunnel Committee, whose president was now Paul Cambon, a former ambassador to Britain, to involve
the Italians by asking the Italian Prime Minister, Signor Facta, to become
a patron of an Italian Committee, was described by one official at the
Foreign Office as 'impudent', and Curzon returned the same answer as
before to the French. Curzon said on this occasion that the answer was a
'dishonest' one: 'The real reason is strategical.'[2] For Curzon the real
reason may, by this time, have become 'strategical', but there is no reason
to think that for Sir Robert Horne the real reason was other than the one
he had just given – financial. A reduction of national expenditure was a
priority at that time: throughout January and February the Cabinet had
been engaged in an examination of the report of Geddes' Committee on
National Expenditure, which has become known by posterity as the
'Geddes' Axe'.

Enthusiasm on the Continent, however, remained high enough for a
Belgian Channel Tunnel Committee to be formed in April 1922. And in
July Fell twice pressed Lloyd George in the House of Commons for
answers. On the first occasion Lloyd George maintained that 'the whole
of the time at our disposal will be required for the discussion of other
urgent questions', and revealed the hostility to the tunnel of 'even
military opinion' at that moment. On the second occasion Lloyd George
stressed 'the financial position of the country', and added: 'Having
regard to the rapid progress being made in aerial science, no useful
purpose could be served by instituting an enquiry by the Committee of
Imperial Defence until it is necessary to take a definite decision on the
question.'[3]

Lloyd George's successor, Bonar Law, told Parliament on 4 December
1922 that he did not think the financial condition of the country
warranted consideration of the Channel Tunnel. Fell immediately wrote
to the new Prime Minister saying that if he could be assured that a Bill
for the construction of a tunnel would be sympathetically considered by
the Government, the Channel Tunnel Company would promote one
that would throw no additional burden upon the budget. The company
was confident, he said, that it could raise all the capital necessary for the
building of the British portion. Hankey, still Cabinet Secretary, drafted
a reply for Bonar Law to make. This read: 'Complex considerations of
national policy are involved in any decision on the part of the Government to construct the Channel Tunnel and the Prime Minister is not
prepared to undertake to reverse the statement he made in the House of
Commons on 4 December that the Government is not at present
prepared to consider the question.' Nevertheless, when Bonar Law

spoke in Parliament ten days later he left the door ajar, for he promised that, if it could be proved that private individuals were ready to start with their own money, he would have the question reconsidered.[4] Bonar Law died in May 1923, however, and was succeeded by Stanley Baldwin.

As had become its habit, the House of Commons Channel Tunnel Committee immediately asked the new Prime Minister to reconsider the matter, only to be told (in June 1923) that he was not prepared to do so. Shortly after this, Arthur Fell relinquished the reins of that committee to Sir William Bull, Conservative M.P. for Hammersmith South from 1918 to 1929 and chairman of the London Unionist MPs since 1910. It was as a result of Bull's efforts that the next significant parliamentary statement by a Prime Minister about the Channel Tunnel was made. It was to be made by Ramsay MacDonald and was to be exactly as drafted for him by Hankey.[5]

On MacDonald's becoming Premier Bull had decided to make another attempt, as he put it, 'to get the Tunnel through'.[6] He organised a deputation from the 400 strong House of Commons Channel Tunnel Committee, which MacDonald received on 26 June 1924. Early that month Departments of State were notified and arrangements made to bring the matter before the CID. Hankey wrote to the Foreign Office, asking whether they would produce a memorandum by 19 June, or whether they would stick to the memorandum of May 1920. MacDonald, who was Foreign Secretary as well as Prime Minister, dealt with this, minuting: 'I have always regarded this project as (a) military and (b) transport and commercial. The F.O. as such ought to have no overriding views.'[7] Given the hostility of the Foreign Office in general (but not of the Permanent Under-Secretary Sir Eyre Crowe, who was so neutral that he professed to be convinced by both sides of the argument) and in particular of the memorandum of 1920, Bull's later speculation that MacDonald 'was thoroughly in favour of the Tunnel' may well be correct.[8]

It was not to be expected that Hankey would fail to prepare his own ground with a view to conditioning the outcome. On 21 June he finished a memorandum which brought up to date the one he had prepared in December 1919. He began with a section on 'The International Aspect':

In its essence the question of the Channel Tunnel appears to depend upon the state of our foreign relations with the Power which possesses the Continental end of the tunnel. If, for example, Northern France were a British Possession, no one would object to the construction of a tunnel, for in that case there would be no serious military danger. Similarly, if it were a loyal Dominion no one would object. On the other hand, if it were in the possession of a people like the Russian Bolsheviks, or even the Germans, no one would suggest the construction of a tunnel at the present time.

So far as the French were concerned, Hankey wheeled out his arguments on the Fashoda crisis and on French policy during the Boer War. As regards the Germans, he recalled that both in August–September 1914 and in April–May 1918 'we have been faced with the possibility of Germany occupying the northern coast of France'. In this connection he was able to draw on Ludendorff's book, *My War Memories*, which had recently been published.

The section on Defence Considerations began:

> The case against the Channel Tunnel from the point of view of Defence may be reduced to this, that the French, or whoever for the time being held the Continental end of the Tunnel, might, by a *coup de main*, seize our end before we had put the Tunnel out of action. The enemy would then be in possession of a bridgehead with a secure military line of communications behind him for the invasion of this country. The *coup de main* might be effected either by a seaborne (or, in the future, possibly an airborne) raid, or by the use of the Tunnel itself, using some *ruse de guerre* or stratagem.

It seems not to have occurred to him that the British might respond by making similar raids, seaborne or airborne, or by utilising the firepower of their Navy and Air Force with a view to attacking the continental end and thereby rendering the military line of communications anything but secure, and effectively isolating the enemy at the bridgehead that it had taken. On the question of raids, whether 'out of the blue' or 'out of the grey', Hankey drew on the conclusion reached by a committee chaired by Lord Salisbury on National and Imperial Defence:

> While the menace of attack from the air has greatly increased and necessitates a strong home defence air-force, as proposed in Part VI of this Report, the three Staffs are agreed that in existing conditions the liability of the country to seaborne invasion has considerably diminished as compared with pre-war standards. As the basis of the Military scheme for home defence it should be assumed that the maximum enemy force which might be landed is 100,000 men, but if, when the home defence scheme is being worked out by the Staffs, it is considered that any change in this assumed basis is necessary, the question should be reconsidered. (CID Paper 463-B)

Hankey stated that the existence of a Channel Tunnel 'might provide a strong incentive for a raid', and contended that 'it is clear from the above extract that the possibility of a seaborne raid cannot be left out of

MID-CHANNEL QUALMS.

Mr. Asquith. "FAR BE IT FROM ME TO UNDERESTIMATE THE MILITARY OBJECTIONS TO A CHANNEL TUNNEL; YET, STANDING AT THIS RAIL, I ASSERT WITHOUT FEAR OF CONTRADICTION THAT THE CIVILIAN ARGUMENTS IN ITS FAVOUR ARE SUBSTANTIAL AND EVEN OVERWHELMING."

The Other Ex-Premiers (*faintly*). "AGREED."

'Mid-Channel Qualms',
Punch, 9 July 1924

account'. He understood that an airborne military raid was not yet practicable, 'but long views are necessary in this question, and it would appear undesirable to exclude it from the range of possible future developments'.

Hankey remained obsessed with the possibilities. He recalled how in the wars of the Dutch Republic it had been a favourite trick of the Spanish forces and of their German mercenaries to drive women and children of Dutch nationality across a bridge as cover to the advancing troops. 'It would not be difficult', he said, 'to adapt this stratagem to the passage of the Tunnel . . . The troop trains might follow the ordinary mail train from a considerable distance and make the passage of the Tunnel, so to speak, under its shelter.' Despite the conclusion of Salisbury's Committee on National and Imperial Defence, Hankey was by no means certain that their conclusion applied to the case of a *coup de main* against Dover:

> Guns are already in existence which can fire from the coast of France far beyond Dover. In the distant future it is by no means impossible that it might be possible to provide a barrage from the French coast to assist a landing . . . The concentration of aircraft which had come from great distances would considerably assist a *coup de main* by causing panic and confusion and by temporarily interrupting the communications by which reinforcements and assistance could be brought. Aeroplanes are already in existence which can carry small bodies of troops. What the future will bring in the form of submarine transports, submarine tanks, aerial transports and aerial tanks it is impossible to foresee . . .

The logic of Hankey's one-sided position was that whatever the future brought, it brought these things only to the enemies of the British, and not to the British themselves, who had, apparently, in this respect, no future of their own. And yet, as Hankey had mentioned on the previous page, 'A landing operation involving the use of Tanks was actually worked out in detail and rehearsed in the later stages of the late war.'[9]

Hankey sent a copy of this memorandum to the Chief of the Air Staff, Sir Hugh Trenchard. This was an appropriate thing to do in view of the aerial aspects addressed. It was also appropriate in another sense, for Trenchard, who had served under Wolseley in the Boer War, had in his possession a letter in Wolseley's hand, dated February 1882 (see Appendix 1). Hankey told Trenchard that the memorandum contained a good deal of material which did not appear in any of the papers circulated officially: 'For the present I am keeping it up my sleeve, for production if the decision should go the wrong way. In that event (which I do not think likely) I shall say that I have some fresh material and ask for an adjournment. I will then dish it up in a form suited to the exigencies of the moment.'[10]

Hankey had taken another precaution. He had induced MacDonald to invite to the CID meeting all the Prime Ministers who had presided over discussions of the scheme and who were still alive – Balfour, Asquith and Lloyd George; Baldwin, whose short-lived first premiership had not included any such discussions, also received, and accepted, an invitation to attend.[11]

Hankey's precautions paid dividends at the CID meeting on 1 July 1924. The First Sea Lord, Lord Beatty, spoke first, repeating the conclusion arrived at by the Chiefs of Staff Sub-Committee, namely that 'The military danger of a tunnel was not serious, but a slight danger must necessarily exist'. That fact alone 'made them feel that the great advantage possessed by this country of being surrounded by water should not be foregone unless there were great advantages to be gained'. From a purely naval point of view he drew attention to the likely disappearance of the cross-Channel steamer services, which 'had been proved to be of great value during the late war and formed an important part of the Naval Reserve'. He also said that the construction of a tunnel 'would probably have an adverse effect on the development of civil aviation and would weaken one of the supports of our Air power'. The CIGS, Lord Cavan, then made a short statement to the effect that the existence of a tunnel 'was bound to add to the anxieties of those in control, was bound to add to our commitments, and consequently was bound to add to our expenditure on defence forces'. Trenchard's points owed much to the memorandum sent him by Hankey. He said that the best laid schemes for putting the tunnel out of action might be dislocated by a determined enemy, that large air forces in being on the Continent made the possibility of a 'bolt from the blue' more probable, 'in which case a small and determined force of the enemy might conceivably gain possession of our end of the tunnel and, supported by a strong concentration of their Air Force, might successfully hold the Tunnel exit for two or three days, during which time the passage of considerable forces could have taken place'.

Both Balfour and Lloyd George admitted to having wavered in their opposition to the tunnel, the former during the late war, and the latter at the end of it, which Lloyd George put down to 'the atmosphere resulting from war'. Lloyd George thought that many of the 400 MPs who supported the project would 'after due reflection and after hearing the objections to the proposal, hesitate to pledge themselves to a scheme which might prove detrimental to the safety of this country'. So far, he said, these MPs 'had only heard one side of the story'. Not only were there military reasons against the scheme, 'but also psychological reasons which would tend to alter the conduct of our foreign policy and our diplomatic negotiations'. He went on to explain:

> The Committee had listened to the views expressed by the naval, military and air experts, who had all agreed that no guarantee could be given with regard to the defensibility of the tunnel. He pointed out that the French experts would in all probability reach the same conclusion, and would advise their Government to that effect, so that the French would always have it in mind that they could strike a sudden blow at this country. If the tunnel was constructed, therefore, it might tend to weaken our diplomacy.

He considered that Trenchard's words added to the arguments against the tunnel. In short, he regarded the tunnel 'as a very dangerous experiment, which should be postponed until all possibilities of conflict with a European nation had disappeared'.

Asquith, Baldwin and Beatty all declared how impressed they were with the sentiments expressed in Balfour's memorandum of February 1920, which had been reprinted for them. Indeed, Beatty had ended his statement by quoting the final sentence of that memorandum: 'So long as the ocean remains our friend, do not let us deliberately destroy its power to help us.' MacDonald, who had started with the assumption that, if no overriding reasons could be adduced against the tunnel, he would be inclined to favour its construction, now joined their ranks. Sidney Webb, the President of the Board of Trade, admitted to having undergone a similar conversion whilst examining the proposal: 'From a trade point of view the existence of a tunnel would dry up the present cross-Channel services and would provide no counter-balancing advantages to trade of an appreciable character.'

It was agreed that the CID recommend that the Channel Tunnel should not be proceeded with, that a communiqué be issued to the press stating that Lord Balfour, Mr Asquith, Mr Lloyd George and Mr Baldwin had been involved in the consideration of the question, and that Balfour's memorandum should be circulated to the Cabinet which would deal with the matter the next day.[12] On 2 July the Cabinet accepted the recommendation of the CID.[13] MacDonald broke the news to Bull, saying, 'I have done my best, but as a Constitutional Prime Minister I am bound to accept the advice of my technical advisers, and there the matter must remain'.[14] A week later MacDonald read out to the House of Commons the statement drawn up for him by Hankey.

Writing immediately after the statement was delivered, Hankey was confident that the Channel Tunnel had been 'flooded out' once and for all.[15] Involving the previous Prime Ministers had been a master-stroke. Balfour in particular had proved what a force he still was in the land.

2. 'The Knife of Common Sense', 1929-30

Hankey's celebration was premature. The next questions in Parliament should be seen against the background of the statement made by Lloyd George at the CID on 1 July 1924, that the tunnel was a dangerous experiment that should be postponed 'until all possibilities of conflict with a European nation had disappeared', for two foreign political developments occurred which at the very least appeared to diminish such possibilities. On the eve of the signature of the Locarno Pact, which guaranteed the Rhine frontier on both sides, Ernest Thurtle, MP for Shoreditch, asked Prime Minister Stanley Baldwin whether, in view of that agreement, and bearing in mind the amount of employment the scheme would provide, the Government would reconsider the question. Baldwin's reply was in the negative.[16]

Three years later Baldwin could not repeat that performance, although he tried initially to do so. The signatories of the Kellogg-Briand Pact of 27 August 1928 renounced war as an instrument of national policy. Following this up, though the Pact was not due to become fully operational immediately, Thurtle again asked Baldwin whether this had made any difference to the Government's attitude to the Channel Tunnel.[17] Baldwin's negative reply of 12 November 1928 caused a furore. Sir William Bull, on announcing that he would call the House of Commons Channel Tunnel Committee together in the following January, described the response amongst his parliamentary colleagues and the press as 'like putting a match to a sun-dried heath'. It seemed to him that 'the psychological moment' had arrived.[18]

In January 1929 the Air Ministry took it upon itself to dust off the views it had expressed in 1924. The concluding paragraph of a memorandum prepared in the Plans Division caught the popular mood:

In this paper no account has been taken of the economic, social and commercial arguments in favour of the Channel Tunnel. It has been assumed – possibly wrongly, but with some justification – that in view of the constantly recurring and very intensive agitation on the part of politicians, businessmen, and Press, the advantages to be gained from the venture are genuinely great. That there are certain military advantages, cannot be dismissed. The freedom of this country from invasion must always be treated as a case of special and supreme importance. But in these days of the League of Nations and Kellogg Pacts, there are factors to be considered other than purely technical defence considerations and such considerations, which had necessarily to be the sole deciding factors in the past, need not and cannot today stand alone in the path of progress and economic development.

Earlier in the memorandum, the writer had found it 'astonishing' that, even forty-six years ago, a soldier of Wolseley's experience could have committed himself to saying that, were a tunnel made, 'England as a nation could be destroyed without any warning whatever when Europe was in a condition of profound peace'. He considered any such *coup de main* as Wolseley, Hankey and others had envisaged as unlikely in 1882, almost inconceivable in 1914, and doubly impracticable in 1929. From his aerial point of view, 'What more ideal target for aircraft, bombers and low flying fighters can be imagined than the entrance and exit of the Tunnel during the passage and detrainment of an invading army?' He was loath to believe that Haig had said that air bombing had increased the danger of a tunnel, in that if the German had reached the Channel Ports they could have bombed a zone round the English entrance and poured troops into England. This he described as 'as good instance of the familiar method of argument which loads the scales against the country and is blind to the other side of the question'. For if it was possible to bomb a zone, it was much easier to concentrate on the smaller target of the tunnel entrance. He had no doubt that if a foreign General Staff had ever seriously contemplated the possibility of an invasion of England by tunnel before 1914, 'they would never dream of doing so now in the face of air opposition'. It followed from this that no very extensive defences were necessary: only strong anti-aircraft defences and 'very elaborate defences against sabotage'. The freedom of action of the Expeditionary Force was not liable to be affected.

He had disposed of the old argument about panic, 'the indirect effect on the public mind'. Over two-thirds of the House of Commons and most of the newspapers were engaged in an active agitation in favour of the tunnel, and there seemed to exist 'a pretty general conviction that the dangers of the scheme exist mainly in the imagination of the Fighting services'. Englishmen as a race, he said, were not prone to alarm or unrest unless there was a strong reason, and the sound common sense of the nation was not likely to be seriously disturbed by a possibility so obviously remote as invasion through a tunnel. The Press, even if so inclined, would find it difficult to arouse great enthusiasm for a cause so unpopular as additional defence expenditure. It was difficult to resist the conclusion 'that if the Press were unable to produce any more formidable bogies than have been conjured up by statemen and soldiers in the past, the tax-payer is not likely to sleep any less soundly in his bed on account of the existence of the Channel Tunnel'.

He had found it impossible to agree with Balfour that the cutting of a tunnel, once built, would be disastrous. Balfour had said that its existence would destroy an immense proportion of the Channel steamers. yet the Board of Trade had concluded in 1914 that the result of the tunnel on the shipping situation would be 'practically negligible'. He had also disagreed with Wilson, Haig and French that a tunnel would adversely affect the strategy of a campaign in defence of France: the tunnel would at most be only one of several lines of communication to France; 'it is even doubtful in these days, with the Tunnel exit presenting the target it would to air bombardment, whether [it] would be counted on as a line of communication at all'.[19]

In a further note of 19 February, the same writer, who later became Air Marshal Sir John Slessor, expounded again his case that 'invasion through the Tunnel is in these days an absolute impossibility', even if the bridgehead had previously been gained by a seaborne attack. He acknowledged that there were objections of a political nature to the tunnel project. One, which had appeared in the *Saturday Review* of 5 January, was that the tunnel would 'deflect the normal course of our policy, giving it a French bias, and subtly undermining the force and independence of our views'. He proceeded to dispose of this objection in no uncertain terms:

> The contention that these two 18 feet tubes from Dover to Calais are going to convert us from an island power to a Continental one again is difficult to understand, primarily because we are already a Continental power and have been for centuries. At intervals it has suited us to adopt an attitude of splendid isolation, to endeavour to set ourselves apart from the affairs of our neighbours, and to pretend that they do not concern us. But this has never been our true position as a thousand years of war on the Continent have proved; nor can it ever be in the future . . .

To the argument that a tunnel would join Britain to France in a marriage from which there could be no divorce, he replied:

> its effect, if any, will merely bring us closer geographically to France, and European history does not encourage us to suppose that geographical proximity entails either close friendship or political interdependence. In any case the

marriage argument seems to imply that the Tunnel will be our only link with European nations of which France is already our nearest neighbour. Moreover in the last decade two circumstances have arisen which established us irretrievably as a Peninsula of Europe. The one is the League of Nations (with its development, the treaty of Locarno) and the other is the rise of air power. We are finally committed in certain circumstances under the League to intervention on the Continent; if our action under the League does not necessarily entail military operations on land, then the construction of the Tunnel can make no differences to that commitment. It is believed that we are hiding our head in sand if we suppose that we can stand by and watch a European war from a position of disinterested neutrality; and if we have to fight France, she can strike us from the air far more effectively than by indulging in the old-fashioned and highly speculative gamble of a land invasion which no enemy has, in fact, attempted since 1066.[20]

Trenchard, to whom this memorandum was sent, turned out to be the ostrich here. Trenchard said that if the economic and social arguments in favour of the tunnel, in terms of its effect on employment or increasing the general prosperity of the country were really strong, he would not consider the military arguments against it sufficiently cogent to stand in the way. However, he believed the economic case for the tunnel to be weak, and existing military disadvantages to outweigh possible military advantages. He would not alter his attitude unless it was proved beyond doubt that there would be genuine and great economic advantages. Amongst the military disadvantages he picked out the military commitments that would be required for the defence of the tunnel, 'human nature being what it is':

> He well remembers the constant cases in the last war where, against all better judgment, we had to give way to appeals by normally intelligent and well-instructed people based on a mass of unintelligent and ill-instructed public opinion. He instanced the cases where airman were stoned because they could not afford complete protection against air raids, and he foresees that if, at a future date, our relations with France became dangerously strained, it will inevitably entail demands even from people like the C-in-C, ADGB and GOC, Eastern Command, for extra measures of defence, a few more aeroplanes or a few more machine guns, which will be very difficult to resist in the fact [sic] of opinion worked up by the Press.

He was definitely opposed to anything that would entail extra expenditure on defence, however small that extra expenditure might be.

As regards the strategic effect of a tunnel on a campaign in France, Trenchard still believed Henry Wilson's arguments of 1919 to be sound. He was 'inclined to think that a British commander would in fact try and stick to the tunnel. There is a natural feeling that it is better to have dry land behind one than to rely on ships . . . ' He was also still persuaded by Balfour of the danger which the tunnel might present:

> He considers that in the case of war in France, the tunnel would be an invaluable line of supply, and the enemy would make every effort to stop it, especially by an air action. One well aimed bomb might block the tunnel, and as the effect of that bomb would be so immense, we should necessarily be committed to measures of defence to prevent that bomb being dropped – which would entail a diversion from the decisive front.[21]

By this time, views expressed in the Press on the other side of the Channel were beginning to have an impact. These views were collected in an article published in the *Manchester Guardian Weekly* on 1 February. The French, for their part, seemed to be concentrating on the political and strategic consequences of a tunnel, which they considered to be both enormous and revolutionary. They regarded a possible invasion of England by such a tunnel as too futuristic to be taken seriously. What impressed them was the permanent possibility that a tunnel would create of a British invasion of the Continent. They had not forgotten that between 1914 and 1918 Great Britain put 6,000,000 armed men on the Continent, and by so doing not only decided the destiny of Europe but revealed herself as potentially a military Power of tremendous proportions. If a tunnel existed, no blockade of British waters could interfere with her power to intervene in Europe: her ability to seek a decision by land warfare would remain intact. A Channel Tunnel could constitute the most tremendous military bridgehead in the world, and a strategic objective of vital importance. It would invite the main attack, and as a simple logical corollary would require the main defence. The military possibilities of the tunnel would displace and distort the whole of the strategic conceptions hitherto governing the continental General Staffs. They would tend to make Great Britain a continental military Power, and to make her army an instrument on the continental model of a conscript nation. Was the British mind as yet ready to face these realities, asked M. Paluel-Marmont of the *Echo de Paris*?: 'This permanent linking up of England and Continental Europe which would be made effectively tangible by the construction of a means of communication so safe and practical as a tunnel, would involve for the British Empire consequences of such a character in the military and economic domain that it hardly seems as if the British people are yet prepared for them.' Or, as the writer for the *Manchester Guardian Weekly* put it, 'Is the

Committee of Imperial Defence prepared to change so vitally the traditional conception of Great Britain's world role? Will British public opinion, when it comes to the test, accept the inevitable burden?[22]

On the British side of the Channel, General Sir Ian Hamilton, who had commanded unhappily at Gallipoli, weighed in against the tunnel and against the French: 'Were the tunnel to take shape, the most vital strategic spot in the world would be no longer Constantinople, but the button which would dominate the tunnel.'[23] General S.S. Long, who had drawn up the supply plans for the late war and been Director of Supplies and Transport until 1916, weighed in against Hamilton. Long found an ally in favour of the tunnel in the form of Major-General Sir E. Swinton, the inventor of the tank. At the Department of Overseas Trade a split emerged between the Government's Chief Economic Advisor, Sir Sydney Chapman, and the writer of a memorandum of which Chapman said: 'He has definitely made up his mind that he doesn't want the tunnel and has completely coloured the memorandum with his personal views. It is not therefore a fair presentment of the case.'[24] Sir William Bull, meanwhile, was conducting a referendum in Parliament, as his predecessor had done on the previous occasion.

It was clear that something had to be done about all this commotion, and on 26 March Baldwin made an announcement. There would be 'an impartial inquiry' into the economic aspects, which had not been examined for several years. If the committee set up for this purpose decided that economically the tunnel was impossible, the question would fall to the ground, 'but if they decided that the economic advantages are considerable, the question for the Government will be to decide whether the economic advantages are such as to outweigh any such military disadvantages as may be put'.[25] Early in April Bull's Parliamentary Channel Tunnel committee issued a report of their own, embodying the findings of their referendum, which were:

	Peers	*MPS*
In Favour	116	232
Neutral	36	94
Against	59	11

The committee set up by Baldwin was a Sub-Committee of the Committee of Civil Research. Its terms of reference were 'To examine and report on the economic aspects of proposals for the construction of a Channel Tunnel or other new form of cross-Channel communication.' The composition of this committee was as follows:

E.R. Peacock (former Director of the Bank of England, now of Baring Brothers and Co.), Chairman

Lord Ebbisham of Cobham (formerly Sir Rowland Blades, Lord Mayor of London, President of the Federation of British Industries)

Sir Clement Hindley (Chairman of the Racecourse Betting Control Board)

Sir Frederick Lewis (of Furness, Withy Ltd., and of twenty-three other shipping and insurance companies)

Sir Henry Strakosch (member of the League of Nations Financial Committee)

Their hearings began immediately, but as they were suspended during the summer recess their report was not finished until February 1930, by which time Ramsay MacDonald had been Prime Minister again for eight months. Peacock's committee, which interviewed over fifty witnesses (see Appendix 6) was the most thorough investigation into the matter since that chaired by Lord Lansdowne in 1883. Peacock and the majority of his colleagues arrived, as had Lansdowne, at a conclusion in favour of the construction of a tunnel. As they put it, 'the construction of a Channel Tunnel, by creating new traffic and thus increasing trade, would be of economic advantage to this country'.[26] Peacock had another experience on the same lines as Lansdowne, although not quite as marked, in that one of his colleagues, Lord Ebbisham of Cobham, disagreed, and wrote a Note dissenting from the Report.

Foreseeing that the second part of the two-part inquiry outlined by Baldwin might be necessary, Hankey had begun to prepare for the worst, from his point of view, as far back as November of the previous year. At various stages in the proceedings of the Peacock Committee he had tried to influence them in what he regarded as the right direction. In April 1929 he had sent them a note on 'The Failure of the French to destroy the Tunnels through the Vosges Mountains in the War of 1870'.[27] In May he had supplied one on 'The Time Required to Cross a Land Frontier', which had led to the writing of many reports by British Consuls on the Continent.[28] In November he had drawn their attention to the text – his text – of MacDonald's public statement of July 1924, and also sent them an extract from the report – his report – of his Home Ports Defence Committee of December 1919, managing to bring the date of this forward to 1921 in order to make it appear more recent than it was.[29] At the end of November he put the finishing touches to the twenty-seven page, forty-two paragraph memorandum called 'The

Channel Tunnel: The Political and Military Aspects' on the same lines as the one he had produced late in 1919.[30]

Two days before the Peacock Committee's report was issued, Hankey redated his latest memorandum to 28 February 1930. On 28 February, to coincide with the publication of the Peacock Report, he sent his memorandum to Major-General J.R.R. Charles at the War Office, saying disingenuously, 'it may amuse you to read it'.[31] On the same day, he also sent it to the Prime Minister. Appreciating that MacDonald might not care to read the whole of so long a document, he drew his attention to the articles of 1 February from the *Manchester Guardian Weekly* which he had tacked on as an appendix. In his covering letter he took the opportunity to stress that before a final decision was reached, a re-investigation of the political and military aspects would have to take place. He suggested new reports be commissioned from the Home Defence Committee and from the Chiefs of Staff, and that representatives of the two political parties be invited to attend a meeting of the CID. Bearing in mind the forthcoming Naval Conference, he wrote: 'I suggest that the procedure should not be very rapid. It would be distinctly embarrassing if you had to announce a rejection of the Channel Tunnel project while French Ministers are in London . . . '[32]

Hankey's covering letter strongly suggests that he believed MacDonald's mind to be already made up against the Channel Tunnel project, which may well have been the case. Hankey's own mind, of course, had been made up long ago. It is worth pointing out that, at this stage, he had not even read the report of Peacock's committee. When he did read it, in the first days of March, he did so with a view to highlighting every reservation, and every qualification, that the text of a report such as this inevitably contained. Not surprisingly, given that he could take advantage of Ebbisham's minority view, he was able to produce a set of critical 'Remarks on the Report of the Channel Tunnel Committee', which enabled him to conclude: 'It is submitted that, quite apart from military and political considerations, the case has not been made out which would justify the Government in encouraging this enterprise.'[33] He sent a summary of his criticisms to MacDonald on 5 March, saying that his study of the report had 'rather altered my views as to the method of handling' it. He now thought that the economic advantages, as disclosed by the report, were 'so slender and so uncertain of realisation' that there could be no justification on economic grounds in giving encouragement to the scheme. He recommended, in contradistinction to his advice of 28 February, that, 'if possible, the scheme should be allowed to fall by its lack of attractiveness on the economic side.'[34]

It was not to be as easy or straightforward as that. Peacock's report had after all been commissioned by the Government. Of those who produced it, only Ebbisham dissented from the conclusions at which it had arrived. Given the terms of reference, it would be distinctly embarrassing to commission another report on economic aspects from another set of people. It would be assumed that a secret agenda had been set for any duplicate committee to adhere to. Criticisms from Hankey, who was not an expert in the economic field, of a report on economic aspects, were not enough. Baldwin, moreover, had announced a certain procedure in Parliament on 26 March 1929, and on 3 March 1930 MacDonald had asked Baldwin and Lloyd George to attend a meeting of the CID on the Channel Tunnel.[35] (Asquith had died; Balfour was terminally ill.)

MacDonald decided that he must adhere to the programme outlined by Baldwin in March 1929. Whilst the service Departments considered their positions, the Economic Advisory Council set up a Channel Tunnel Policy Committee. This consisted of Sir Andrew Duncan (Chairman), Mr E. Bevin, Sir John Cadman, John Maynard Keynes, Sir Alfred Lewis and G.C. Upcott (Deputy-Controller of Supply Services, Treasury). This committee met twice, on 17 and 25 March, to consider a Treasury memorandum of 14 March on the economic aspects of the Channel Tunnel. In the Treasury Hankey found, in effect, a most important ally. The Treasury considered that, if construction of the tunnel was commenced, it was certain that there would be a loss of capital at present profitability employed, and probable that there would be no increase in employment. They damned the Peacock Committee's Report as 'a triumph of hope over evidence'. They noted that Peacock's majority was considerably more optimistic as to the feasibility of construction than were the consulting engineers, and predicted that, if the Government favoured or acquiesced in the proposals of the report, strong pressure would be brought upon it to make itself responsible for the exploratory work. They concluded that the conclusion of the majority of the Peacock Committee was 'not supported by any evidence of concrete and substantial advantage. No case had been made out on economic grounds which would justify the Government in encouraging the enterprise'.[36]

The Economic Advisory Council's Channel Tunnel Policy Committee agreed with the Treasury. The phrasing of its short report, of 25 March, owed much to Keynes: 'If private enterprise can provide funds, H.M. Govt. should not withhold consent. Otherwise, we are of the opinion that the evidence in the Report regarding the advantages of the Channel Tunnel to the country as a whole is not sufficient to justify H.M. Govt. either (a) constructing the Tunnel itself or (b) giving financial assistance to enable it to be constructed.'[37] When on 15 April the Cabinet dealt with this second report, the Prime Minister informed his colleagues that he had referred the Peacock Committee report to the CID for examination, and reminded them of their undertaking that they would not allow military to override economic considerations. This rather odd statement produced from the Chancellor of the Exchequer, Philip Snowden, the remark: 'That had regard to a situation in which the balance of economic advantages were convincingly in favour of construction. That was not the case in the Report.' The Cabinet agreed to a suggestion that Hankey had made to the Prime Minister beforehand, that the Peacock Report be sent to Departments concerned in the economic aspects of the tunnel so that they might express their views.[38]

As the view taken by the Treasury, the most important of such Departments, is already clear, I shall confine myself at this stage to citing that produced by the Board of Trade on 13 May. William Graham, the President of the Board of Trade, wrote:

> I can see no prospect of a balance of advantage over such a period as the Government in present circumstances ought to take into account – although in a distant future it might be realised.
>
> I fear that at the outset the facilities afforded by a tunnel would at what might still be a difficult time, add to our economic difficulties – and the more so having regard to Continental tariff policies. Beyond that we need not look for the purpose of framing a decision, and I do not think that a further inquiry would serve any useful object.[39]

Although hampered by the holding of the Naval Conference in London, the British defence establishment had, by this time, decided what line to take. The Home Defence Committee, under Hankey, had taken as their basic assumption, in regard to invasion, that the situation might be as in 1914, when according to Ludendorff's memoirs six brigades of specially mobilised troops were sent to affect a *coup de main* against Liège. That committee suggested that such a situation was one against which the defence organisation of any tunnel should provide. It also recommended the use of steel in the construction, on the grounds that steel tubing would be far less liable to damage by an explosive charge than cast iron, which the consulting engineers preferred because it was less liable to deterioration by rusting. Finally, it had recommended a scale of air defence which the Air Ministry in due course considered too high. The Air Ministry's counter-arguments brought out the extent to which France was being posited as the most likely enemy. As Douglas Portal put it, the sixteen 4.7 inch AA guns and twenty AA searchlights were unnecessary because

(a) In the case of invasion . . . the French air operations, by both bombers and fighters, would probably be carried out at such a low height that AA fire would be ineffective.

(b) In the case of invasion, it would be unnecessary to provide AA defences for the tunnel mouth and exchange station, as the French would gain little or nothing by bombing them.

(c) In the case of invasion the French aircraft could not be used by night in close support of their troops in the tunnel area, and therefore AA searchlights would not be required.

(d) In the case where we should want to use the tunnel ourselves, we agreed that strong AA defences for the tunnel area and exchange station would be required *but* we think that the necessary guns and lights could be found from the Home Defence force since by hypothesis we should be allies, not enemies, of France.[40]

(Portal also picked up an attempt by Hankey to misrepresent the views of Air Vice-Marshal Sir Sefton Brancker, the Director of Civil Aviation at the Air Ministry, who when interviewed by the Peacock Committee in July 1929 had told them that civil aviation had nothing to fear from a Channel Tunnel; as Portal put it: 'it therefore seems that Hankey was under a misapprehension when he stated at Chiefs of Staff on Monday that the conclusion of the Economic Committee in this respect was contrary to the evidence of the civil aviation witnesses'.)[41]

The Air Force, however, kept its head down when it came to the full CID meeting, which was held on 29 May, and said nothing whatsoever. The meeting began with the Prime Minister asking the CIGS, Sir George Milne, for his views as to the desirability of locating the Tunnel mouth at Shepherdswell instead of at Folkestone. Milne replied that the Shepherdswell site had several advantages. Because it was inland, the danger of its being captured by a raiding force landed on the coast was reduced, as was the possibility of bombardment from the sea. A further advantage was the reduction in the cost of the field defences. Shepherdswell being behind Dover, it would be practicable to utilise the existing Dover defences for covering the tunnel, whereas, if the exit of the tunnel were behind Folkestone, new seafront defences would be needed. Milne prefaced and followed these remarks by making it clear that the Chiefs of Staff still agreed with the views expressed by their predecessors in

1924. He could not see any great advantage in the tunnel in the event of Britain being engaged in a war on the Continent. He considered that Henry Wilson's opinion of 1919 that it might save forty-eight hours in the despatch of the Expeditionary Force to France could no longer be justified: 'it required some 70 to 80 trains to move a division complete; this would tax the tunnel possibly beyond its limits, whereas if we had a number of ports from which to send our expeditionary force, as in 1914, there was little likelihood of delay'.

Even more important was the strategical effect of the existence of a tunnel: 'Great Britain had always relied on its sea power to change its bases to meet the varying strategical conditions of war, and he considered that this policy was one we should follow and not bind ourselves to a line of communication such as the Tunnel might provide.' Milne's comment that 'Although France was friendly at the present time we could not always depend upon a friendly Power being in control of the Continental entrance to the Tunnel, and, although it might suit our strategical requirements in one situation, it would not necessarily do so in another', was backed up by Sir Robert Vansittart, the Permanent Under Secretary at the Foreign Office. Vansittart said that he must speak with reserve as he was not in possession of the views of the Foreign Secretary: 'Subject to this the Foreign Office considered that the construction of a Tunnel would tend to incommode us in our relations with Continental Powers. He believed that both Germany and France would consider the construction of a Tunnel as a definite link and bond between Great Britain and France, and this would seriously embarrass us in the diplomatic sphere.' For the Admiralty, the First Lord, Mr A.V. Alexander, said that the tunnel would result in a serious reduction in the cross-channel services, and the silting up of certain ports: 'As it would be impossible to rely entirely upon the Tunnel for the transport of troops, munitions and stores . . . this deterioration of sea facilities in the Channel might have serious consequences.'

The politicians spoke towards the end of the meeting. Baldwin was even more against the scheme than he had been in 1924: 'It appeared to him that Britain was to gain nothing by the construction of the Tunnel, and would have to accept additional responsibilities. We were already carrying a heavy burden of defence on account of our world-wide responsibilities, and he would be most reluctant that any more should be added.' Regarding the diplomatic side of the question, he revealed that he was most impressed by the extract from the *Manchester Guardian*, already referred to, which Hankey had incorporated into the revised version of his memorandum of 28 February: 'The French would, without doubt, consider the Tunnel to be a tie between Great Britain and themselves, and this might result in their trying to pull us into their orbit, both political and military.' Lloyd George, for his part, considered Hankey's latest memorandum to be 'unanswerable': 'We had nothing to gain by its construction, and it presented considerable dangers.' He reminded the meeting that

> In 1914 there was a good deal of doubt as to whether we should enter the War, and a decision was not taken until war had actually begun. All kinds of difficult and conflicting considerations arise at such a time. In these circumstances, a Government would always be reluctant to take so decisive an action as to flood the Tunnel during the period before war broke out.

In his view, however, the most important consideration of all was 'the psychological effect upon the people of the country':

> It might be possible to persuade seven or eight experts that no danger of invasion existed, but it was a different thing to persuade 45,000,000 people that invasion was impossible. The Existence of the Tunnel might well cause a panic in the country and influence a movement towards the maintenance of military forces on a scale existing on the Continent. It might appear to the people of this country to be anything but satisfactory for us to have an army of 100,000 men if we were connected by means of a Tunnel with a continental Power possessing a huge army of two or three million men, particularly if, in the event of trouble in India or elsewhere we had to reduce our home forces to some thirty or forty thousand . . .

MacDonald made a fair summary of the proceedings:

> From the Economic Advisory Council's report [chairman Sir A. Duncan] it was clear that the Tunnel would give to Great Britain no economic or financial advantages; from a diplomatic point of view it must embarrass us as it would tend to tie us to the policy that France desired; from the military standpoint it added to our responsibilities without in any way adding to our strength; the present Report of the Chiefs of Staff showed that the military objections to the scheme were even greater than those visualised in the 1924 Report.[42]

Well before the CID's negative conclusion was formally arrived at, MacDonald had been considering how best to overcome the opposition likely to manifest itself in Parliament. In April, Hankey had been anxious to delay the announcement of a negative decision, because the French were 'keen on the Tunnel for reasons shown in my own Memorandum, and it would not have a good effect to announce its rejection during the [Naval] Conference'; the most tactful procedure would be to argue a case against the tunnel on a mixture of economic and military considerations.[43] At some point in May, MacDonald instructed Hankey to prepare a statement which he, as Prime Minister, would in the first instance put before the Cabinet. Hankey tried to convert his latest memorandum into the statement required, but his idea of 'a balance of considerations' did not square with what MacDonald had in mind. As Hankey wrote to Sir John Salmond, the Chief of the Air Staff, on 30 May, enclosing a copy of the statement which MacDonald was going to submit to the Cabinet:

> For your personal information I should like to say that the Prime Minister has cut about a half of that portion of the draft which I originally put up dealing with the military aspect. Personally I regret this, as I wanted to make a rather convincing case on military grounds on this occasion. I suspect however that the P.M. is doing this for political reasons, of which he is a better judge than any of us.[44]

Despite MacDonald's excisions, the Cabinet on 4 June found the draft statement, which the Prime Minister told them he intended to show to Baldwin and Lloyd George and then read in the House of Commons before the Whitsuntide recess, to be too long. The Cabinet agreed instead that it should be published as a White Paper. They also agreed that 'if any strong opposition to the rejection by the Government of the Channel Tunnel proposal should manifest itself in Parliament, the Prime Minister should have authority to offer the appointment of a committee drawn from all Parties in the House of Commons, which would be given access to the voluminous material at the disposal of the Government'. Margaret Bondfield, the Minister of Labour and the only woman in the Cabinet, who in mid 1924 had been quoted in the press as saying 'I believe in a Channel Tunnel because it will facilitate international transport and international trade and will destroy another fetish of the military mind', asked the Prime Minister on this occasion, 'in publishing the Statement as a White Paper, to include a mention of the fact that the men employed in excavating the tunnel could not be drawn from the unemployed owing to the specialist character of the work'.[45]

The Government's (or rather MacDonald's reduction of Hankey's) statement of policy was issued as a White Paper immediately. On the economic side, it latched onto the fact that one of the members of the Peacock Committee had dissented from the majority report, and was opposed to the scheme on economic grounds. It maintained that the weight of the majority conclusion was diminished by 'important qualifications and hesitations', that there were doubts and uncertainties, and that support from trade and industry was really rather lukewarm. It stressed the view of the consulting engineers (Livesey, Son, and Henderson; Mott, Hay and Anderson; Rendel, Palmer and Tritton) that the feasibility of construction was not yet proven, and that only a pilot tunnel, estimated to cost £5,600,000 and to take five years to complete, would remove doubts on that score; and further pointed out that the infrastructure required would considerably exceed the £30,600,000 estimated for the pilot and main tunnels. No overwhelming case, it was maintained, had been made out on economic grounds. On the military side, MacDonald retained Hankey's summary of the views of the Government's military advisers, namely Balfour's statement, 'So long as the ocean remains our friend, do not let us deliberately destroy its power to help us'.[46]

Sir William Bull, of the Parliamentary Channel Tunnel Committee, valiantly but vainly wrote a memorandum in reply to the White Paper, and sent it to Baldwin.[47] MacDonald's Government allowed the House of Commons a free vote on a motion to proceed with the Channel Tunnel scheme on 30 June. The Government announced beforehand, however, that whatever the result of the vote it would not change its mind. This example of parliamentary democracy in action, together with the forceful repetition of the arguments against the tunnel by MacDonald, by Sir Samuel Hoare, who reminded the House of Kitchener's pre-war opposition ('it will bias our policy in time of peace, and it will dominate our policy in time of war if a tunnel is built') and by Herbert Morrison, the Minister of Transport, caused parliamentary support for the scheme to slump to 172; 179 voted against.[48]

Hankey credited himself with killing the scheme 'with the knife of common sense', having dwelt on its 'lack of economic attractiveness' rather than on purely military considerations. Hankey's knives were always out for the Channel Tunnel; whether they were the knives of common sense even he was inclined to doubt, as the next chapter will demonstrate. As we now know, however, it was MacDonald rather than Hankey who was responsible for the final balance of the White Paper. As for common sense, that remained what fanatics, of whatever persuasion, find only amongst their own kind. Hankey also claimed that MacDonald's experience of the French during the recent Naval Conference had caused him to have no wish to be 'tied to the leg' of that nation.[49] If MacDonald's mind was already made up before the conference met, however, as suggested above, then his experiences there could have at best confirmed him in the correctness of his views. The outcome on this occasion was rather a result of that happy little band of Little Englanders, the insiders of Whitehall and of the old services, who were afraid of new commitments and new demands, who were, not to put too fine a point on it, afraid of change *per se*, completely outmanoeuvring the relative outsiders represented by and interviewed by the Peacock Committee, who in turn found their evidence misrepresented and turned round against them. It was a classic conspiracy, finely executed, and the role of the committee on which Keynes sat was crucial, in that it got the MacDonald Government off the hook which the Baldwin Government appointed Peacock Committee had placed it on.

3. Epilogue: An Imaginary German Tunnel, 1940–42

From this point, with the death of Sir William Bull in 1931, the going into liquidation of the Channel Tunnel Company, and the worsening of the recession, the question of the Channel Tunnel was absent from the political agenda for the rest of the decade. News arrived from the Continent from time to time suggesting that cheaper schemes, or alternative cross-Channel communications, were still being considered there. The Foreign Office politely turned them away.[50] In January Mr W. Collard, of London and Paris Railway Promoters Ltd, wrote to the Foreign Secretary, Sir Anthony Eden, suggesting that in view of the present political tension and the French fear of a closer understanding between Italy and Germany, the construction of a Channel Tunnel and of electric railways between London and Paris would be a spectacular assurance of solidarity and support on the part of Great Britain and, allied with a low tariff treaty, would regain France's warm co-operation with the League of Nations. One of Eden's minions minuted:

> From an economic point of view there is probably even less to commend the Channel Tunnel scheme than there has been in the past. Passenger traffic is more or less adequately catered for by the air services and by the train ferries which the Southern Railway are shortly to put into operation while, as regards goods traffic, in these days of economic nationalism the aim is to discourage rather than to facilitate international trade. There is little likelihood of the French being induced to contemplate a low tariff treaty.[51]

Later in the same year sir Robert Vansittart's brother Guy, who worked in Antwerp, forwarded a question from the Belgian Government. Count Renaud de Briey, who had been charged unofficially with the re-examination of the question, but in this case of a tunnel to Belgium instead of France, wanted to know if the objections of 1930 still held good. Vansittart made some informal enquiries, and replied that it was unlikely that the scheme would be favourably received.[52]

Still later in 1936, on 30 November, Lord Kilmaine asked a series of parliamentary questions about the Channel Tunnel. He particularly stressed that the development of air power made it increasingly important that there should be communication between England and the Continent that was immune from air attack. The same negative answer was given.[53]

There was still time for Neville Chamberlain to add his name to the list of the twentieth-century British Prime Ministers who had turned down the scheme. This occurred in November 1938, when Chamberlain asserted that nothing had occurred since June 1930 such as to cause the Government to reconsider its views.[54] The coming to power in Germany of the Nazi Party, the conversion of Germany into a totalitarian state, her withdrawal from the League of Nations, her reoccupation of the Rhineland, her annexation of the Sudetenland – even cumulatively, all this was as nothing. Or, possibly, it was 'balanced' in Neville Chamberlain's mind by the Munich Agreement made two months before. The imminence of war and, finally, war itself, made no difference to Chamberlain in this respect.[55]

Within the time-frame of this book, however, two bizarre incidents deserve to be mentioned. The first of these occurred in the summer of 1940, when the managing director of KLM, the Dutch airline, approached the Foreign Office with a proposal for a peace treaty between the Third Reich and the British Empire. This approach maintained that so great a trust would be developed between Germany and Great Britain as to enable the completion of a Channel Tunnel. The Foreign Office officials who saw this document made no comment.

The second incident was of rather longer duration. It turned the clock back 140 years, to the period when those of an imaginative disposition could envisage the French tunnelling under the Channel in preparation for an invasion of the United Kingdom. At the beginning of 1941 it was rumoured that the Germans might be engaged in that very activity. The Chief Engineer of Home Forces, Major-General King, was sceptical, but referred the matter to the President of the Institute of Civil Engineers, Sir Leopold Savile, who was of the same mind. So were those involved on the Geophysics Sub-Committee of the Advisory Council on Scientific Research and Technical Development. At this stage Hankey, who was now Paymaster General and Chairman of the Cabinet's Scientific Advisory Committee and Engineering Advisory Committee, entered the fray. Maintaining that he was impressed with the possibility that the Germans might be employing a method for converting rubble into slurry which had been recommended by the French engineer

Fougerolles, thus reducing the amount of time required for the operation, Hankey suggested in May 1941 that the question be examined by the Joint Intelligence Committee.[56] The JIC summarily dismissed Hankey's scaremongering, leaving him to express the hope that someone would keep an eye on the area around Sangatte for 'unusual dumps of debris'.[57]

Hankey was not yet finished. His obsessional hostility to a Channel Tunnel had been revived. Perhaps thinking that it was dormant rather than dead, he saw a chance to injure any future prospects that a reappearance of the scheme might have by exaggerating the feasibility and practicability of it from the German point of view at this stage of the war. Hankey's opportunity was provided by a memorandum by R.B. Bourdillon of the SAC, entitled 'Notes on the Importance and Difficulty of Detecting German-Built Channel Tunnels before Completion', dated 22 October 1941, in which it was maintained that, by using the latest technology in the form of tungsten-carbide cutters and Fougerolles' technique of soil removal, the Germans could complete a tunnel in only sixteen months. Bourdillon sent his memorandum to Sir Henry Dale, another member of the SAC. Dale was distinctly unimpressed, as is clear from the covering letter in which Dale passed the memorandum on to Hankey, describing the author of it as 'a colleague of mine, for whose ability I have, in fact, more respect than for his judgement in many matters'. Hankey took his chance with typical economy for the truth: in pushing for a joint investigation by the EAC and SAC, he rendered Dale's view of Bourdillon into 'a colleague, for whose ability he [Dale] has respect'.

The question was referred to the Vice-Chiefs of Staff; Bourdillon produced another memorandum, in which he expressed concern about the likelihood of multiple exits from a German tunnel; and a joint panel of members of the EAC and SAC was set up, in November 1941, as Hankey had wished. Hankey himself chaired the first meeting of this panel, in January 1942; R.A. Butler, the President of the Board of Education, chaired the rest, the last of which was in November 1942. The panel of eminent scientists and engineers was remarkably receptive to some of Bourdillon's ideas. It acknowledged that recent extensions to the London Underground had demonstrated that 'In most tunnelling work the rate of advance is governed by the time needed to dispose of soil'; it also considered it possible that the Germans had the machinery to implement the ideas of Fougerolles for soil disposal. It took note of a finding of the Deputy Director of Torpedoes and Mines that it had been established that any tunnelling activity could be heard with certainty above 200 yards, and under favourable conditions at up to 1,000 feet. The report of the panel recommended routine listening along a ten-mile stretch of the South Coast.[58] As a result, a handful of Royal Engineers spent a part of the Second World War burying microphones in sand and chalk. The stretch of coast selected ran for five miles to the east and five miles to the west of Dover's Shakespeare Cliff, where borings had been made many decades earlier. Nothing was heard.

Chapter 9

'Intangible and Psychological' Factors

Paragraph 150 of the report of the Peacock Committee of February 1930 noted that two of the witnesses interviewed by them had been opposed to the Channel Tunnel scheme on other than economic and military grounds. The non-economic and non-military grounds were that a Channel Tunnel would create a land frontier and that this would produce 'undesirable reactions of a social and moral kind'.

One of these witnesses was the Right Hon. the Earl of Crawford and Balcarres KT. Crawford's interview took place on 14 October 1929. He said that he had certain statements and allegations to make. His hypothesis was that the Channel crossing, 'the worst short sea journey in the world', was a great deterrent to personal transit between England and the Continent, and that a Channel Tunnel would greatly increase the number of foreigners visiting this country. His determination was to keep the situation as it was, because dislike of the Channel was 'our chief protection from . . . the obscenity of . . . Continental towns':

> I am a xenophobe, particularly as regards the French. I look upon France as a corrupt and corrupting influence, and that the less the personal intercourse between Britain and France the better for Britain.

He did not, however, limit this xenophobia to France alone:

> Crime in England is largely the crime of British subjects of foreign extraction. Their numbers are relatively small, their percentage of crime is actually high, the percentage of crime is far higher in proportion to their numbers. That is to say the most criminal element of our population is the least British element.

He listed several items of crime which were, according to him, on the increase: the White Slave Traffic ('It is quite exceptional for any English person to be convicted in any White Slave case'); the drug traffic ('I think that in 80 per cent of the cases in this country those who are caught are of foreign extraction'); undesirable publications, obscene publications, pornography ('It is notorious that that is not so easily carried on here as a trade as it is abroad'); betting ('You know, of course, that betting has got into the hands of British subjects of non-British extraction').

He recalled how, nearly forty years ago, when he had been interested in founding Workman's Clubs in the East of London,'we had to exclude Jews because of their corrupting influence in gambling'. 'The Jew', he said, 'was an inveterate gambler', and he handed the committee a police court report of March 1929 of forty-five men charged with gambling in a gambling house in Edgware Road. 'That is remote, of course, from the Jewish centre', he said, and then proceeded to construe almost every name as Jewish. Only the names John Bridges, Henry Osborn, Frederick Pearse and Reginald Crabb conveyed nothing to him.

He proceeded to illustrate the 'corrupt and corrupting' manifestations of these kinds of crime in France itself:

> This Spring there were certainly three and perhaps four plays in Paris dealing with incest alone – all running at once. The theatre and the music hall – which is of course nothing more nor less than an exhibition of nudism – are, I think, notorious.

He contended that on the Continent the authorities were quite unable to check obscene publications: 'I was greatly struck in Germany last year by the dangerous and sinister direction of the indecent aspect of German thought towards homo-sexuality – the commerce of man with man, or of woman with woman . . . ' He had noticed 'a queer thing in England, at any rate, that the risqué publications that are taking place are taking place with people, again, who have names like those of the gamblers – non-British names'. 'I have made out a list', he said, 'It is a very curious and queer list.' It included reproductions of the work of a man called Lawrence. He insisted on giving a French example of obscene pictures and books to the committee:

> These were published last week and I have torn them out. They publish their advertisements of their publications without any pretension of concealment, and I notice how typically French it is. Here is one. They tell you to ask for 'Miss So and So' in the shop – 'Demandez Mlle Sousa, – Mlle Grot, – Mlle Jeanne, – Mlle Louisa, – Mlle Josette; 'le plus charmant accueil' – the most kindly reception is promised. These are photographs – 'prises sur le vif' – taken from life – 'realiste'. '40 poses vivantes'. '33 poses troublantes' – exciting, moving.

There are any number more. They are advertised with the addresses. I will give you the prices . . .

A few minutes earlier he had stated, 'I am not a prude myself'. All these things, as well as the advertising of abortion facilities, were going on 'in all these Continental capitals': 'These degenerates are allowed, in effect, complete toleration, and, as I say, it is the blackguard type of crime ('It is the vileness of the foreign and Continental vice that is so horrible. It is not honest in its viciousness, it is vile') that is so offensive about the whole thing.'

He wondered what powers of resistance England had:

We have fortunately at present the Channel crossing which has kept these people from coming to London to ply their trade. We have a police which I believe to be incorruptible. The fact that two or three were caught taking bribes from these very people – foreigners, mind you – is, in my opinion, the proof of their incorruptibility as a whole. It cannot go on. You can be corruptible for six weeks or a month, but you are only really corruptible when it goes on continuously, as it does in France . . . But the attack is very insidious . . . backed by the immense profits . . . and I think that if once this country . . . got into the way of this style of thought and practice, the results here would be far more serious than they are in the older and less susceptible Latin civilisations, where they have a tradition of extreme vice which to some extent inoculates them against the disaster and catastrophe that this sort of thing would produce on our people here.

Sir Clement Hindley asked Crawford if he had not, perhaps, underestimated 'our powers of resistance'. Crawford answered: 'Well. I wonder. The readiness with which we accept the modern practices is very striking. If you compare the ordinary illustrated newspaper and the pictures of the prize bathing girls with, shall I say, 1913, before the war, there is an apparent revolution in the public outlook regarding these things.' Hindley, who was as well travelled as Crawford, having gone backwards and forwards to India for years, persisted. So did Crawford: 'the attack is being intensified. The scale and extent of it has enormously increased in France, in Berlin and Brussels, and to some extent in Milan and Madrid, and our powers of resistance are not so great as they were, especially as our blood becomes more and more mixed as time goes on. There it is'.

Crawford felt so strongly that he would have prohibited the Channel Tunnel because of this consideration alone. He had drafted a statement which he wanted the committee to integrate into their report. It ran: 'A Channel Tunnel will create a land frontier. This will probably/inevitably have social/moral results. We were not invited to discuss this aspect of the

problem, but the subject requires/deserves/demands careful consideration by His Majesty's Government.'

At the end of the interview Peacock, who said that Crawford's illust-
ration regarding bathing 'is a very striking one', said, 'You have set us an
interesting problem, Lord Crawford. We shall certainly consider it.
What we can do about it we shall have to see. We are very much obliged
to you, and I hope you will feel that the time has not been wasted'.
Crawford said, 'It is very kind of you to say so'.[1]

David Alexander Edward Lindsay, 27th Earl of Crawford and 10th
Earl of Balcarres, had been conservative MP for North Lancashire
(Chorley) from 1895 to 1913, had been Conservative Chief Whip before
the First World War, had been President of the Board of Agriculture
and Fisheries from July to December 1916, Lord Privy Seal December
1916 to January 1919, Chancellor of the Duchy of Lancaster January
1919 to April 1921, and First Commissioner of Works April 1921 to
October 1922. In 1923 he became Chancellor of the University of
Manchester; in the same decade he became a Trustee of the National
Portrait Gallery and of the British Museum, and helped found the
Council for the Preservation of Rural England. He had described
himself to the Peacock Committee as a 'criminologist'. His only publications were *Donatello* (1903) and *The Evolution of Italian Sculpture* (1910).

On 23 May 1930, less than a week before the CID was due to meet,
Hankey wrote to J.M. Clynes, the Home Secretary, saying that the Prime
Minister had asked him to draw Clynes' attention to paragraph 150. He
went on to say that he had happened to meet Crawford shortly after the
publication of the Peacock Report, and that Crawford had told him
about his evidence and expressed the hope that the Government would
not overlook it. Hankey wrote: 'The PM thinks it would be a good thing
if you would see Crawford and hear what he has to say. You could then
mention it to the Cabinet if you thought fit, with such observations as you
might deem advisable.'[2] Clynes duly saw Crawford, and wrote in his turn
to MacDonald on 2 June. Clynes agreed with Crawford's first proposition, that the general moral standards of most of the European countries
and especially France were lower than those obtaining in England; he
also said that it was 'certainly true that while our records here do not
show that any undue proportion of crime generally is attributable to our
alien population, the traffic in women, drugs and obscene publications
. . . is foreign in origin'.[3]

It is not at all unlikely that it was Hankey who drew MacDonald's
attention to paragraph 150, and got Clynes involved, rather than the

A RELIC OF THE INSULAR AGE.

BOY OF THE FUTURE. "WHAT'S THAT FUNNY PICTURE MEAN?"
MR. PUNCH. "WELL, YOU'LL HARDLY BELIEVE IT, MY BOY, BUT THAT'S HOW WE USED TO GO TO FRANCE IN THE QUAINT OLD DAYS BEFORE THE TUNNEL."

'A Relic of the Insular Age',
Punch, 23 January 1929

other way round. For it was Hankey who was the other witness referred to in that paragraph. Hankey had been interviewed on 11 November 1929. The interview had begun conventionally enough in his case, with his trying to frighten the committee with the danger of the tunnel's being in private hands – 'it is much easier for the Government to destroy its own property than a Company's property'. He then told a story of how during the 1920 enquiry he had approached some of the Channel Tunnel group of that day, asked for definite details of how the tunnel would be flooded, and of how one of them had said, 'Yes, I will put the English engineers in touch with the French'. As he put it, 'If you have an arrangement of that kind you want it to be a secret arrangement, and the first thing they did was to consult the French engineers!' Both for him and for Sir Henry Wilson, he said, that very much bore out one of Wolseley's main points, 'that you never could keep the secrecy of the thing'.

Hankey then embarked on a statement on 'another aspect of the subject which has been in my mind for some time'. This aspect was neither defence nor economics – it was 'one of those subjects slightly intangible which falls between the two and is apt to be lost sight of'. It was 'the sort of instinctive repugnance' that he had found, amongst a very large number of people, to the Tunnel:

> When I say that I say it of ex-Prime Ministers, I say it of many Cabinet Ministers, a great many soldiers and sailors, people like Lord Fisher, Lord Haig, and Lord Kitchener, and business men, and all sorts of people, who have a sort of prejudice, a sort of instinctive feeling against the Tunnel.

He then told the story of an Admiral (Beauvoir Brock in 1920) to whom were given the staff papers and minutes on the Tunnel: 'He read the papers, and his minute was this – "I cannot see any specifically naval reasons which enable me to put up a case against the Tunnel, but I remain invincibly opposed to its construction" '.[4]

Hankey professed to have been wondering for a long time what was the cause of this response. He professed to have found the the answer in a recent conversation with a very distinguished Japanese. The Japanese had said, in effect, 'We Japanese, we live on an island and we think we have built up a civilisation of our own in Japan which is quite different from and superior to the rest of Asia, and we should view with horror any physical connection with the mainland'. Hankey must have known that this hardly squared with Japanese imperialist ambitions in Manchuria, Korea and, most recently, China. That was not his point:

If you want to be brutal about it you can call it sheer insularity, but I think there is a feeling amongst a great many people that the British civilisation is quite different from Continental civilisation, that we are much more different from our Continental neighbours than the Continental neighbours are from one another . . .

There were many differences:

There is our mental attitude, our moral attitude, our literature, our press and our sports, and our own way of life; in fact I think a good many people feel that living on an island we have been able to take from the Continent what we think best in the Continent without getting too much of it, to develop on our own lines and what we think are better lines all round.

He did not think that getting to know the Continent better would produce better relations:

If you take the great International hatreds – France and Germany, countries adjacent to one another, with admirable communications between them; Italy and France; Italy and Austria; Germany and Poland; even to my astonishment as I found out at the Hague Conference, Belgium and Holland who seem not to understand one another. Where you get peoples very close to one another, where you get them mixed up as in the Balkans, or in India or Palestine or Poland, or Silesia, you get absolute hatred and loathing. On the other hand, the great International friendships are the very reverse – England and Japan, Austria and Spain, France and the U.S., France and Russia. Distance seems to lend enchantment to the view.

He had another point which he thought 'rather in the same order of ideas'. It was to do with getting the English to realise the importance of sea power – not in a military sense but 'in the sense of the importance of maritime communications and depending on the sea and what we are to the sea and to the Empire imports, exports, and so on'. To his mind the Channel crossing was a most important element in the education of the English on this subject:

The majestic Dover Cliffs and the Harbour; the men of war; the crossing of the trade route, the more impressive because it is so narrow, so concentrated – one is always struck by that; and then the feeling you have, except in the finest weather, of the vastness of the ocean.

Hundreds of thousands of people, he claimed, underwent this experience every year. It made a massive impression on them – 'young people, all these children, boys and girls you see going over to complete their education and all these people from the Midlands and the North going out in great masses under Cooks and Lunns tours'. With the Tunnel, that impression would be lost:

> Now, you are going to send them down a drain, and they are never going to see the sea at all! Many of them never will see the sea in that aspect or in any aspect except the nigger minstrels or whatever the modern equivalent thereof is at the seaside.

At the end of the interview Peacock said that the committee were indebted to Hankey and Crawford 'for a certain addition of light on aspects of the question that perhaps do not come so strongly before us'. Hankey's final comment was: 'It is a little intangible and psychological.'[5]

Hankey's statement was much more eloquent, even poetic, than Crawford's. It had been carefully prepared beforehand with sub-titles in the margins beside each paragraph: 'Neither Defence nor Economics', 'Instinctive Repugnance', 'Distinctiveness of British Civilisation' etc. The 'Story of the Admiral Invincibly Opposed' had been carefully rehearsed.[6] Fundamentally, however, their attitude was the same. Crawford's diary for 9 November 1933 records: 'I had an amusing talk with Maurice Hankey, whose views on politics (especially the Alien question in all its bearings) coincide with my own – and we therefore like to compare notes.'[7] Moreover, Hankey had tried the sort of thing he tried in relation to paragraph 150 on a previous occasion. Exactly ten years earlier, on 27 January 1920, the day before redating his memorandum of November 1919, he had written to the then Home Secretary, Edward Shortt:

> I do not know whether you have ever considered the possible effect of the Channel Tunnel on immigration . . . If a Tunnel is constructed, presumably it would lead to an enormous increase in the number of persons entering from the Continent. How would it affect immigration and alien restrictions? . . . Would it not be very difficult to ensure that persons travelling from the Continent do not settle permanently? If this happened would it not be very undesirable and lead to the entry of a considerable criminal population? I have often observed in the newspapers how the magistrates in some parts of London complain of the huge proportion of aliens appearing in their courts.[8]

Shortt's officials thought that the point Hankey had thought it worth-while to bring to the Home Secretary's attention did not constitute any serious argument against the Tunnel, and Shortt agreed with his officials, In his reply, he gave Hankey no shrift at all.[9]

In 1919 Hankey had stated that he would stop at nothing to prevent the building of a Channel Tunnel.[10] In 1929 he had professed to being profoundly disquieted 'at the reaction of the Tunnel on Imperial Defence'.[11] So far as Hankey is concerned, the question is whether his playing of the aliens card in 1920 and in 1929-30 was an example of how far he would go in an instrumental way to prevent what he saw as a danger to the country, or whether it revealed the real danger, the thing of which he was most afraid. As already indicated, this writer has come to the conclusion that the second of the alternatives just stated is really the case. More than that: I am inclined to adapt the explanation given by Hankey himself, Lloyd George's 'insular Englishman', for the opposition to the tunnel of so many other eminent people. For Hankey's efforts to define what he called 'a kind of common denominator to all objectors in this instinctive repugnance'[12], continued. On the eve of the release of the Peacock Committee Report, possibly Hankey's severest test, in February 1930, Hankey penned another memorandum. His definition of 'psychological' factors was of a different order from that ostensibly held by Lloyd George, which involved panic and popular pressure on governments for expenditure and even for conscription. In this untitled memorandum, which to the best of my knowledge was not circulated, Hankey peels away even from his hero Wolseley the layers of self-censorship with which so many of the public figures in this book covered their true feelings, and reveals the arguments they put forward in their official capacities for the superstructure, the façade, the screens, that they really were. Apart from Hankey, only Crawford, Repington in certain of his articles,[13] and Ewart in his diaries of 1906-7,[14] had exposed themselves in quite this honest way. It makes a fitting end.

> The question of the Channel Tunnel is one that is apt to arouse rather strong feelings, with the result that both its advocates and its opponents tend to exaggerate their case. This applies both to the military and civil aspects of the question. The passionate vehemence of Lord Wolseley's opposition must have been due to something more than mere apprehension of military risk; while the reply of those who say that 'We were able to defend some hundreds of miles in France against the German army; cannot we defend a hole in the ground a few feet in diameter?' shows considerable lack of perspective. It appears desirable at the outset to consider what is the fundamental reason for this violent difference of opinion. To some extent the reason would seem to be psychological.
>
> Those who support the Tunnel cannot understand why Great Britain should be deprived of a means of communication with their nearest neighbour which exists between nearly all the countries of the Continent, provided the physical difficulties can be overcome. If France and Switzerland are willing to drive

tunnels through the Alps and to that extent to weaken the military value of the Alpine barrier, what logical argument is there for refusing to make a tunnel under the Channel? Why, they ask, should we continue to expose ourselves quite unnecessarily to the discomforts and limitations of a sea voyage that is often very rough and which involves transhipment at either end, when the whole journey might be carried out through a tunnel without changing one's seat?

The opponents of the theory, on the other hand, are animated by an objection that is probably instinctive, but which has not been defined in the public controversy on the subject, against the abandonment or partial abandonment of our insular position. Put into words this instinctive objection might perhaps be stated in some such terms as the following: Great Britain has always been an island. To its insularity it probably owes its peculiar institutions. It has always been able to adopt so much of Continental civilisation as it thought wise and desirable. In fact, however, it has adapted rather then adopted. The result is something quite unique. British civilisation, as American and Canadian travellers often point out, is much more different from Continental civilisation than is one Continental country from another. Thus British characteristics have developed themselves in partial isolation from the rest of the world and have, indeed, made a contribution which is perhaps greater than that of any other country to the civilisation of the world.

Probably the strongest opponent of the Channel Tunnel would not claim that peculiar features of British life would disappear if the Tunnel were constructed. The barrier of the Channel would still exist even though communication by land were established. He would say, however, that Great Britain would lose something of that insularity which he prizes so highly, partly owing to the increased mixing with natives of Continental countries and partly because the travelling public (which is so large in these islands) would lose that personal contact with the sea which, though brief, makes such an indelible impression upon most people's minds.

This historical sense of insularity, this pride in the distinctive features of British civilisation, this belief in the influence of the sea upon British character, is a factor which ought not to be overlooked in any examination of the problem of the Channel Tunnel.[15]

Appendix 1

Letter by Lieutenant-General Sir Garnet Wolseley, 5 February 1882 (PRO, AIR 8/75)

As long as England remains unconnected by a tunnel with France, we could always recover from the effects of a successful invasion.

Granted that an Army of 150,000 or 200,000 ever land in England and march on London: they could claim any price in money they wished – we might be forced to pay off the national debt and to surrender our Fleet, but still, if we be a people worthy of freedom and worthy of independence, we could recover ourselves as the Prussians did after Jena.

The French could not forever occupy England: when we had paid for our folly, we should have a fresh start, and the French once returned to their own shores we could – if any national spirit such as that which burned in the breasts of our forefathers remained to us – build a new fleet and we could raise and organise an army large and powerful enough to obtain our revenge, and to take back from France all she had forced from us. Of course, we could only do so by submitting to enormous sacrifices: but for the sake of argument let us suppose that we had enough manliness and patriotism left in us to enable us to do all this, and we are bound to admit that we might recover all that we had lost.

But, if the tunnel is ever made, and such a national misfortune should ever befall us, we fall like Lucifer – never to rise again: the tunnel would enable France to hold Dover in perpetuity as a material guarantee against our ever again daring to raise our heads or attempt to raise another army or create a new fleet: the tunnel would rivit [sic] our chains upon us, and convert us into the position of being the helots of France for ever.

And where is the soldier whose opinion is worth having who will presume to say that the successful invasion of England is an impossibility? If such exist, he must be wiser than the great Napoleon.

Appendix 2

Memorandum on the Proposed Channel Tunnel by Lieutenant-General Sir John Adye, Surveyor-General of the Ordnance, May 1882

The instructions of the technical Committee of which Sir Archibald Alison was the Chairman, purposely limited the Committee to a consideration of the means by which (supposing the Channel Tunnel completed) its use could be interdicted to an enemy in time of war.

A perusal of their report brings to notice that the military precautions necessary to provide against such a contingency almost naturally divide themselves into two parts:

1 The defence or command of the exit by means of batteries and fortifications.
2 The closing or destruction of the tunnel itself, either temporarily or permanently, both as regards its land and submarine portions.

The Committee have dealt with both points in some detail. As regards the former they urge, that whilst the land portion of the tunnel should be constructed in the vicinity of a fortress, it is also important that its exits should lie outside but under the full command of the batteries in the outworks of the fortress itself. With respect to the partial closing or entire destruction of the tunnel, both in its land and submarine portions, the Committee have entered into various details, and have made numerous proposals by which, if necessary, these objects may be accomplished.

According to my judgment their recommendations, both as to defence and closure, are sound and practical, can be carried out without great cost or difficulty, and will amply suffice for the objects in view. I agree with them that the general line of the land portion of the tunnel had better be constructed not far from the lines of a fortress, whilst the exit should also be under the command of the guns of its outworks. Such a disposition of the tunnel will facilitate the arrangements in respect to the preparation of mines, &c., whilst a full command of the mouth will render its use or occupation by an enemy practically impossible.

The various details and proposals of the Committee as to obstruction and closure, partial or permanent, are such as, I think, will commend themselves to Engineers, civil or military, as being efficacious for the purpose; and I would further point out that whilst they are comparatively simple, it is evident they can be multiplied indefinitely, and have the further advantage, that the possession of the tunnel and its exit by an enemy would not prevent their being carried into effect; and even should some of them fail, such a contingency would not necessarily entail the failure of others. The means of obstruction, in short, are not only various but are independent of each other, and many of them could be improvised or multiplied even at the last moment. Nothing, indeed, is more obvious than the facility with which the tunnel can be denied to an enemy, by means which no vigilance on his part could prevent or remove.

Appendix 3

Memorandum by Field-Marshal Sir John French, 9 July 1914 (CAB 38/28/34)

In discussing the relative advantages and disadvantages of a Channel Tunnel, I wish to put forward a view of the strategic aspect of the question which is based largely upon recent developments in aircraft and submarines.

It is often, if not generally, held that the risk of invasion is largely reduced by these innovations. In this paper I propose to give some reasons for differing from that opinion.

I believe the danger to be greatly increased, and although my ideas may, at the present moment, be considered unwarranted, and even Utopian, I venture to hope the views expressed may meet with a certain amount of serious consideration.

2   The relative fighting value of the submarine and the battleship has been lately under discussion in the press and elsewhere.

Whichever view of that controversy may be taken, I think it will be allowed that, in a war between ourselves and a great continental Power which is in possession of the Eastern Channel coast-line between Dunkirk and Boulogne, submarines, assisted by aircraft, would effectually deny the passage of the Straits of Dover to any war vessel which was not submersible. In fact, the command of the sea, in so far as this part of the Channel is concerned, would not depend upon the relative strength of the opposing navies, but would remain in dispute until one side or the other effected practical destruction of its adversary's aircraft and submarines.

The way would then lie open to the Power which had gained this advantage to move an invading force of any size in comparative safety across the Straits and threaten a landing at any part of the coast between (say) Ramsgate and Dungeness on the one side, and Dunkirk and Boulogne on the other.

The command of these Straits would be a contest between submarines and aeroplanes.

If we gained such command, the advantage would only lie in the possibility of denying the use of the Channel to our enemies, as we have no army of a sufficient size to embark on continental invasions single-handed.

If, however, the continental Powers secured the command, they would possess the further great advantage of menacing us with a twentieth-century edition of the stroke Napoleon intended to deal against us from Boulogne in 1805.

3   In considering the possible circumstances in which one side or the other may gain the ascendancy, it is to be remarked, in the first place, that the element of chance would enter far more into the problem than it does in most operations of war, and further, that if the contest is to be in the nature of a gamble, we should be staking far more than the enemy.

It is said that the submarine is impervious to attack, but when dealing with so vital a question as this is, it is surely unsafe to accept this as true in the absence of any real war experience. New developments and fresh ideas will assuredly evolve some method of counter-action.

4   If, then, the command of the Straits of Dover can be attested and secured by success in a trial of strength between forces composed of submarines plus aircraft, and it is conceded that the very nature of the opposing forces introduces a much greater element of chance than any other kinds of contest, it may be safely assumed that a much greater relative superiority of force is necessary to ensure reasonable safety than would be the case in any other form of warfare.

5   Approaching the question of what might be opposed to us in such a condition of affairs, I propose to imagine a very possible situation.

The case of a war between the Triple Alliance and the Triple *Entente* has gone against us. France has been compelled by overwhelming circumstances to submit to terms which places the coast line under discussion entirely in German hands, another condition being the cession to the latter Power of all the French naval and air forces.

In such circumstances as these, it is conceivable that three parts of the available submarine and air craft power in possession of all the great

European Powers might be concentrated on the Eastern Channel coast line opposite the Straits of Dover, whilst the factories and arsenals of such Powers (including France) would be available to reinforce and make good losses.

As regards ability to concentrate such a force of submarines in these particular ports, it must be remembered that our command of the sea elsewhere than in these waters will not hinder such a concentration. Submarines can be moved by canals or rivers, or carried by rail to their base ports.

Having regard to these facts, our own existing resources and the most liberal estimates of future construction, we might in such circumstances find ourselves, although in full naval command of the North Sea and the Atlantic, yet fatally weak at what would then be the vital point, namely the Straits of Dover.

6   To put the matter briefly: I hold that the Straits of Dover, regarded as a military obstacle to the invasion of this country, will in the not far-distant future altogether lose their maritime character, and the problem of their successful passage by an invading force will present features somewhat resembling those involving the attack and defence of great river lines or operations on the great lakes in a war between Canada and the United States.

The main object to be attained in trying to secure the passage of a great river line is to gain possession of the opposite bank and establish a strong bridge-head.

In accordance with the views enunciated in this paper, I apply the same principle to the Straits of Dover, and hold that the only reliable defence against a powerful attack by hostile aircraft and submarines in vastly superior numbers, is to possess a strong bridge-head on the French coast with an effective means of passing and repassing across the Straits, which would only be secured by the projected Channel Tunnel.

7   Supposing such a tunnel to be in existence with a powerful 'Tunnel' (bridge) head completely fortified and secure from any sudden attack; consider its effect in the case of a war between the Triple Alliance and the Triple *Entente*.

In the event of disaster to the Franco-British armies, such a complete and indestructible line of communication between the two countries would provide France with an effective *point d'appui*, enable her to hold the neighbouring terrain, and deny the use of the ports to hostile submarines. We should then have reasonable grounds to throw aside any fear that France could be so overwhelmed as to necessitate the sacrifices most disastrous to this country contemplated in paragraph 5 of this paper.

8   Experience, however, proves that alliances and *ententes* are not everlasting, and I would take the case of the existence of a Tunnel with an unfriendly France. France is, and always has been, very anxious to build the Tunnel, and has shown throughout all the negotiations a studious regard for the susceptibilities of all shades of opinion in this country; and it would seem to be not altogether outside the bounds of possibility to secure agreements, which in certain contingencies would give this country the right to hold the French side of the Tunnel. Of course, this is a matter which has to be judged by diplomatists; but, speaking personally, I should not despair in the present state of feeling of arriving at an arrangement by which we could permanently do so.

If, however, no such arrangement with France is feasible, the existence of the Tunnel would not, from a military point of view, make our situation any worse. In case of an unfriendly France, it would probably have to be rendered temporarily ineffective.

9   It is not my purpose here to discuss the question of the construction of a Channel Tunnel in its wider aspects, or to answer the many military objections to it which have from time to time been made by the most distinguished soldiers.

The whole of these objections were made and, in my opinion, conclusively refuted so far as they apply to the present day, in an address which was read by Lord Sydenham to the House of Commons Channel Tunnel Committee on the 29th June last.

I firmly believe the danger to be a very real one, but owing to the difficulty of putting on paper apprehensions which I instinctively feel I have some fear that the views expressed herein may seem to many somewhat fantastic. If there is, however, even some substratum of reasonable possibility in these ideas, I submit them in the hope that one more argument may be added to the many advanced by those who ardently desire to see the Tunnel a *fait accompli*.

Appendix 4

Memorandum by Field-Marshal Sir Henry Wilson, CIGS, 23 December 1919 (CAB 3/3)

The Probable Effect which the Channel Tunnel Would Have Had on the Recent War

1   It is not easy to say what would have been the general effect, had the Channel Tunnel been in existence before the recent war began; but it would certainly have influenced the general mobilization and concentration when hostilities opened, and also the subsequent strategy on both sides.

2   As regards mobilization, there would have been a gain of at least 48 hours in the Expeditionary Force reaching the French coast if the Channel Tunnel had existed, but it must be remembered that approximately four days were lost in 1914 owing to delay in coming to a decision as to whether the Expeditionary Force was to mobilize or not. The daily detail of train loads to Southampton in 1914, and the corresponding numbers through the Tunnel are shown in Appendix 'A'. In judging the comparative figures it must be remembered that the subject is a complicated one. The daily number of trains in 1914 was affected by various factors:

(a) The number of units ready to move.
(b) The accommodation for trains at Southampton and home ports
(c) The shipping ready at Southampton and home ports.
(d) The wharfage available at the French ports.
(e) The trains available in France.

In considering the Channel Tunnel there are only two factors, the units ready to move and the capacity of the Tunnel to take them.

As a general rule the saving of 48 hours is, or should be, of great importance in any scheme to mobilization, more especially for war on the Continent.

Furthermore, the bulk of the force would have entered France much closer to the Belgian frontier than they did in 1914, and would therefore have been able to concentrate further forward.

After the concentration the Tunnel would have been available for the main line of supply, and a considerable amount of cross-Channel shipping would have become available for other purposes.

3 From the enemy's point of view the Channel Tunnel would have formed a strategic objective of the first importance; of such importance indeed that we may safely conclude that the original deployment of the German armies would have been so far modified as to include Calais and the Tunnel mouth in the first onward sweep of their projected advance. For it must be borne in mind that the existence of the Channel Tunnel must affect cross Channel shipping, and we should have relied on the Tunnel as the chief means of transporting the Expeditionary Force to France, as the main line of supply for that Force once landed, and as the line of retreat should such a movement become necessary.

It is hardly too much to say therefore, that the Germans might have concentrated their initial effort on the capture and occupation of Calais and the Tunnel mouth, and probably Boulogne, prior to an advance on Paris. In so doing they would have provided themselves with bases west of the Straits of Dover from which their submarines would have made our cross-channel supply and maintenance services increasingly precarious; and might well have throttled our military effort long before it had grown to maturity. Thus the Tunnel would have acted as a magnet drawing the enemy in the direction which would have proved most fatal to the Allies.

4 From the Allied point of view too, the existence of the Channel Tunnel would or certainly should have, modified profoundly the initial strategic concentration.

In the first place, from the point of view of Great Britain, it would have been essential that the strategic rôle allotted to our Expeditionary Force was such as to be compatible with covering and securing our main line of supply, (*i.e.*, the Tunnel Mouth). Consequently, we should hardly have consented to any operations which left the Tunnel mouth uncovered.

Unless, therefore, the French had been willing to modify their plans so as to ensure that the left of their forces always kept in touch with our troops, instead of our right keeping in touch with their left, a fundamentally different conception, the result would have been that the Expeditionary Force would have been separated from the French Army and would have been independent of it.

Such an event would have had grave military disadvantages, as co-operation and mutual support would thereby have been lost, and if the opening weeks of the campaign turned out as unfortunately as they actually did in 1914, we should have run a grave risk of losing the greater part of the Expeditionary Force and the exit of the Channel Tunnel as well. With a force of only six divisions, under the conditions given and under the opening moves of the campaign in 1914 as they actually took place, it is not too much to say that the existence of the Tunnel in that year would have lost us the campaign.

5   It is probable, however, that the French would have realized in advance the enormous importance of the Channel Tunnel, and would have remodelled their plan of campaign accordingly.

Actually in 1914 the French plan of campaign was based on three main hypotheses, none of which presumably would have affected their plans had the Tunnel been in existence. These were:-

(a) That the German Army would not cross the Meuse north of Namur, since this would involve such an infraction of Belgium neutrality, as could not be tolerated either by Belgium or by Great Britain.

(b) That owing to the uncertain attitude of Belgium, no definite plans could be concerted with that country, no reliance could be placed on any understandings which might exist, and that French troops could not advance into Belgium until invited to do so.

(c) That absolute reliance could not be placed on the timely intervention of the British Army.

Following on the above assumptions the French placed their concentration too far to the south and east, and when the full extent of the German advance through Belgium became apparent they were unable to transfer their reserves to the threatened flank in time, and in consequence the general retreat began which was only stopped outside the walls of Paris.

Had the Channel Tunnel existed, it may be assumed that our obligation to France would have been of a more definite nature, and one which would have exerted a stabilizing effect on the attitude of Belgium. Presumably the actual line of the German main advance would also have been estimated more correctly by the French, and taken in conjunction with the existence of the Tunnel it is reasonable to conclude that the initial concentration of the French forces would have been entirely changed, and that they would have concentrated their striking force somewhere on the northern frontier of France, with the dual object of attacking the enemy should he advance either towards Calais or Paris, and at the same time of ensuring the maintenance of contact between the British and French Armies.

Had some such plan been substituted for the one actually adopted it is probable that a battle of first importance would have taken place somewhere in Belgium.

On the result of this battle would have depended the subsequent course of the campaign, and further speculation is really idle, as it is impossible to say how it would have gone. If we assume that, as in the majority of battles on the Western Front, neither side was strong enough to obtain any decisive results, it would be fair to conclude that the line of trenches would have run approximately along the French frontier as far as Belgium and then somewhere through Belgium to the north.

Whether Brussels and Antwerp would have been in our hands or the Germans, the line would almost certainly have been to the east of the line Charleroi – Ostend.

A further point to note is that if the Channel Tunnel had been long in existence the French would probably have constructed a fortress round Lille in order to cover Calais from a German advance coming south of Brussels. Before the Channel tunnel could be seriously attacked, this fortress would have to be invested if not taken, as otherwise the German communications would be in jeopardy.

6   In general, therefore, it is reasonable to conclude that the existence of the Channel Tunnel would have eliminated the delay in mobilization caused by the uncertainty in the minds of the Government, the subsequent speed of concentration would have been increased by two or three days, and the first battles of the campaign would have been fought when the Allied Forces had been fully concentrated in Belgium, and consequently in circumstances less unfavourable than actually occurred in 1914. Had the battle ended decidedly in our favour the whole strategy and possibly the duration of the campaign would have been

altered, whilst, if it had been indecisive there is some reason for supposing that the end of 1914 would have found the Allies holding a line considerably in advance of the one actually occupied, and the resources of the areas which include the coal and iron products from Bruay to Charleroi would have accrued to the Allies instead of to the Germans. If, however, the Allies had suffered a decisive defeat, there is every reason to suppose that the British Army would either have been driven past the exits of the Tunnel and left the enemy established at Calais and Boulogne, or that the British and French Armies would have retreated in different directions. In either case it is difficult to see how we could have escaped disaster.

7   Looking to the future, the French frontier has been pushed forward in Alsace and Lorraine so as to form a pronounced salient, suitable enough as a jumping off ground for an army, capable, like that of Napoleon, of conducting an offensive against an inferior Germany, but a great source of weakness to one which is outnumbered and forced to act on the defensive. There appears no great probability of Belgium maintaining an army capable of holding its own against Germany and so closing the widely opened left flank of France. Nor does there seem any greater prospect that a British Army will be in being on a scale sufficient to repair the deficiencies of the Belgians within the time required. On the other hand, assuming that Germany recovers far more quickly than Russia, a period will come when, free from anxiety as to her Eastern front, she will be in a position to throw her full weight against France. In such conditions, it will be necessary for England to exert her whole strength from the earliest moment. The Channel Tunnel is merely one item in this problem, and it would be unwise to suppose that it would prove anything but an anxiety at the commencement of any future campaign unless our military forces are commensurate with the magnitude of the task in view. If, however, our forces are proportionate to our responsibilities, the Channel Tunnel would have an important economic and military value.

Appendix 5

Memorandum by A.J. Balfour, 5 February 1920 (CAB 3/3)

The problem of the Channel Tunnel has come up in a new shape and under new conditions. Undoubtedly the results arrived at by previous enquiries must be revised. Whether they should be reversed or not is a different question. On the whole, after considerable hesitations and some vacillation of opinion, I am inclined to think that the old decision should be upheld.

My reasons are the following:

It is of the first importance that the country should be secure from invasion; it is almost as important that if it is secure, it should think itself so. For only thus can we avoid the perpetual agitation and the recurrent alarms which are inevitable if our existence as a nation is in doubt.

Before the Defence Committee came into existence some twenty years ago there was no pretence of agreement between the Army and the Navy on this subject. The Navy always declared that it could protect us from serious invasion; but the Army never even pretended to believe them. Discussions in the Defence Committee between the heads of the two Services and the statesmen of the day effected at least the appearance of agreement. The Army conceded that while we retained command of the sea invasion on a conquering scale was impossible; the Navy, for its part, conceded that it could not guarantee our shores against a raid; each side perhaps making its concession with some slight mental reservations.

It was in this state of affairs that repeated decisions against the Channel Tunnel were arrived at after long discussions and duly recorded.

Since then what has occurred to change our views?

1 Our alliance with France has made us feel that anything which would facilitate the rapid transfer of British troops to French soil is in

the interests of both countries. This argument, as far as it goes, is, I think, a good one; though I must observe that there is some doubt whether a Channel Tunnel would always secure the object aimed at. Its very existence would destroy an immense proportion of the cross-Channel steamers on which we had so largely to rely during the war in order to maintain our communications with France. Once destroyed, they would be extremely difficult to replace, and we should have no temptation to replace them so long as the Channel Tunnel was in good working order. But if, either by accident or design, through the blunder of an official or deliberate sabotage, the tunnel was put out of action, our means of communicating with the Continent would be worse than they have ever been within living memory. If such a calamity occurred at some critical moment in the fortunes of a British army engaged in a continental war the effects would be disastrous.

2   Railway communications with France would make the blockade of this country by raiders and submarines far more difficult than it is. This, I think, may be admitted; but I fear that we must not exaggerate the advantage we should thus secure. If we were fighting for our lives against a strong naval Power and France were a neutral, the advantage of the railway, from the supply point of view, would, I doubt not, be very considerable. But this is a somewhat improbable contingency; and if France were either our friend or our enemy, the advantage would be almost negligible. This is quite obvious if France were our enemy; but it would also be true if France were our ally, for in that case she would herself be a large importer of food, of raw materials, and of munitions. Her railways would be choked with moving troops, and her rolling-stock would be required for her own purposes. We should get nothing.

3   Some of the precautions for rendering the railway useless for purposes of invasion, which were suggested before the war, and which were even then thought inadequate, are now impossible. The viaduct connecting the tunnel with the interior, which was to be so arranged as to be vulnerable to gun-fire from the sea, might, under existing circumstances, be more useful to the enemy than to ourselves. They could bombard it from submarines as well as we; and I have already explained how perilous it would be to have our communications through the tunnel interrupted at a time when the railway might be the main line of communication between our home bases and our forces at the front.

4   The possibility of a raid has always been admitted: and it would be unreasonable to assert that if a raid is possible elsewhere along our coasts, it could not be effected where that coast approaches most nearly the shores held by an enemy. No doubt it would be within our power to station sufficient forces in the neighbourhood of Dover to repel any raid which was lucky enough to elude our Navy. But this would involve, I suppose, the construction of new barracks and the permanent locking-up, in peace as in war, of a considerable body of regular troops. This would be expensive, and from a purely military point of view extremely inconvenient. Nor would it be made more attractive by the fact that modern artillery can easily keep Dover under fire from the French shore, can make the harbour useless, and the barracks untenable.

5   I do not dwell upon the risks which are inseparable from the most cunningly devised schemes for denying, at the right moment, the use of the tunnel to an enemy. All such schemes may be defeated by some accident happening to a complicated machine, or a nervous official losing his head. I do not say that such a contingency is likely; I only say that it is remotely possible: and this, for my argument, is sufficient. On the other hand, what is not only possible, but relatively easy, would be the destruction of the tunnel by sabotage, at a moment when military operations based upon its use were being carried out on the other side of the Channel.

6   The dangers I have adverted to are known, and in a certain sense are calculable, but I am even more afraid of the dangers which are not known and which are not calculable. All that has happened in the last five years in the way of military and naval development – submarines, aircraft, and long-range guns – have tended without exception to render ·the Channel Tunnel a more dangerous experiment. These have all made it more difficult for us to be sure that it will be open when we want it to be open, and closed when we want it to be closed.

And have we the least ground for thinking that the process is going to be reversed? And if it is not, if after the economic and sound habits of the world have adjusted themselves to this new mode of access to the Continent we find that it is fatal to our safety, what are we going to do? Destroy the tunnel in times of profound peace? Impossible. Wait till its dangers have been proved by a disastrous war? Still more impossible. The riddle will be insoluble.

It may of course be said that the unknown dangers which I fear, may possibly be of a kind which will put an end to our position as an island Power, and make the command of the sea useless as a means of defence. It may be so; but let us wait till it is so, and so long as the ocean remains our friend do not let us deliberately destroy its power to help us.

Appendix 6

List of Witnesses, Sub-Committee of the Committee of Civil Research, 1929-30

LIST OF WITNESSES

Date of Meeting	Name	Description of Witness
19 April 1929	Sir Cyril Hurcomb, KBE, CB	Secretary, Ministry of Transport
	Col. Sir John Pringle, CB	Chief Railway Inspecting Officer, Ministry of Transport
	Mr E.W. Rowntree, CBE	Assistant Secretary, Ministry of Transport
	Lt Col. A.H.L. Mount, CBE	Railway Inspecting Officer, Ministry of Transport
	Mr T. Shirley Hawkins, OBE, M.Inst CE	Civil Engineer, Ministry of Transport
26 April 1929	Sir Sydney Chapman, KCB, CBE	Chief Economic Adviser to His Majesty's Government
29 April 1929	Mr John Pringle (on behalf of Sir John Flett, KBE)	Senior Geologist, Geological Survey of Great Britain
3 May 1929	The Rt Hon. Sir William Bull, Bart, MP	Chairman of the Channel Tunnel Parliamentary Committee
	Sir Arthur Fell	Late Chairman of the Channel Tunnel Parliamentary Committee
	Accompanied by	
	Mr Robin B. d'Erlanger	
6 May 1929	Baron Emile B. d'Erlanger	Chairman, Channel Tunnel Company
	Mr Robin B. d'Erlanger	
10 May 1929	Sir Brodie Henderson, KCMG, CB, M.Inst CE	President, Institution of Civil Engineers
13 May 1929	Sir Herbert Walker, KCB	General Manager, Southern Railway
	Accompanied by	
	Mr W. Bishop	Solicitor to the Southern Railway
24 May 1929	Mr C.E.R. Sherrington	Secretary, Railway Research Service
27 May 1929	Mr Basil Mott, CB	Partners in Messrs Mott, Hay and Anderson, Consulting Engineers
	Mr David Hay	

Date of Meeting	Name	Description of Witness
31 May 1929	Mr Carrol Romer, MC	Editor, *The Nineteenth Century and After*
3 June 1929	Sir Ernest Moir, Bart, M.Inst CE	Partner in Messrs S. Pearson and Son, Ltd, Contractors for Public Works
1 July 1929	Air Vice-Marshal Sir Sefton Brancker, KCB, AFC	Director of Civil Aviation, Air Ministry
5 July 1929	Sir Ralph Wedgwood, CB, CMG	Chief General Manager, London and North-Eastern Railway
	Accompanied by Mr H. Allaway	Assistant General Manager (Shipping), London and North-Eastern Railway
8 July 1929	Sir Charles Howell Thomas, KCB, CMG	Permanent Secretary, Ministry of Agriculture and Fisheries
	Accompanied by Mr R.C. Hinton	Marketing Investigator, Ministry of Agriculture and Fisheries
11 July 1929	Monsieur P.E. Javary	Managing Director of the French Channel Tunnel Committee and General Manager, *Chemins de fer du Nord*
	Accompanied by Monsieur J. Rieter	*Correspondent à Londres, Chemins de fer du Nord*
12 July 1929	Sir Herbert Walker KCB	General Manager, Southern Railway
	Accompanied by Mr C.W. Cooper	Deputy Continental Assistant, Southern Railway
15 July 1929	Mr H.H. Dalrymple-Hay, M.Inst CE	Civil Engineer
4 October 1929	Sir William Lobjoit, OBE, JP	Chairman of the Fruit and Vegetables Committee of the National Farmers' Union
	Mr A.G. Linfield	Chairman of the Glasshouse Growers' Sub-Committee of the National Farmers' Union
	Accompanied by Mr E.C. Boughton	Secretary of the Fruit and Vegetables Committee of the National Farmers' Union
	Sir Evan D. Jones, Bart	Governing Director, Messrs. Topham Jones and Railton (1926) Limited, Public Works Contractors
14 October 1929	The Right Hon. the Earl of Crawford and Balcarres, KT	
16 October 1929	Sir Josiah Stamp, GBE	Chairman and President of the Executive, London, Midland and Scottish Railway
4 Nov. 1929	Mr G. Ellson	Chief Engineer to the Southern Railway
	Monsieur Garcey	Head of the Commercial Branch. *Compagnie internationale de Wagons-Lits*

Date of Meeting	Name	Description of Witness
	Accompanied by Mr Stanley Adams	Director of Messrs Thomas Cook and Sons
11 Nov. 1929	Mr C.T. Everest	London Manager, Bennett Steamship Company, Ltd. (nominated by the Chamber of Shipping of the United Kingdom)
	Accompanied by Mr P. Maurice Hill	Assistant General Manager of the Chamber of Shipping of the United Kingdom
	Dr Isserlis	Chamber of Shipping of the United Kingdom
	Col Sir M.P.A. Hankey, GCB, GCMG	Secretary, Committee of Imperial Defence
25 Nov. 1929	Mr Harold Cox	
	Mr W. Collard	Governing Director, The London and Paris Railway Promoters, Ltd

	Accompanied by
	    Mr Theodore Stevens
	    Mr Lennox Stanton	

20 Dec. 1929	Captain Paolo Coridori
	Accompanied by
	    Signor Joseph Grassi
	    and Mr T.W. Graham	

3 Feb. 1930	Sir Herbert Walker, KCB	General Manager, Southern Railway
	Accompanied by Mr C.W. Cooper	Deputy Continental Assistant, Southern Railway

Notes

Chapter 1
Prologue, 1850–1906

Chapter 1 is based on three sets of Parliamentary Papers: 'Correspondence relating to Channel Tunnel', C1206, *Accounts and Papers*, 31 (1875); 'Correspondence with reference to the Proposed Construction of a Channel Tunnel', C3358, *Accounts and Papers*, 17, (1882); 'Report from the Joint Select Committee of the House of Lords and the House of Commons on the Channel Tunnel', *Reports, Committees*, xii (2) (1883).

[1] *Illustrated London News*, vol. 19, 22 November 1851, pp. 612–13.
[2] See *The Railway News*, 5 May 1906, for a full account of this project.
[3] *Railway News*, 24 May 1913.
[4] Albert Sartiaux in *Revue politique et parlementaire*, 10 July 1906.
[5] Gladstone to Granville 21 June, Granville to Gladstone, 28 June 1873, in A. Ramm (ed.), *The Political Correspondence of Mr Gladstone and Lord Granville, 1868–1876*, Camden 3rd Series, (London, 1952), nos 845, 848.
[6] G.E. Buckle (ed.), *The Letters of Queen Victoria*, second series (London, 1926), ii, pp. 380–81; Derby diary, 11 February 1875.
[7] War Office to Treasury, 13 March 1875, WO 32/6269.
[8] War Office to Treasury, 1 April 1875, ibid.
[9] Notes by Nugent for Stanley, undated but mid April 1875, ibid.
[10] See A.A. Jackson, *London's Metropolitan Railway* (Newton Abbot, 1986) p. 334.
[11] See M. Partridge, *Military Planning for the Defence of the United Kingdom, 1814–1870* (New York, 1989), pp. 9, 13–14, 18, 31.
[12] Watkin to Wolseley, 7 January 1882, Wolseley MSS.
[13] Notes by Tenterden and Dilke, 5 March 1882, Tenterden MSS, FO 363/5.
[14] Note by Tenterden, 8 March 1882, ibid.; memorandum by Hertslet, 13 March 1882, FO 881/4601.
[15] Memorandum by Tenterden, 17 March 1882, FO 881/4652. The papers by Hertslet and Tenterden are both printed in K. Bourne and D.C. Watt (general editors), *British Documents on Foreign Affairs: Reports and Papers from the Foreign Office Confidential Print*, part

I, series F, vol. 10, (ed. J.F.V. Keiger), documents 47, 48 (University Publications of America, 1989).

[16] Minute by Granville, March 1882, Tenterden MSS, FO 363/5; draft by Granville, February 1882, Granville MSS, PRO 30/29/118.

[17] Note by Childers, 22 February 1882, WO 32/6269.

[18] WO 33/39.

[19] Cambridge to Wolseley, 17 January 1882; Childers to Cambridge, 14, 16 February 1882, Cambridge MSS; Dunsany in *The Nineteenth Century*, (February 1882), pp. 288–304.

[20] Knowles to Cambridge, 15 February 1882, Cambridge MSS.

[21] *The Nineteenth Century*, xi, nos 61, 62, 63: March to May 1882.

[22] Shipton's evidence to Joint Select Committee, p. 127.

[23] Chamberlain in the House of Commons, 15 August 1882, *Hansard*, 3rd Series, vol. 272, cols 1816-17.

[24] Gladstone in the House of Commons, 3 April 1883, ibid., vol. 277, cols 1373–76.

[25] Ibid., cols 1383–84.

[26] Gladstone in the House of Commons, 5 June 1890, ibid., vol. 345, cols 41–42.

[27] Kimberley in the House of Lords 6 April 1883, ibid., vol. 277, col. 1630.

[28] Ibid., vol. 282, cols 285–86; J.L. Garvin, *Life of Joseph Chamberlain* (London, 1932), i, p. 432.

[29] *Hansard*, 3rd Series, vol. 345, cols 45–49, 5 June 1890.

[30] Ibid., vol. 277, cols 1375–76, 3 April 1883.

[31] H. Cunningham, 'Jingoism in 1877–78', *Victorian Studies*, 14 (1971), pp. 429–53.

[32] Cambridge to Wolseley, 17 January 1882, Cambridge MSS.

[33] Holland to Wolseley, 8 August 1883, Wolseley MSS.

[34] Minutes of 31 January, 1 February; War Office to Treasury 19 February 1894, WO 32/6269.

[35] Repington's evidence at CID sub-committee on Invasion, November 1907, CAB 16/3, pp. 33–34, Repington's italics.

[36] H. Moon, 'The Invasion of the United Kingdom: Public Controversy and Official Planning 1888–1918' (unpublished University London PhD thesis, 1968), pp. 678–79.

[37] Ibid., pp. 680–81.

[38] Ibid., pp. 681–82.

[39] Ibid., pp. 684–5, 688.

[40] Intelligence Department memorandum, April 1902, 'Manoeuvres in Austria-Hungary, France, Germany, Holland, Roumania, Russia, Servia and Switzerland, 1901', WO 33/225, pp. 20–22.

[41] Moon, 'The Invasion of the United Kingdom', pp. 686–87.

[42] See above, note 35; C. à C. Repington, *The First World War* (London, 1920), i, p. 10.

[43] Moon, 'The Invasion of the United Kingdom', p. 689.

[44] Ibid., p. 690.

Chapter 2
The Committee of Imperial Defence

1 *The Times*, 31 May, 8 June 1906.
2 Lord Sydenham [Sir George Clarke], *My Working Life* (London, 1927) p. 205.
3 Clarke to Esher, 9 June, 16 July 1906, Esher MSS 10/39.
4 Memorandum by Clarke, 'The Channel Tunnel', 18 June 1906, CAB 3/1/37A, para. 5.
5 Ibid., para. 6.
6 Ibid., para. 7.
7 Ibid., paras 9–12.
8 Ibid., paras 13, 14.
9 Ibid., para. 19.
10 Ibid., para. 22.
11 Ibid., para. 24.
12 CAB 3/1/40A.
13 Notes by H. Llewellyn Smith, 3 August 1906, BT 65/12.
14 Clarke to Campbell-Bannerman, 2 January 1907, Campbell-Bannerman MSS 41213.
15 Clarke to Esher, 30 December 1906, Esher MSS 10/40.
16 Note by Clarke, 'The Channel Tunnel Bill', 31 January 1907, CAB 3/2/41A.
17 *The Times*, 2, 3 January 1907; Clarke to Esher, 3 January 1907, Esher MSS 10/40.
18 Sartiaux's article was reprinted from *Revue politique et parlementaire*, 10 July 1906. Quotations are from pp. 26 and 27 of the Channel Tunnel Company publication of February 1907 already mentioned in the text.
19 *The Nineteenth Century and After*, 360, February 1907, pp. 176–81.
20 *Hansard*, 3rd Series, vol. 169, cols 514, 515.
21 ADM 116/866B/014, January 1907. All the papers printed for the CID on this question between 1906 and 1914 are in CAB 18/25.
22 WO 32/5299.
23 Ewart Diary 8, 13 January 1907, quoted in Moon, 'The Invasion of the United Kingdom', pp. 695–6.
24 Memorandum by General Sir H.H. Wilson, March 1914, paras 2–5, WO 32/5300.
25 Minutes of 96th CID, 28 February 1907, CAB 2/2.
26 Clarke to Esher 2 January 1907, Esher MSS 10/40.
27 Clarke to Esher 18 July 1906, Esher MSS 10/39.
28 Minutes of 125th CID, 3 March 1914, CAB 2/3.
29 CAB 16/5; and see R. MacKay, *Fisher of Kilverstone* (Oxford, 1973) pp. 404–7.
30 J. Gooch, 'Sir George Clarke's Career at the Committee of Imperial Defence, 1904–7', *Historical Journal*, 18 (1975), pp. 555–69.
31 Campbell-Bannerman to the King, 20 February 1907, CAB 41/31; see also Sir S. Lee, *King Edward VII* (London, 1927), ii, pp. 467–68.
32 Esher to M. Brett 21 March 1907, in M.V. Brett and Esher (eds), *Journals and Letters of Reginald, Viscount Esher* (London, 1934–38), ii, p. 230; Lloyd George on 12 November 1919 in reply to Deputation of Members of the Channel Tunnel Committee of the House of Commons, CAB 24/93, CP 119.
33 An article in *The Times* on 17 January 1907, 'Channel Ferry *v.* Channel Tunnel', had suggested that, as a ferry service could be established at a small fraction of the cost of a tunnel, the former should be given precedence and serve as a sort of trailer for the latter,

which might follow when the ferries showed signs of being overwhelmed by the volume of traffic generated.

[34] *Hansard*, 3rd Series, vol. 171, cols 1203–4, 1208–9.

[35] Ibid., cols 1204, 1210–11.

[36] Ibid., col. 1673, 26 March 1907.

Chapter 3
The Committee of Imperial Defence, 1913–14

[1] Under-Secretary of State for Foreign Affairs to Secretary, CID and to DMO, 5 Nov. 1912; Conan Doyle to Hankey, 18 Dec. 1912, 17 January 1913, CAB 17/34.

[2] *Hansard*, 5th Series, vols 51, cols 1164, 1624; 52, cols. 522-23.

[3] Fisher to Churchill, 10 Mar. 1913 and note by Churchill, in R.S. Churchill (ed.) *W.S. Churchill*, vol ii, Companion vol. iii, (London, 1969) p. 1936; FO to Admiralty and DMO, 28 April; Admiralty to FO, 10 June; FO to Army Council, 25 June, 19 July, 5 Aug. 1913, WO 32/5300.

[4] A verbatim account of the meeting is in CAB 17/34.

[5] Minute by Wilson, 15 May 1913, WO 32/5300.

[6] *The Times*, 6 Aug. 1913, p. 4 col. 2.

[7] Lichnowsky, Prince Karl Max von, *Heading for the Abyss* (London, 1928), pp. 351–52.

[8] Seely to Nicholson, 10 Sept., Nicholson to Seely, 13 Sept. 1913, WO 32/5300.

[9] Hankey to Asquith, 3 Oct. 1913, and minute by Asquith; Hankey to FO, 3 Oct. 1913, CAB 17/34.

[10] Crowe to Hankey, 11 Oct. 1913, ibid.

[11] Memorandum by French, undated but October 1913, in WO, 32/5300.

[12] Notes by French for Secretary of State for War, undated, ibid.

[13] Minute by Wilson, 8 April 1914, ibid.

[14] CAB 38/25/35 and 36.

[15] CAB 38/26/1.

[16] CAB 38/26/9.

[17] Minutes of 125th CID, 3 March 1914, CAB 2/3.

[18] Wilson Diary, 3 March 1914.

[19] Memorandum by Wilson, March 1914, WO 32/5300, Wilson's emphasis.

[20] 'Policy and the Army', pamphlet by Wilson for private circulation, 1 January 1913, Wilson MSS 3/7/1, pp. 52–54. The full argument was that if Britain had such an Army as would enable her to intervene with effect, 'she would almost certainly never be called on to intervene.'

[21] Memorandum by Wilson and minute by Wilson, 8 April 1914, WO 32/5300.

[22] Minutes by Wilson, 21 April 1914, ibid.

[23] Minutes by Wilson, 24 April, 1 May 1914, ibid.; CAB 38/27/26.

[24] CAB 38/26/15.

[25] Fisher to Asquith, May 1914, in A.J. Marder (ed.), *Fear God and Dread Nought*, ii, (London, 1956) p. 504; see also R. MacKay, *Fisher of Kilverstone*, p. 451; a paper by Hankey summarising the naval, military and strategic reasons for and against the tunnel, which had three papagraphs in favour and six against, was apparently held back, CAB 38/27/18.

[26] Minutes of 126th CID, 14 May 1914, CAB 2/3.

[27] CAB 38/27/24, 19 May 1914.

[28] Hankey to Harcourt, 21 May 1914, Harcourt MSS 511.

[29] CAB 37/120/69, 12 June 1914.

[30] CAB 38/27/18; Proceedings and Reports of the two CID enquiries into Oversea Attack are in CAB 16/3 and CAB 16/28A and B.

[31] Draft memorandum by Hankey, 1 July 1914, CAB 17/34.

[32] Note by the Secretary, 6 July 1914, CAB 38/28/33.

[33] Memorandum by Seely, 1 July 1914, CAB 38/28/29.

[34] French to Hankey, 1 July 1914, Hankey MSS 4/6.

[35] Lord Sydenham *Proposed Channel Tunnel: Military Aspect of the Question*. On receiving the text of the proceedings of the deputation of August 1913, he had written: 'In the thirty years that have elapsed since I first supported the Tunnel scheme, there has been a wholesome change of opinion towards the question. The military arguments against it would never stand the least examination, and are opposed to all the experience of war. They rest upon wild conjectures, in which imbecility on the part of the Government and of the people of this country is gratuitously assumed. I think that the military objectors are now less numerous. At the same time, the need for the Tunnel is becoming more apparent to our commercial men, and your position may be strengthened by the fact that you can now depend wholly on Electric Traction, which in certain respects alters the conditions . . . if the French would agree to have the generating plant on this side of the Channel, the fears of the "old women of both sexes" might be allayed.' Sydenham to H.H. Spiller 16 August 1913, in *Channel Tunnel – Deputation to the Prime Minister* (London, 1913) p. 35.

[36] Memorandum by French, 9 July 1914, CAB 38/28/34.

[37] Minutes of 128th CID, 14 July 1914, CAB 2/3; Lord Hankey, *The Supreme Command* (London, 1961), p. 109. Kitchener had also spoken to Fisher: Fisher to Spender, 9 July 1914, in Marder, *Fear God and Dread Nought*, p. 509.

[38] Esher to Hankey, 20 July 1914, Esher MSS 4/5. In 1907 Esher had failed to respond to Clarke's call for a Royal Commission.

[39] Minutes of 128th CID, CAB 2/3.

[40] Fisher to Spender, 9 July 1914, Marder, *Fear God and Dread Nought*, p. 509.

[41] Fisher to Corbett, 1 Dec. 1913, ibid., p. 495.

[42] J. Buchan, *Lord Minto: A Memoir* (London, 1924) p. 252.

Chapter 4
The First World War, 1914–18

[1] *Daily Chronicle*, 22 Nov. 1913.

[2] *The Times*, 13 Dec. 1913.

[3] *Daily Chronicle*, 15 Dec. 1913.

[4] *The Globe*, 17 July; *The Universe*, 23 July 1915.

[5] *Yorkshire Post*, 17 April 1916.

[6] *Daily Graphic*, 23, 24 April 1916.

[7] *Observer*, 14 May 1916.

[8] *The Star*, 25 May 1916.

[9] Ibid., 27 May 1916.

[10] Turner Perkins to Hankey, 1 June 1916, CAB 17/139.

[11] *Yorkshire Post*, 10 June 1916.

[12] 'The Channel Tunnel: Recent Parliamentary History', Curzon MSS, IOLR, Eur. F112/233.

[13] *Glasgow Herald*, 26 June 1916.

[14] *Daily Chronicle*, 8 July 1916.

[15] *Daily Graphic*, 10 July 1916; *The Channel Tunnel and the World War* (London 1917) pp. 60–62.

[16] *Daily Chronicle*, 28 July 1916.

[17] *Morning Post*, 29 July 1916.

[18] See for instance *Dundee Advertiser*, 29 July; *Manchester Daily Dispatch*, 29 July; *Financial Times*, 31 July; *Shipping World*, 2 Aug. 1916; there were of course dissenting voices – see letters from Admiral de Horsey and Rear-Admiral (retired) S. Eardly Wilmot, in *Morning Post*, 27 and 29 July 1916.

[19] Fell to Asquith, 10 Aug. 1916, Appendix I in memorandum by Hankey, 23 Oct. 1916, CAB 3/3.

[20] C. à C. Repington, *The First World War, 1914–18* (London, 1920) i, pp 298–99, 308–9.

[21] Brade to Hankey, 2 Sept. 1916, Appendix II in memorandum by Hankey, 23 Oct. 1916, CAB 3/3.

[22] Repington, *The First World War*, i. pp. 313, 322.

[23] Minute by Marwood, 30 Sept. 1916, BT 65/13.

[24] Llewellyn Smith to Hankey, 5 Oct. 1916, Appendix III in Hankey memorandum, 23 Oct. 1916, CAB 3/3. A letter of the same date from Turner Perkins to the CID gave some hostages to the fortunes of the tunnel: 'In the absence of cooperation on the part of the State, the financial advisers of the Company doubt whether, for some time after the conclusion of peace, it would be possible to raise in this country the sum of £8 millions required for the construction of the British portion of the Channel Tunnel. No such difficulties are anticipated for the French.' Turner Perkins to Longhurst, 5 Oct. 1916, CAB 17/139.

[25] *Hansard*, 5th Series, vol. 86, col. 201, 12 Oct. 1916.

[26] Repington, *The First World War*, i, pp. 308, 311.

[27] Murray to Hankey, 21 Oct. 1916, Appendix IV in memorandum by Hankey 23 Oct. 1916, CAB 3/3. See also ADM 1/8466/211.

[28] Memorandum by Hankey, 23 Oct. 1916, CAB 3/3.

[29] Memorandum by Hankey, 25 Oct. 1916, CAB 17/139.

[30] 'The Channel Tunnel and the World War', pp. 1–11.

[31] Note by Hankey, 31 Jan. 1917, Appendix III to minutes of War Cabinet 51, CAB 23/1.

[32] War Cabinet 51, item 11, 1 Feb. 1917, ibid.

[33] *Hansard*, 5th Series, vol. 92, col. 1504, 17 Apr. 1917.

[34] CAB 24/18.

[35] War Cabinet 188, item 10, CAB 23/3.

[36] Memorandum by Robertson, 20 July 1917, GT 1458, CAB 24/20.

[37] Repington, *The First World War*, i, p. 467; Greene to Hankey, 26 July 1917, CAB 24/22.

[38] Fell to Lloyd George, 13 Aug. 1917, Appendix III in GT 1702, CAB 24/23.

[39] Memorandum by Moggeridge, 14 Aug. 1917, BT 65/13.

[40] War Cabinet 216, item 5, 15 Aug. 1917, CAB 23/3; GT 1702, Appendixes I, II, CAB 24/23.

[41] A. Fell, *The British Government and the Channel Tunnel* (London 1917).

[42] *The Times*, 19 Dec. 1917. The source was retired Vice-Admiral Kirchhoff, in *Das Grössere Deutschland*.

[43] See above, note 12.

[44] D'Erlanger, *The Channel Tunnel* (London 1918).

[45] 'Summary of Sir Francis Dent's Evidence in regard to the Channel Tunnel, given before the Select Committee on Transport, on 16 October 1918', BT 65/12.

[46] E. Geddes to Lloyd George, 18 Nov. 1918, Lloyd George MSS, F/18/2/27. I am obliged to Dr K. Grieves for bringing this to my attention.

Chapter 5
The Paris Peace Conference, 1919

[1] WC 538A, 28 Feb. 1919, CAB 23/15.

[2] *Hansard*, 5th Series, vol. 113, col. 878, 10 Mar. 1919.

[3] *The Times*, 11 March 1919.

[4] Ibid., 12 March 1919.

[5] House Diary, xv, pp. 92–93, cited in H. Nelson, *Land and Power: British and Allied Policy on Germany's Frontiers, 1916–1919* (Newton Abbot, 1971), p. 220.

[6] Morning Post, 12 March 1916.

[7] Ibid., 13 March 1919.

[8] *The Times*, 13 and 14 March; *Morning Post*, 14, 15 March 1919.

[9] *The Times*, 18 March 1919; d'Erlanger to Churchill, 18 March 1919, WO 32/5301.

[10] Amery to Churchill, 18 March 1919, WO 32/5301.

[11] Creedy to Amery, 20 March 1919, ibid.

[12] Extract from Report of French Committee of Enquiry, 23 March 1919, BT 65/12.

[13] Wilson Diary, 22 March 1919.

[14] Ibid., 23 March 1919.

[15] Ibid.

[16] Ibid.

[17] Memorandum by Hankey, 23 March 1919, Hankey MSS 8/11. This went so much against the grain that, many years later, Hankey attempted to erase the sentence, 'The British Government . . . will cooperate' by going over the typescript heavily with a ball-point pen. As presently preserved, it can be read from behind with the help of a torch and a mirror and three pairs of hands. The Fontainebleau Conference is not covered in the extant version of Hankey's diary.

[18] *Hansard*, 5th Series, vol. 113, col. 1721, 17 March 1919.

[19] A.S. Link (ed.) *The Papers of Woodrow Wilson*, lvi (Princeton, 1987), pp. 446, 455–56. In his treatment of this meeting Nelson, *Land and Power*, p. 227, n.2, confuses 'numbers' with 'speed' (*rapidité*). It was a question of doubling the latter. See P. Mantoux (ed.), *Les délibérations du Conseil du Quatre* (Paris, 1955), i, p. 95. Both Foch and the French War Minister favoured a tunnel. The latter had written to the Minister for Public Works on 7 March: 'The existence of a tunnel under the Channel would greatly facilitate military transportation in the case of a war in which the British armies cooperated with the French, and would not present any danger to France in any other eventuality.' Extract from Report of French Committee of Enquiry, 23 March 1919, BT 65/12.

[20] Wilson Diary, 31 March 1919.

[21] Fleuriau to Foreign Office, 9 April 1919, BT 65/12.

[22] Cubitt to Admiralty, 22 April, Churchill to d'Erlanger, 23 April 1919, WO32/5301.

[23] Cubitt to Secretary, HPDC, 9 May; Secretary, Air Ministry to Secretary, HPDC, 13 May 1919, ibid.

[24] Summary of French Report of 23 March 1919, by E.J. Elliot, 30 April 1919,, BTC 13, BT 65/12. He even contemplated, given that the Government's attitude to the revival of the scheme might be sympathetic, passing on the French Report to the Channel Tunnel Company which, he said, 'appear to have an unrivalled status in the matter': note by Elliot, 7 May 1919, ibid.

[25] Minute by Carlill, 15 May 1919, ibid.

[26] Lloyd George at B.E.D.30, 5 May 1919, CAB 29/28.

[27] Note by Clement Jones, 17 May 1919, WCP 797, Curzon MSS, F112/233.

[28] Notes by Elliot, 27 May, and Carlill, 27 June 1919, BT 65/12.

[29] W. Turner Perkins to Creedy, 17 May 1919, WO 32/5301.

[30] Notes by the General Staff, 20 June 1919, ibid.

[31] Elliot to Rissik (FO), 8 Aug. 1919, BT 65/12.

[32] Elliot to Hill, 13 Aug.; note by Carlill, 19 Aug. 1919, ibid.

[33] Memorandum by Elliot, 'The Board of Trade Memorandum on the Channel Tunnel of January 1914', 15 Aug. 1919, ibid.

[34] Note by Carlill, 22 Aug. 1919, ibid.

[35] Spicer (FO) to Secretary, Board of Trade, 25 Aug.; note by Elliot, 4 Sept. 1919, ibid. The Foreign Office replied to the French on 20 September.

[36] Fountain (BT) to Secretary, War Ofice, 19 Sept. 1919, WO 32/5301.

[37] War Office to Board of Trade, 28 Sept. 1919, ibid.

[38] War Cabinet 616A, 15 Aug. 1919, CAB 23/15.

Chapter 6
Hankey-Pankey

[1] A. Sharp, 'Britain and the Channel Tunnel, 1919–1920', *Australian Journal of Politics and History*, 25 (1979), pp. 210–15. Sharp did not have access to the Hankey Diary and other papers. In his book *The Versailles Settlement: Peacemaking at Paris, 1919* (London 1991), p. 191, Sharp tends to attribute to 1919 a sentiment which was much more a feature of 1920. He also relies too heavily on Kerr, whose advice was by no means always taken by Lloyd George.

[2] Secretary, Admiralty to Secretary, HPDC, 16 Oct. 1919, CAB 132/2. See also ADM 167/59.

[3] P. Cambon to Curzon, 30 Oct. 1919, BT 65/12; CAB 23/18, 5 Nov. 1919.

[4] Note by Hankey, 10 Nov. 1919, CAB 24/92.

[5] Note by Hankey, 10 Nov. 1919, enclosed in Hankey to Balfour 10 Nov. 1919, Balfour MSS, GD 433/2/17.

[6] Hankey Diary, 16 Nov. 1919, Hankey MSS 1/5.

[7] CAB 23/18, 11 Nov. 1919, item 4.

[8] Hankey to Lloyd George, 11 Nov. 1919, CAB 63/25.

[9] Hankey Diary, 16 Nov. 1919, Hankey MSS 1/5.

[10] Ibid.

[11] Deputation of Members of House of Commons Channel Tunnel Committee to Prime Minister, 12 Nov. 1919, Report of PM's reply, CAB 24/93.

[12] WO 32/5302.

[13] 'Rough Notes', HPDC/4, 18 Nov. 1919, para. 1, CAB 13/2.

[14] Major-General Sir P.P. de B. Radcliffe (DMO), Lt Col. P.K. Lewes (Assistant-Director of Artillery), Col. E.P. Brooker (Assistant-Director of Fortifications and Works), Major-General C.F. Romer (Chief of the General Staff, Forces in Great Britain).

[15] 'Rough Notes', HPDC/4, 18 Nov. 1919, para. 6, CAB 13/2.

[16] Hankey Diary, 16, 23 Nov. 1919, Hankey MSS 1/5.

[17] Minutes of 33rd meeting of HPDC, 21 Nov. 1919, p. 3, CAB 12/1.

[18] Ibid., pp. 5–6.

[19] Ibid., p. 4.

[20] Ibid.

[21] Ibid., pp. 7–8.

[22] Ibid., p. 8.

[23] Hankey Diary, 23 Nov. 1919, Hankey MSS 1/5.

[24] Draft notes by Hankey, 22 Nov. 1919, CAB 63/25.

[25] Minutes of 34th meeting of HPDC, 16 Dec. 1919, CAB 12/1.

[26] Hankey Diary, 29 Dec. 1919, Hankey MSS 1/5.

[27] Ibid.

[28] Memorandum by HPDC, 17 Dec. 1919, CAB 13/1. Para. 5 is a possible choice: 'The experience of the war and the new conditions created thereby do not afford any grounds for modifying the views previously held, and in this connection it is necessary to remember that from time to time the political relations of countries inevitably change, and that, although under existing conditions the exit of a tunnel on the Continental side would be in the hands of a Power with whom England is on terms of closest friendship, there can be no guarantee that it will at all times in the future be in friendly hands. On the other hand the tunnel once constructed will be always there until destroyed; and, even though great changes may take place in the future in the International situation, it is almost inconceivable that the destruction of a tunnel costing anything from £30m to £50m to build, will be contemplated except in the last emergency, and when war with the Power in possession of the other end is imminent, or has even broken out. It is essential, therefore, that means should exist for putting the tunnel both temporarily and permanently out of service at a moment's notice.'

[29] Hankey Diary, 29 Dec. 1919, Hankey MSS 1/5; notes by Hankey, one dated 17 Dec. 1919, in CAB 63/25, ff. 50–56.

[30] Note by Thomas Jones, Acting-Secretary to the Cabinet, 21 Jan. 1920, CAB 24/26.

[31] Admiralty to Hankey, 24 Jan. 1920, CAB 3/3. See also ADM 1/8579/14.

[32] Note by Hankey, 28 Jan. 1920, CAB 63/26, f.17.

[33] See Report of HPDC, 17 Dec. 1919, CAB 13/1, para. 5; and note by Elliot, 14 May 1919, where the highest figure was £16,000,000, BT 65/12.

[34] Memorandum by Hankey, 28 Jan. 1920, para. 1, CAB 63/26.

[35] Ibid., paras 15, 16.

[36] Ibid., paras 24, 25.

[37] Ibid., para. 32.

[38] Ibid., para. 44.

[39] Ibid., para. 47.

Chapter 7
Departmental Decisions

[1] Secretary, Air Ministry, to Hankey, 22 Nov. 1919, 31 Jan. 1920, CAB 3/3.

[2] ADM 1/8579/14.

[3] A.F.C. de B. St. Aulaire, *Confession d'un vieux diplomate* (Paris, 1954) p. 779.

[4] HPDC Report, paras 11, 12.

[5] Memorandum by Balfour, 5 Feb. 1920, CAB 3/3.

[6] Hankey to War Office 4 Feb.; minute by Churchill, 8 Feb. 1920, WO 32/5302; Hankey to Bonar Law, 9 Dec. 1922, CAB 63/33.

[7] Hankey to Army Council, 12 Nov., to Wilson, 27 Nov. 1919, WO 32/5302.

[8] Memoranda by Wilson, 16, 23 Dec. 1919, CAB 3/3, Wilson's italics.

[9] Churchill to Wilson, 5 Jan. 1920, WO 32/5302.

[10] Minutes by Wilson, 7 and 13 Jan., by Churchill, 8 Jan. 1920, ibid.

[11] Note by Churchill, 15 Jan. 1920, ibid.

[12] Note by Radcliffe, 24 Jan. 1920, ibid.

[13] Notes by Wilson, 29 Jan., 4 Feb.; by Churchill, 31 Jan. 1920, ibid.

[14] Churchill to Wilson 4 Feb.; Wilson to Churchill 6 Feb. 1920, ibid. A few days later Wilson told Foch, who wanted to know what answer the British were going to give about having conversations between the military chiefs of England, France and Belgium about the defence of the two latter countries, that he had written to Curzon on this, that he

(Wilson) would represent England as he had before the war, but that the Cabinet 'were inclined to bargain about this': Wilson Diary, 11, 12, 14 Feb. 1920.

[15] Note by Churchill, 9 Feb. 1920, CAB 3/3.

[16] Memorandum by Chamberlain, 26 Feb. 1920, ibid.

[17] Memorandum by Barstow, 2 Feb. 1920, T186/13.

[18] MT 6/3512.

[19] E. Geddes to Hankey, 10 Feb. 1920, CAB 3/3.

[20] Memorandum by Addison, 4 March 1920, ibid.

[21] Note by Elliot, 27 Feb. 1920, BT 65/12.

[22] Memorandum by Elliot, ?27 Feb. 1920, ibid.

[23] Memorandum by Carlill, 16 March 1920, ibid.

[24] Minutes of 55th meeting of Board of Trade Council, 16 Mar. 1920, ibid.

[25] Memorandum by Geddes, 17 Mar. 1920, CAB 3/3.

[26] Memorandum by Crowe, 21 Mar. 1920, FO 371/3765/187042.

[27] Derby to Curzon, 29 Mar. 1920, copy in BT 65/12. M. Marsal's positive views appeared in an article in the *Star* on 9 April 1920.

[28] Minute by Curzon, 7 April 1920, FO 371/3765/187042.

[29] Memorandum by Hardinge, 25 April 1920, ibid.

[30] Memorandum by Foreign Office, undated, sent to Cabinet by Curzon 1 May 1920, Curzon MSS, IOLR Eur. F.112/233.

[31] J.D. Goold, 'Lord Heritage as Ambassador to France', *Historical Journal*, 21 (1978), 913–27.

[32] Hardinge of Penshurst, *Old Diplomacy* (London, 1947), pp. 248–49. He also claimed to have said that the question of security had been transformed by the progress of aviation, and that it would become easier to seize the entrance to a tunnel by a *coup de main* carried out by soldiers landed in aeroplanes. There is no mention of aviation in his memorandum.

[33] Hankey to Lloyd George, 13 May 1920, Lloyd George MSS F/24/2/34.

[34] Note by Hankey for Lloyd George, 10 June 1920, CAB 63/28; A. Sharp, 'The Foreign Office in Eclipse, 1919–1922', *History*, 61 (1976), pp. 198–218; R.M. Warman, 'The Erosion of Foreign Office Influence on the Making of Foreign Policy, 1916–18', *Historical Journal*, 15 (1972), pp. 135–59.

[35] These conditions were: '(i) The provision of such naval, military and air defence as will make it extremely improbable than an enemy will ever try to seize the British end; and it is thought that this will entail, in addition to the provision of guns firing on the British end, an extended naval defence, the garrisoning *at all times* of a mobile force in the vicinity of the tunnel exit; the provision of an efficient air and anti-aircraft defence (ii) The duplication of the tunnel exits, and all important machinery; the construction under-ground so far as practicable of all machinery installations for putting the tunnel out of service as also those vital to its use; the provision of obstacles and electric lights (iii) The construction of the tunnel at such a depth below the bed of the sea as to make it immune from submarine attack (iv) The provision of means of temporary flooding and for permanent flooding by letting in the sea in the last resort.'

[36] Hankey to Bonar Law, 9 Dec. 1922, CAB 63/33.

[37] *The Contemporary Review*, 118 (1920), pp. 30–38; J.M. McEwen, 'Lloyd George's Acquisition of the *Daily Chronicle* in 1918', *Journal of British Studies*, 22 (1982), pp. 127–44; for more on the anti-French bias of Curzon as Foreign Secretary, see 'Making Germany Pay: Gwynne's Conspiracy against Lord Curzon in 1923', chapter 7 in K.M. Wilson, *A Study in the History and Politics of the Morning Post, 1905–1926* (Lewiston and Lampeter, 1990) pp. 193–228.

[38] Sharp 'The Foreign Office in Eclipse', pp. 214–5.

[39] Sharp, *The Versailles Settlement*, p. 191.

[40] Asquith to Grey, 7 Sept. 1908: 'He [Clemenceau] is ignorant if he imagines we are going to keep here a standing army of 500,000 to 750,000 men, ready to meet the Germans in Belgium if and when they are minded to adopt that route for the invasion of France. As you point out, he completely ignores the existence – from a military point of view – of his Russian ally.' Grey MSS, FO 800/100. See K.M. Wilson, *The Policy of the Entente* (Cambridge 1985), pp. 80–81. As Churchill reminded the CID in 1925, 'We haven't got the Russians now as we had before the war': minutes of CID, 19 Feb. 1925, CAB 24/172.

[41] K. Jeffery and P. Hennessy, *States of Emergency: British Governments and Strikebreaking since 1919* (London, 1983); A. Rothstein, *The Soldiers' Strikes of 1919* (London, 1980); G. Dallas and D. Gill, *The Unknown Army: Mutinies in the British Army in World War I* (London, 1985), pp. 89–140.

[42] P. Mantoux *Les délibérations du Conseil du Quatre*, i, p. 319; S. Marks, *The Illusion of Peace* (London, 1976) p. 24; T.A. Bailey, *Woodrow Wilson and the Lost Peace* (New York, 1944) pp. 357-58; G.W. Egerton, 'Britain and the "Great Betrayal": Anglo-American Relations and the Struggle for United States Ratification of the Treaty of Versailles, 1919–1920', *Historical Journal*, 21 (1978), pp. 885–911.

[43] K. Jeffery, *The British Army and the Crisis of Empire, 1918–1922* (Manchester, 1984).

Chapter 8
Between the Wars

[1] CAB 3/3. Between June 1920 and July 1922 no full meetings of the CID were held.

[2] Minutes by Tyrrell and Curzon, 19 April 1922, FO 371/8265/W3271.

[3] *Hansard*, 5th Series, vol. 156, cols 563, 821–822, 6 and 10 July 1922.

[4] Ibid., vol. 159, cols 1198–99, 2356–57, 4 and 11 December 1922; note by Hankey for Bonar Law, 9 December 1922, CAB 63/33.

[5] Note by Hankey, 'Channel Tunnel: Statement in Parliament Prepared for the PM by Secretary', CAB 63/36.

[6] Bull interview with Economic Advisory Council, 3 May 1929, CAB 58/123.

[7] Hankey to Crowe 3 June, minute by MacDonald 11 June 1924, FO 371/10544/W4634.

[8] As note 6 above.

[9] Memorandum by Hankey, 21 June 1924, CAB 63/36.

[10] Hankey to Trenchard, 24 June 1924, AIR 8/75.

[11] Hankey, *Diplomacy by Conference* (London, 1946) p. 98.

[12] Minutes of 186th meeting of CID, 1 July 1924, CAB 2/4.

[13] CAB 23/48, 2 July 1924.

[14] As note 6 above.

[15] Roskill, *Hankey, Man of Secrets*, ii, pp. 522–23; *Hansard*, 5th Series, vol. 175, cols 1782–86, 7 July 1924.

[16] FO 371/11050/W10752, 19 November 1925.

[17] FO 371/13351/W10789.

[18] As note 6 above.

[19] Memorandum by Slessor, 26 January 1929, AIR 8/75.

[20] Memorandum by Slessor, 19 February 1929, ibid.

[21] Slessor, 'Notes of Conversation with CAS on the Channel Tunnel', 24 February 1929, ibid. On the other hand, Trenchard considered that the Channel Tunnel would be 'an absolutely invaluable line of supply' supposing Britain was fighting with Germany against Russia.

[22] *Manchester Guardian Weekly*, 1 February 1929.

[23] *Nottingham Guardian*, 13 February 1929.

[24] Chapman to Meredith (Parliamentary Secretary) 14 February 1929, BT 60/22/6.

[25] Baldwin in the House of Commons 26 March 1929, *Hansard*, 5th Series, vol. 226, col. 2258.

[26] Cmd. 3513, in *Parliamentary Papers: Reports, Commissioners etc.*, xii (1929–30).

[27] Note by Hankey, 9 April 1929, CAB 63/41.

[28] See BT 60/22/6.

[29] Note by Hankey, 6 November 1929, CAB 63/42. He admitted only that it was 'more than five years old'.

[30] Memorandum by Hankey, November 1929, ibid.

[31] Hankey to Charles, 28 February 1930, CAB 63/43.

[32] Hankey to MacDonald, 28 February 1930, PREM 1/98.

[33] Memorandum by Hankey, 4 March 1930, CAB 63/43.

[34] Memorandum by Hankey, 5 March, and Hankey to MacDonald 5 March 1930, PREM 1/98.

[35] MacDonald to Baldwin and to Lloyd George, 3 March 1930, ibid.

[36] Treasury memorandum, 14 March 1930, CAB 58/144.

[37] Report of Economic Advisory Council's Channel Tunnel Policy Committee, 25 March 1930, ibid.

[38] CAB 23/63, 15 April 1930; Hankey to MacDonald, 14 April 1930, PREM 1/98.

[39] Memorandum by Graham, 13 May 1930, BT 60/22/6.

[40] Note by Portal, 2 May 1930, AIR 8/75.

[41] Note by Portal, 28 May 1930, ibid.

[42] Minutes of 248th meeting of CID, 29 May 1930, CAB 2/5.

[43] Hankey to MacDonald, 1 and 14 April 1930, PREM 1/98.

[44] Hankey to Salmond, 30 May 1930, AIR 8/75.

[45] CAB 23/64, 4 June 1930; Bondfield quoted by the columnist Callisthenes of the *Daily Telegraph*, 20 June 1929; see also BT 60/22/6.

[46] Cmd. 3591, in *Parliamentary Papers: Reports, Commissioners etc.*, xii (1929–30).

[47] Memorandum by Bull, 24 June 1930, Baldwin Papers, ii, ff. 400–4.

[48] *Hansard*, 5th Series, vol. 240, cols 1608, 1698–1742, 30 June 1930.

[49] Roskill, Hankey, Man of Secrets, ii, pp. 522–23.

[50] FO 371/15648/W1476; FO 371/17674/W7760.

[51] FO 371/19868/C44.

[52] FO 371/19868/C5528.

[53] FO 371/19868/C8525.

[54] FO 371/21608/C198.

[55] CAB 21/732.

[56] J. Farquharson, 'After Sealion: A German Channel Tunnel?', *Journal of Contemporary History*, 25 (1990), pp. 414–15; ADM 1/11924.

[57] Farquharson, 'After Sealion', p. 415.

[58] Ibid. pp. 416–21.

Chapter 9
'Intangible and Psychological' Factors

1 Typescript of Crawford interview, HO 45/13708.
2 Hankey to Clynes, 23 May 1930, ibid.
3 Clynes to MacDonald, 2 June 1930, PREM 1/89.
4 See above, Chapter 7, note 2.
5 Typescript of Hankey interview, CAB 58/125.
6 Memorandum by Hankey, 6 November 1929, CAB 63/42.
7 John Vincent (ed.), *The Crawford Papers* (Manchester, 1984) p. 551.
8 Hankey to Shortt, 27 January 1920, HO 45/13708.
9 Shortt to Hankey, 14 February 1920, ibid.
10 See above, Chapter 6, note 16.
11 Memorandum by Hankey, 6 November 1929, CAB 63/42, f.41.
12 Ibid.
13 See above, Chapter 5, note 7.
14 See above, Chapter 2, note 23.
15 Memorandum by Hankey, February 1930, CAB 63/43.

Bibliography

PRIMARY SOURCES

(a) *Private Papers*

Baldwin Papers, Cambridge University Library.
Balfour Papers, British Library and Scottish Record Office.
Bull Papers, Churchill College Cambridge.
Cambridge Papers, University of Leeds (microfilm).
Campbell-Bannerman Papers, British Library.
Channel Tunnel Company Papers, Churchill College Cambridge.
Curzon Papers, India Office Library and Records.
Derby Papers, Liverpool City Archives.
Esher Papers, Churchill College Cambridge.
Fisher Papers, Churchill College Cambridge
Gladstone Papers, British Library.
Granville Papers, Public Record Office.
Hankey Papers, Churchill College Cambridge.
Lansdowne Papers, Bowood House, Bowood, Wiltshire.
Lloyd George Papers, House of Lords Record Office.
Sydenham Papers (Sir George Clarke), British Library.
Tenterden Papers, Public Record Office.
Wilson Papers, Imperial War Museum.
Wolseley Papers, University of Leeds (microfilm).

(b) *Official Papers at the Public Record Office*

Admiralty: classes ADM 1
ADM 116

Air Force: class AIR 8/75

Board of Trade: classes BT 60
BT 65

Cabinet Office: classes CAB 23
CAB 24
CAB 37
CAB 41
CAB 58
CAB 63

Committee of Imperial Defence: classes CAB 2
CAB 3
CAB 12
CAB 13
CAB 16
CAB 17
CAB 18
CAB 29

Foreign Office: classes FO 27
FO 371
FO 881

Home Office: class HO 45

Ministry of Transport: classes MT 6
MT 9
MT 10

Prime Minister's Office: class PREM 1

Treasury: classes T11
T 175
T 186

War Office: classes WO 32
WO 33

(c) *Parliamentary Papers*

C1206, Correspondence relating to Channel Tunnel, *Accounts and Papers*, 31, (1875).

C3358, Correspondence with reference to the Proposed Construction of a Channel Tunnel, *Accounts and Papers*, xvii, (1882).

Report from the Joint Select Committee of the House of Lords and the House of Commons on the Channel Tunnel, *Reports, Committees*, xii(2) (1883).

Cmd 3513, Report of a Sub-Committee of the Committee of Civil Research, *Reports, Commissioners*, xii (1929–30).

Cmd 3591, The Channel Tunnel: Statement of Policy, *Reports, Commissioners*, xii (1929–30).

Hansard's Parliamentary Debates, Series 3, 4, 5.

(d) *Newspapers and Periodicals*

Daily Chronicle
Daily Graphic
Daily Telegraph
Financial Times
Glasgow Herald
Globe
Illustrated London News
Manchester Guardian
Morning Post
Nineteenth Century
Observer
Pall Mall Gazette
Punch
Railway News
Spectator
Star
The Times
Westminster Gazette
Yorkshire Post

SECONDARY SOURCES

Books and Articles

Bailey, T.A., *Woodrow Wilson and the Lost Peace* (New York, 1944).

Bonavia, M., *The Channel Tunnel Story* (Newton Abbot, 1987).

Brett, M.V. and Esher, Viscount, *Journals and Letters of Reginald, Viscount Esher* (London, 1934–38).

Buchan, J., *Lord Minto: A Memoir* (London, 1924).

Buckle, G.E. (ed.), *Letters of Queen Victoria*, second series (London, 1926).

Churchill, R.S., *Winston S. Churchill* (London, 1969).

Cunningham, H., 'Jingoism in 1877–78', *Victorian Studies*, 14 (1971), 429–53.

Dallas, G. and Gill, D., *The Unknown Army: Mutinies in the British Army in World War I* (London, 1985).

Desbrières, G. (ed.), *Projets et tentatives de débarquement aux Îles Brittaniques* (Paris, 1900–1902).

Egerton, G.W., 'Britain and the "Great Betrayal": Anglo-American relations and the Struggle for United States Ratification of the Treaty of Versailles 1919–1920', *Historical Journal*, 21 (1978), pp. 885–911.

Farquharson, J., 'After Sealion: A German Channel Tunnel?' *Journal of Contemporary History*, 25 (1990), pp. 409–30.

Fell, Sir A., 'The Channel Tunnel', *Journal of the Royal Society of Arts*, 62 (1913), pp. 88–95.

—, *The Channel Tunnel and Food Supplies in Time of War* (London, 1913).

—, *The Position of the Channel Tunnel Question in May, 1914: Statement on Behalf of the House of Commons Channel Tunnel Committee* (London, 1914).

—, *The British Government and the Channel Tunnel* (London, 1917).

—, *The Channel Tunnel: Its Position in October 1921* (London, 1921)

Forbes, Lord, 'Shall We Have a Channel Tunnel?' (Aberdeen, 1883).

Fox, Sir F., 'Geographical Aspects of the Channel Tunnel', *Geographical Journal*, 50 (1917), pp. 106–16.

Garvin, J.L., *Life of Joseph Chamberlain* (London, 1932).

Gooch, J., 'Sir George Clarke's Career at the Committee of Imperial Defence, 1904–1907' *Historical Journal*, 18 (1975), pp. 555–69.

—, *The Prospect of War* (London, 1981).

Goold, J.D., 'Lord Hardinge as Ambassador to France', *Historical Journal*, 21 (1978), pp. 913–27.

Hankey, Lord [Sir Maurice], *Diplomacy by Conference* (London, 1946).

—, *The Supreme Command* (London, 1961).

Hardinge, Lord, *Old Diplomacy* (London, 1947).

Hawkshaw, J.C., 'The Channel Tunnel and its Early History', *Journal of the Royal Society of Arts*, 62, pp. 592–604.

Jeffrey, K., *The British Army and the Crisis of Empire, 1918–1922* (Manchester, 1984)

Jeffrey, K., and Hennessy, P., *States of Emergency: British Governments and Strike Breaking since 1919* (London, 1983).

Lee, Sir S., *King Edward VII* (London, 1927).

Lichnowsky, Prince K.M. von, *Heading for the Abyss* (London, 1928).

Link, A.S. (ed.), *The Papers of Woodrow Wilson*, lvi (Princeton, 1987).

McEwen, J.M., 'Lloyd George's Acquisition of the Daily Chronicle in 1918', *Journal of British Studies*, 22 (1982), pp. 127–44.

Mackay, R., *Fisher of Kilverstone* (Oxford, 1973).

Mantoux, P. (ed.), *Les délibérations du Conseil du Quatre* (Paris, 1955).

Marder, A.J. (ed.), *Fear God and Dread Nought* (London, 1956).

Marks, S., *The Illusion of Peace* (London, 1976).

Matthew, H.C.G. (ed.), *The Gladstone Diaries*, x (Oxford, 1990).

Maurice, Sir F., and Arthur, Sir G., *The Life of Lord Wolseley* (London, 1924).

Nelson, H., *Land and Power: British and Allied Policy on Germany's Frontiers, 1916–1919* (Newton Abbot, 1971).

Partridge, M.S., *Military Planning for the Defence of the United Kingdom, 1814–1870* (New York, 1989).

—, 'Wellington and the Defence of the Realm, 1819–52', in Gash, N. (ed.), *Wellington: Studies in the Military and Political Career of the Duke of Wellington* (Manchester, 1990), pp. 238–62.

Perkins, W.T. (ed.), *Channel Tunnel: Reports by British and French Engineers; Papers on National Defence* (London, 1907).

Ramm, A. (ed.), *The Political Correspondence of Mr Gladstone and Lord Granville, 1868–1876*, Camden Third Series (London, 1952).

Repington, C. à C., *The First World War, 1914–1918* (London, 1920).

Roskill, S., *Hankey, Man of Secrets* (London, 1970–74).

Rothstein, A., *The Soldiers' Strikes of 1919* (London, 1980).

St-Aulaire, A.F.C. de B., *Confession d'un vieux diplomate* (Paris, 1954).

Sartiaux, A., *Revue politique et parlementaire*, July 1906.

Sharp, A., 'The Foreign Office in Eclipse, 1919–1922', *History*, 61 (1976), pp. 198–218.

—, 'Britain and the Channel Tunnel, 1919–1920', *Australian Journal of Politics and History*, 25 (1979), pp. 210–215.

—, *The Versailles Settlement: Peacemaking at Paris, 1919* (London, 1991).

Spiers, E.M., *The Army and Society, 1815–1914* (London, 1980).

Sydenham, Lord [Clarke, Sir George], *My Working Life* (London, 1927).

—, *Proposed Channel Tunnel: Military Aspect of the Question* (London, 1914).

Valbert, G., 'L'agitation Anglaise contre le tunnel de la Manche', *Revue des Deux Mondes*, 51 (1882), pp. 675–86.

Vincent, J. (ed.), *The Crawford Papers* (Manchester, 1984).

Warman, R.M., 'The Erosion of Foreign Office Influence on the Making of Foreign Policy, 1916–18', *Historical Journal*, 15 (1972), pp. 135–59.

Whiteside, T., *The Tunnel under the Channel* (New York, 1962).

Wilson, K.M., *The Policy of the Entente* (Cambridge, 1985).

—, 'Missing Link: the Channel Tunnel and the Anglo-American Guarantee to France in March 1919', *Diplomacy and Statecraft*, 5 (1994), pp. 73–80.

—, 'Hankey's Appendix: Some Admiralty Manoeuvres during and after the Agadir Crisis, 1911, *War in History*, 1 (1994), pp. 81-97.

THESES

Moon, H., 'The Invasion of the United Kingdom: Public Controversy and Official Planning, 1888–1918' (unpublished Ph.D. Thesis, University of London, 1968).

Index